IMAGES
of America

OAKDALE

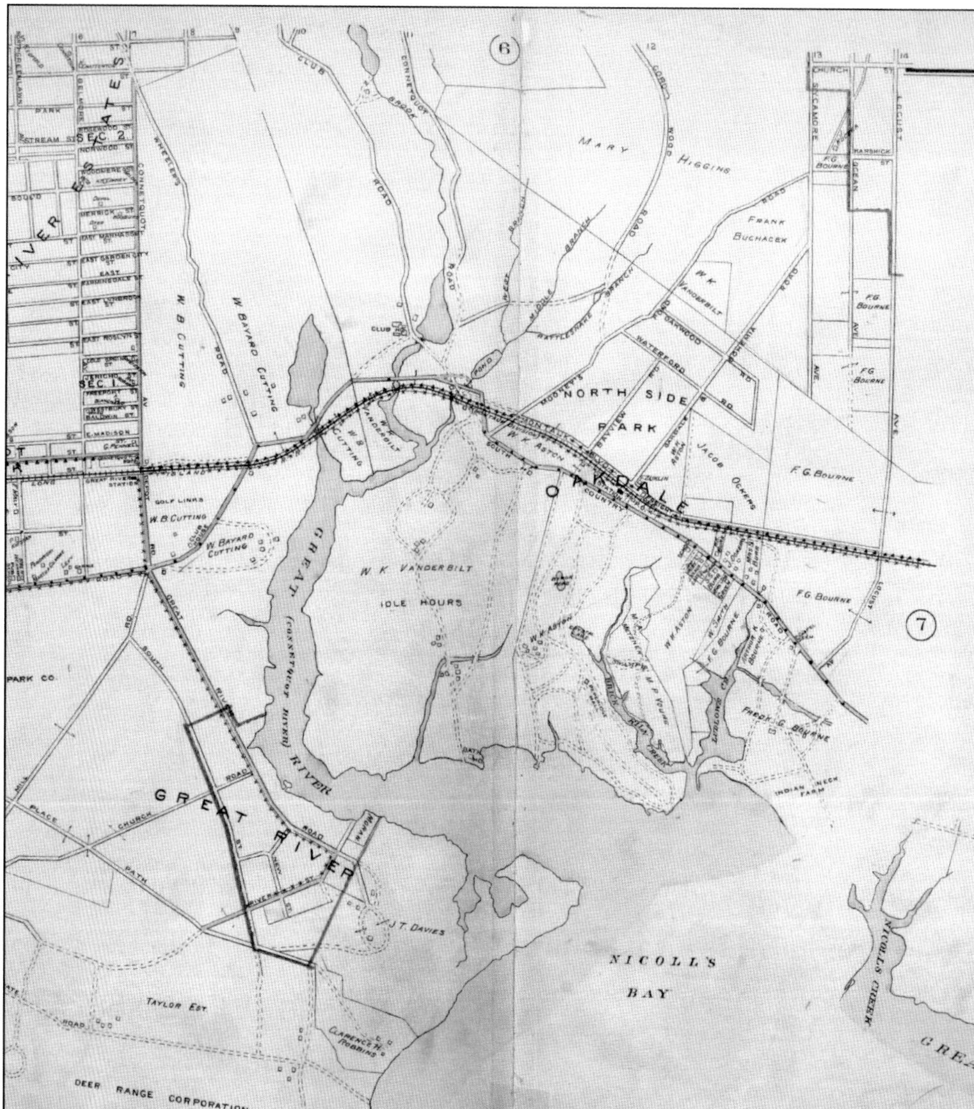

The names that dominate this map of Oakdale from the 1915 Belcher Hyde Atlas are the names of the men and institutions that dominated the previous 50 years of the village's development. To the northwest are the lands of the South Side Sportsmen's Club, the magnet that first attracted many wealthy New Yorkers. William Bayard Cutting's Westbrook sat across the river from William K. Vanderbilt's Idle Hour, both millionaire farmers' estates, where cows and sheep shared space with yachts and private golf courses. Frederick Bourne's farm and Indian Neck Hall straddled Montauk Highway and stretched east into West Sayville. Sandwiched between Bourne and Vanderbilt, the former estate of Christopher Robert was renamed Pepperidge Hall and developed by W. K. Aston. Jacob Ockers maintained a home on the north side of Montauk even though his lucrative oystering business relocated to the east. (Courtesy of the Milstein Division of U.S. History, Local History, and Genealogy, the New York Public Library, Astor, Lenox, and Tilden Foundations.)

On the Cover: Frederick Bourne and his extended family posed on the lawn of his Indian Neck Hall estate around 1913. (Courtesy of the Long Island Maritime Museum.)

IMAGES
of America

OAKDALE

Diane Holliday and Chris Kretz

ARCADIA
PUBLISHING

ISBN 978-0-7385-7239-0

Published by Arcadia Publishing
Charleston, South Carolina

Printed in the United States of America

Library of Congress Control Number: 2009933574

For all general information contact Arcadia Publishing at:
Telephone 843-853-2070
Fax 843-853-0044
E-mail sales@arcadiapublishing.com
For customer service and orders:
Toll-Free 1-888-313-2665

Visit us on the Internet at www.arcadiapublishing.com

In memory of Lavern Wittlock, avid collector of Long Island South Shore history, and to all who have collected and preserved Oakdale's story.

Contents

ACKNOWLEDGMENTS

There are really three authors of this book so thanks must first go to our colleague, Suzanne Garrison Terry, for helping see this through. Also special thanks to Gilbert Bergen, park manager at Connetquot River State Park Preserve; Joy Kaminsky, director at Bayard Cutting Arboretum; Amy Surak of the Manhattan College Archives; Arlene Balcewicz, registrar of the Long Island Maritime Museum; Barbara Forde, librarian of the Long Island Maritime Museum; Fran Monaco of the Long Island Diocese of the Episcopal Church; Ray Dimaria, local resident; fellow history seeker Sally Kachel; and the many who went before us in researching and reporting on the fascinating history of Oakdale. This area has not only accrued quite a fascinating history, it has inspired a great number of local historians and writers to delve into its past. We also want to thank Kristen Nyitray of the Stony Brook University Special Collections for early advice and our editor Rebekah Collinsworth for patience and dedication.

Unless otherwise noted, all images appear courtesy of the Dowling College Library Archives and Special Collections.

We have included a bibliography to list the major sources we consulted in compiling this book. In addition, we should note past issues of the *Long Island Forum* as a valuable asset as well as the online availability of contemporary newspapers such as the *Suffolk County News* and the *Brooklyn Daily Eagle* made possible through digitization efforts by the Suffolk County Libraries and the Brooklyn Public Library, respectively.

Introduction

"Along the shore of Great South Bay, on Long Island, hidden in dense scrub oak, is a colony of exiles." So begins Alexander Kidd's article "Country Homes on the Connecquot River" published in *Outing: An Illustrated Monthly Magazine of Recreation* in April 1901. The colonists in question were millionaires seeking a retreat from the hectic demands of life in New York City, and the verdant fastness they had discovered was called Oakdale.

Oakdale is located in the town of Islip, some 60 miles east of New York City. As Kidd goes on to relate, the forest was not all that dense, as much of the original timber on the island had long since been chopped down and sold for cordwood. For much of its early history, however, the area was fairly remote and sparsely settled. The modern origins of Oakdale date to the late 1600s with William Nicoll, an Englishman well-connected in the new British colony. He began acquiring land in the vicinity, first from the local Secatogue Indians in 1683 and later through grants from the government. The Nicoll Patent, as it was finally configured, contained much (but not all) of the town of Islip, including the area along the bay that became known as Oakdale.

It is hard to say when exactly the name Oakdale was first applied (around 1870), but the honor is usually given to William H. Ludlow, a Civil War veteran and New York state assemblyman. He married into the Nicoll family in 1846 and subsequently inherited the remaining Nicolls lands east of the Connetquot River. Early maps show a strong diffusion of forest, primarily the above-mentioned scrub oak, so it is not hard to see how the name arose.

Even before Oakdale had a name, however, New Yorkers were finding their way to it along South Country Road (the current Montauk Highway, one of the three main thoroughfares the English laid out to traverse the island from east to west). What these early travelers were seeking was not so different from Kidd's colonists. They wanted to get out of the city and enjoy the pleasures of nature. More specifically, they wanted to hunt and fish. Despite the South Country Road, the area in the early 1800s before the coming of the Long Island Rail Road was sparsely settled and overgrown. Numerous small streams ran south to the bay, forming marshes and inlets that made travel difficult. Making it to Oakdale was an exercise that involved many changes of horse and the hazarding of mud, swamps, and thickets. Another periodical account, this one from the *New York Mirror* dated November 15, 1837, recounts what awaited the intrepid traveler when he did make it to Oakdale: "The Connetquut [*sic*] Hotel is a good old-fashioned Dutch inn, of a corpulent form, with an open space around it partly covered with turf. An immense elm stands on the west side, which is a marked object, famous for having had more fat bucks tied up to it than any other tree in the country." This hotel, established in 1820, was run by Eliphalet "Liff" Snedecor and his hospitality, as well as the quality of the hunting and fishing in the surrounding forests, made a name for the area among the cognoscenti. It was such wealthy outdoorsmen from New York, appreciative of the relative uniqueness of an unspoiled preserve within a day's journey from the city, who would purchase Snedecor's establishment and its environs, forming the South Side Sportsmen's Club in 1866.

The sportsmen's club serves as the well spring for much of the next 50 years of Oakdale's history. Even though the South Side Railroad finally reached Oakdale in 1869, it was the sportsmen's club that attracted the men who would build the great estates for which the village became known. It was the Gilded Age, so-named by Mark Twain to denote an era when great fortunes were made and spent on ostentation and extravagant exteriors. New families of wealth came to prominence in New York City, with fortunes derived not from inheritance but built from transportation, trade, and industrialization. This new class of aristocracy found many ways to spend their money but perhaps the most enduring was the creation of ever larger and more lavish estates.

And so, in quick succession, Kidd's colony of millionaires filled in along the south shore of Oakdale. William Bayard Cutting built his Westbrook estate on the west bank of the Connetquot in 1886. Although this places him in what is now known as Great River, Cutting and Westbrook are inextricably linked to the history of Oakdale and the neighboring estates. Christopher Robert occupied the land on which he would build his Pepperidge Hall as early as 1882. Establishing himself between the two was William K. Vanderbilt, who built his first mansion in Oakdale in 1882. The last major landholder would be Frederick Bourne, who began acquiring land in the area in earnest around 1889.

Although among the four of them these men held much of the land in Oakdale, their story is not the only history. Much was happening long before they arrived. William Nicoll had a water mill in operation in the 1750s, near where Liff Snedecor's hotel would take root. In 1765, Nicoll also built Charlotte Church. Although rebuilt in 1784 and again in 1843, the renamed St. John's Episcopal Church is one of the oldest in the county. Early census records show that the houses, which lined the main street, were occupied by sea captains, free blacks, and beginning with the Hage family in 1849, the first Dutch immigrants to the area. The Dutch were vital to the development of the oyster industry on the Great South Bay. In fact, the one hill overlooking Main Street, the highest point in an otherwise flat landscape, was topped by the home of Jacob Ockers, a Dutchman who grew his world-famous Blue Oysters Company in the shadow of the great estates.

This book takes the history of Oakdale into the 1940s. At that time, the age of the great estates had well passed, most of the wealthy families had moved on, and the houses they left behind met varying fates. We leave off with Pepperidge Hall destroyed. The Idle Hour mansion is tenantless, but the lands of the Idle Hour estate serve as home to a thriving residential community. The Westbrook estate remains in the Cutting family while Indian Neck Hall is now in the hands of the Christian brothers as the home of their La Salle military academy. The millionaire's colony is on its way to becoming a community. The post–World War II development boom will see New Yorkers once again discovering Oakdale but this time with families of the middle class departing the city to leave their mark on the south shore.

One

THE SPORTING MEN

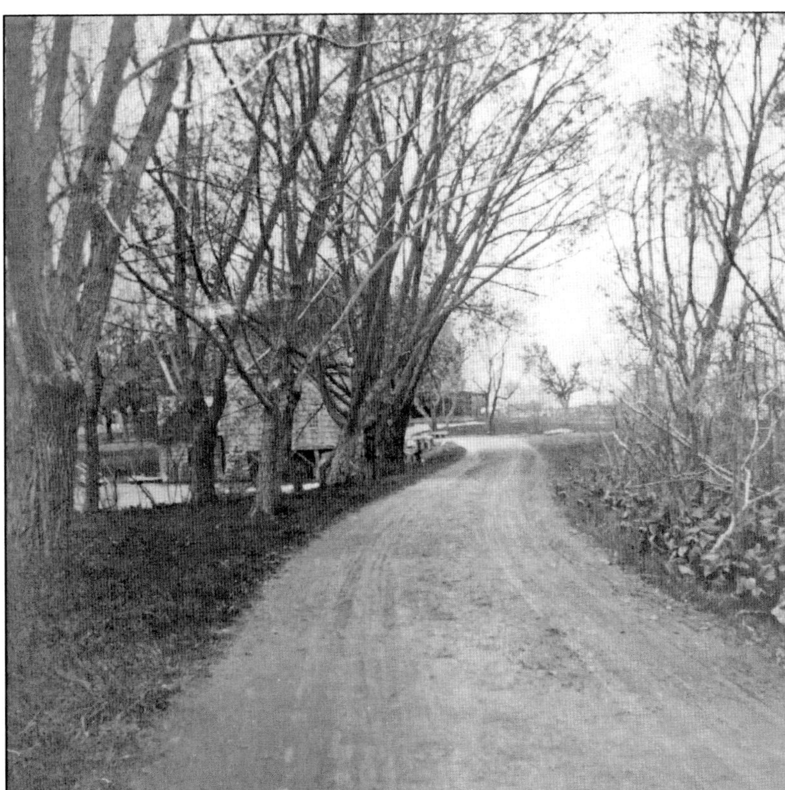

This is how Montauk Highway appeared in 1902. It is shown here running between the mill, seen on the left, and the South Side Sportsmen's Club, which is just out of the picture on the right-hand side. The highway, originally known as the South Country Road, was the main thoroughfare for travel along the south shore of Long Island.

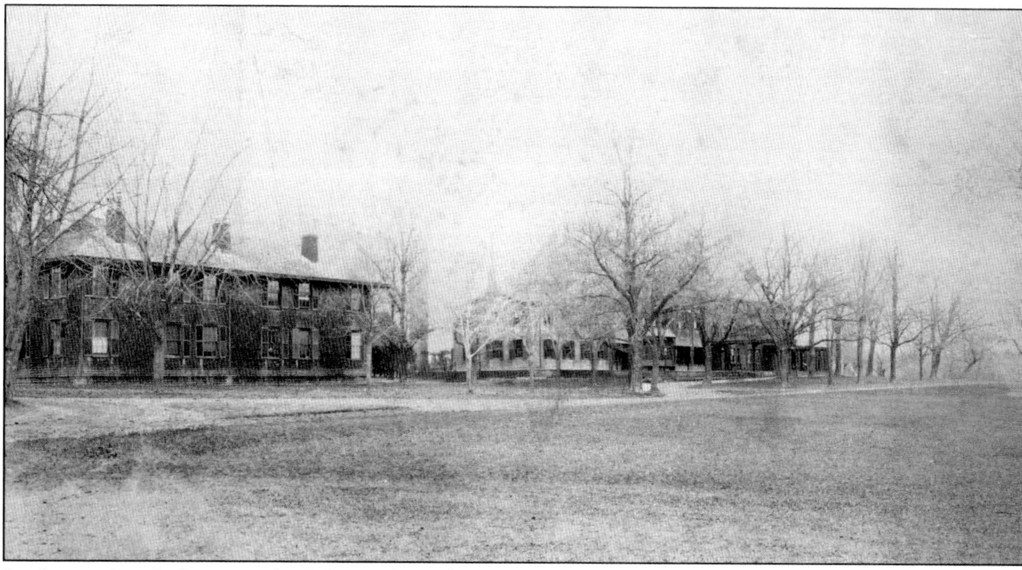

In this undated photography, Montauk Highway is the road running in front of the main clubhouse of the South Side Sportsmen's Club on the right and the old annex on the left. The architect of the old annex is not known. It was built in 1878 to accommodate the growing club.

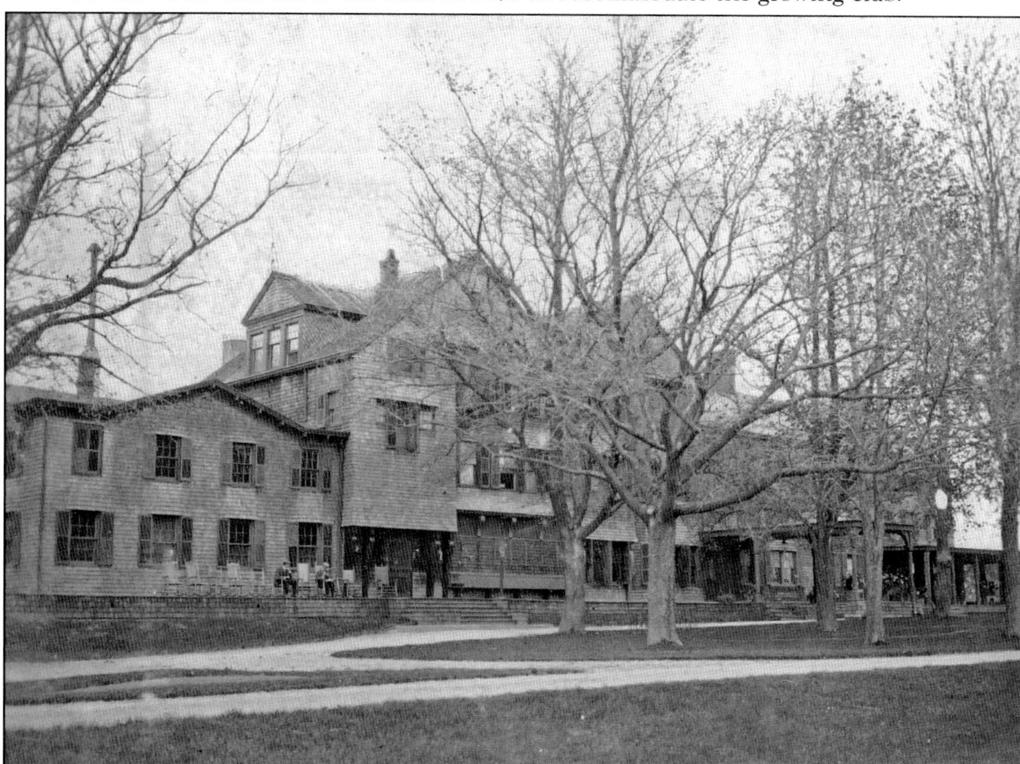

This is an April 1903 view of the sprawling main clubhouse of the South Side Sportsmen's Club. The four-story middle section was designed by the New York architect Bradford Gilbert in 1888. The two-story structure to the left of the 1888 addition contains the billiards room and was part of an earlier edition that was moved over to make room for the 1888 addition.

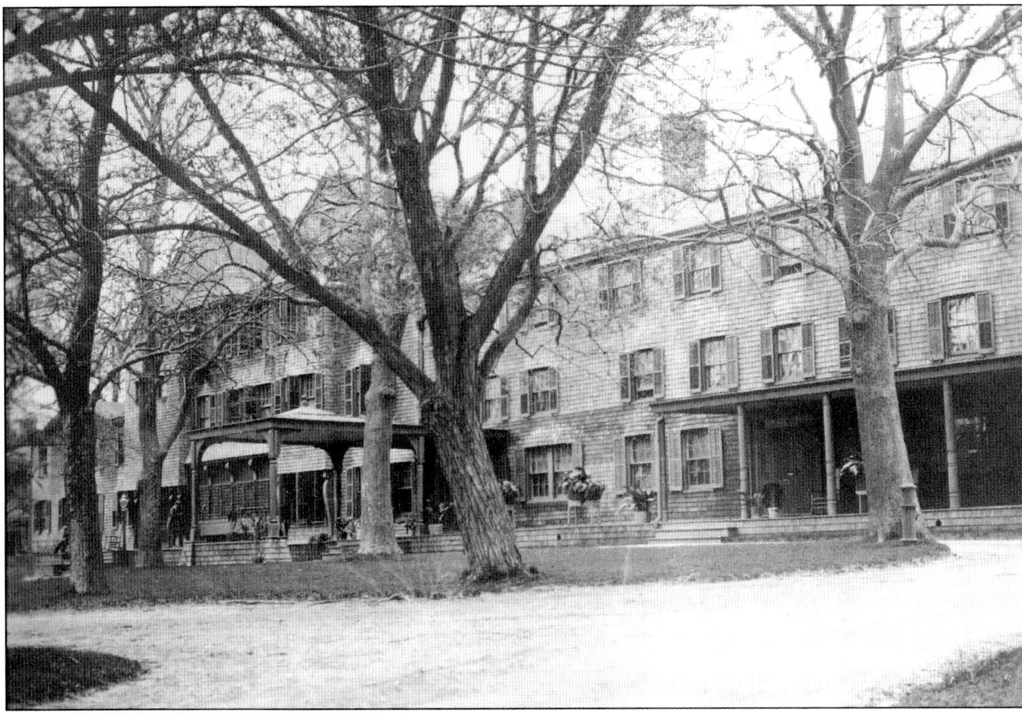

The main clubhouse of the South Side Sportsmen's Club was originally known as Snedecor's Tavern. Originally built in 1820 as a small house, the clubhouse was expanded several times to accommodate its members. This sprawling building is how it appeared in 1904.

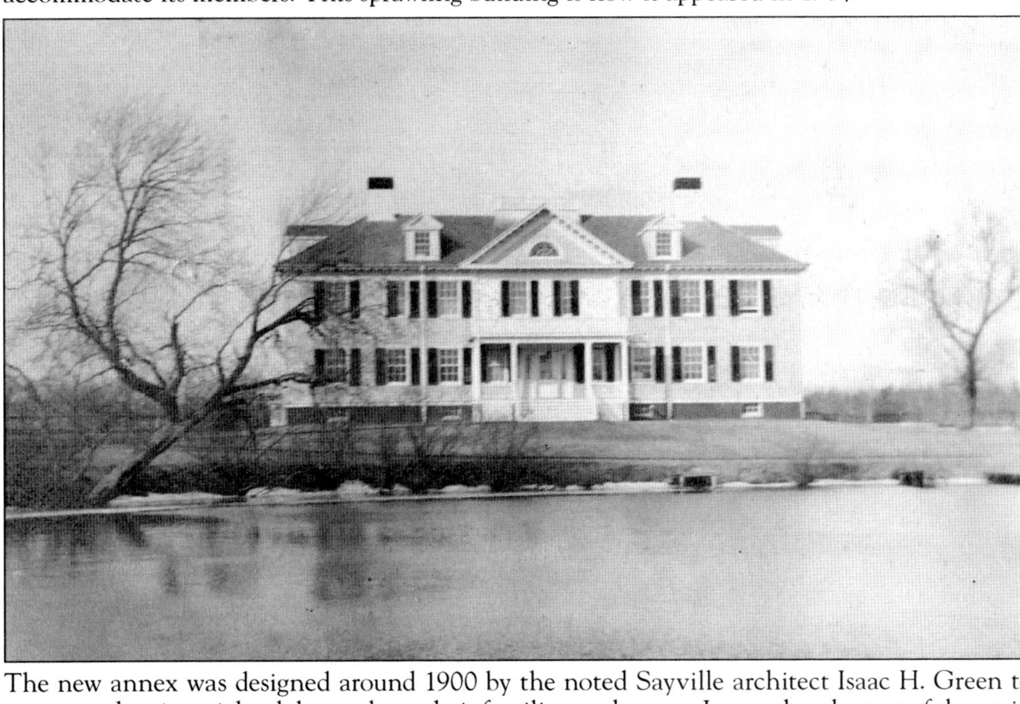

The new annex was designed around 1900 by the noted Sayville architect Isaac H. Green to accommodate just eight club members, their families, and guests. Located to the east of the main clubhouse, this is how the building appeared in 1904.

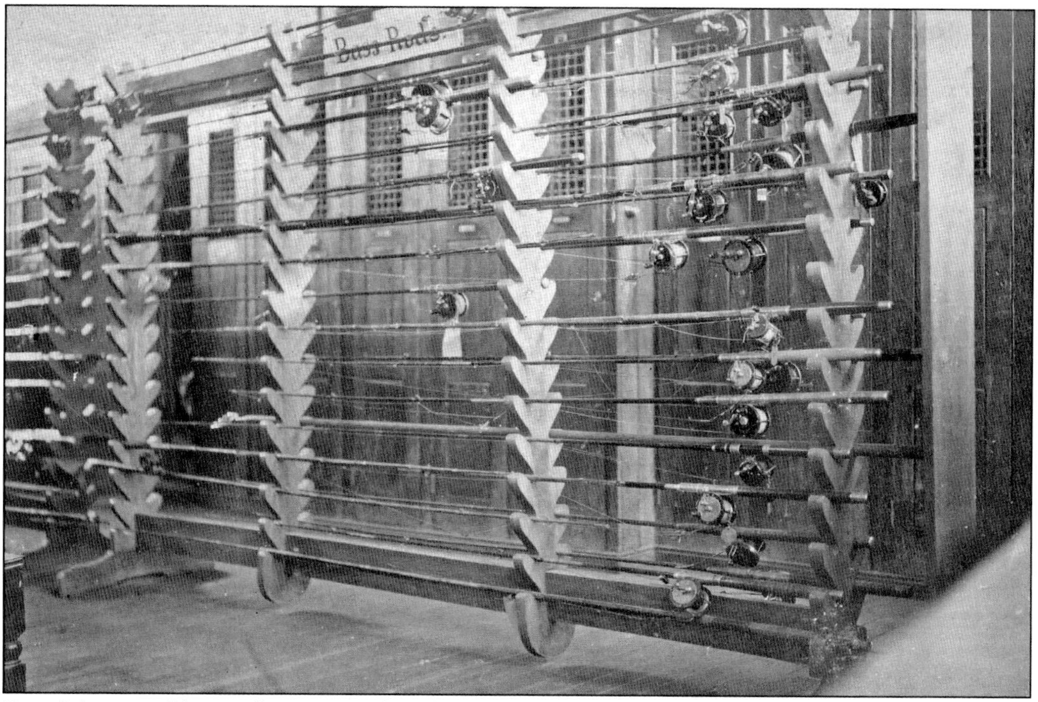

Bass fishing tackle are shown stored on large wooden racks inside the locker room at the South Side Sportsman's Club. Each member had his own locker, as seen in the background of this February 1902 photograph. The lockers, still extant, measure approximately 80 inches high by 18 inches wide by 28 inches deep and are made of a hard and well-seasoned wood. The locker room furnishings date to around 1886.

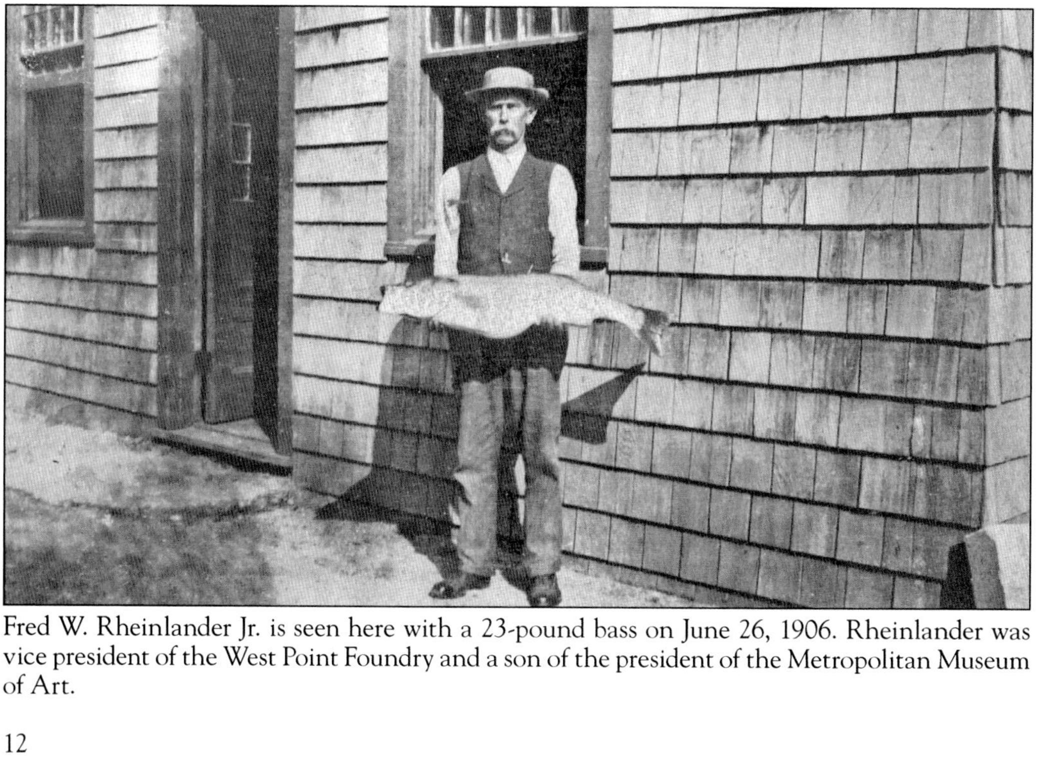

Fred W. Rheinlander Jr. is seen here with a 23-pound bass on June 26, 1906. Rheinlander was vice president of the West Point Foundry and a son of the president of the Metropolitan Museum of Art.

Fishing at the South Side Sportsmen's Club is Fred W. Rheinlander Jr., and Edgar, a club guide, around 1902. Fishing was accomplished in ponds, brooks, and streams that line the 3,473-acre club property. A bass hole was maintained for club members in the Connetquot River, near William K. Vanderbilt's Idle Hour estate.

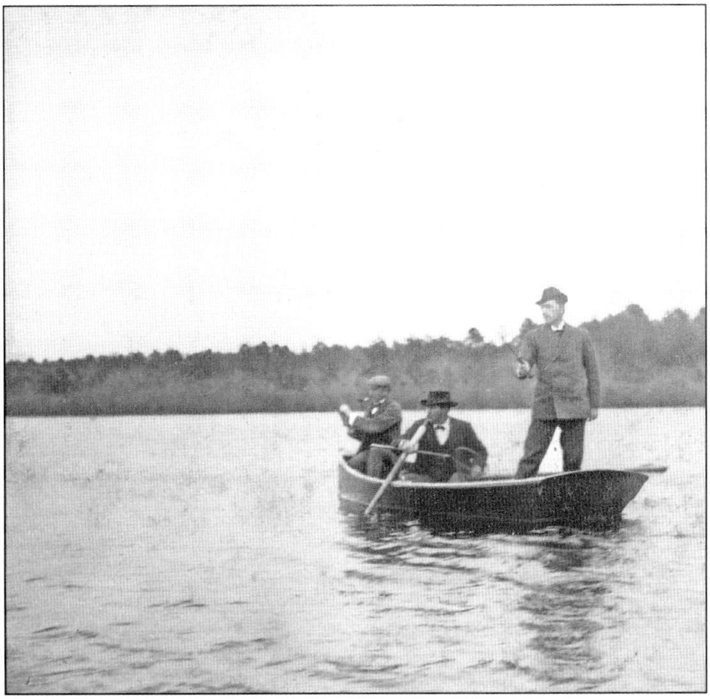

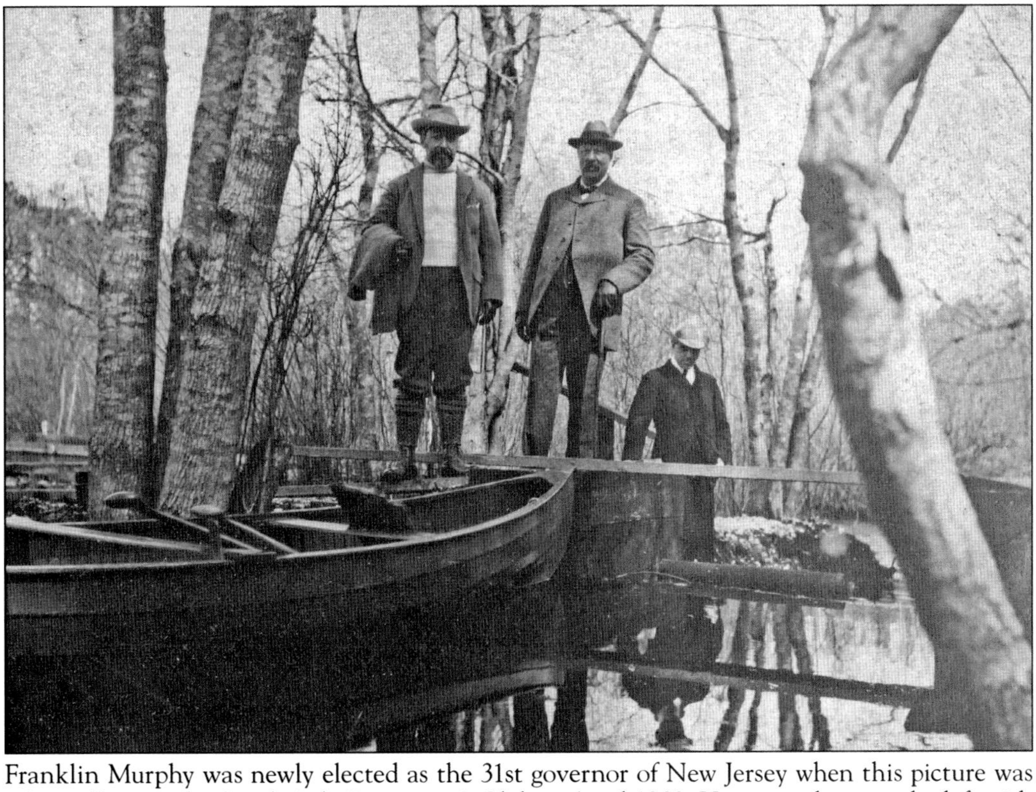

Franklin Murphy was newly elected as the 31st governor of New Jersey when this picture was taken of him at the South Side Sportsmen's Club in April 1902. He is seen here on the left with the club president, George P. Slade, center, and Frank Murphy Jr., his son on the right.

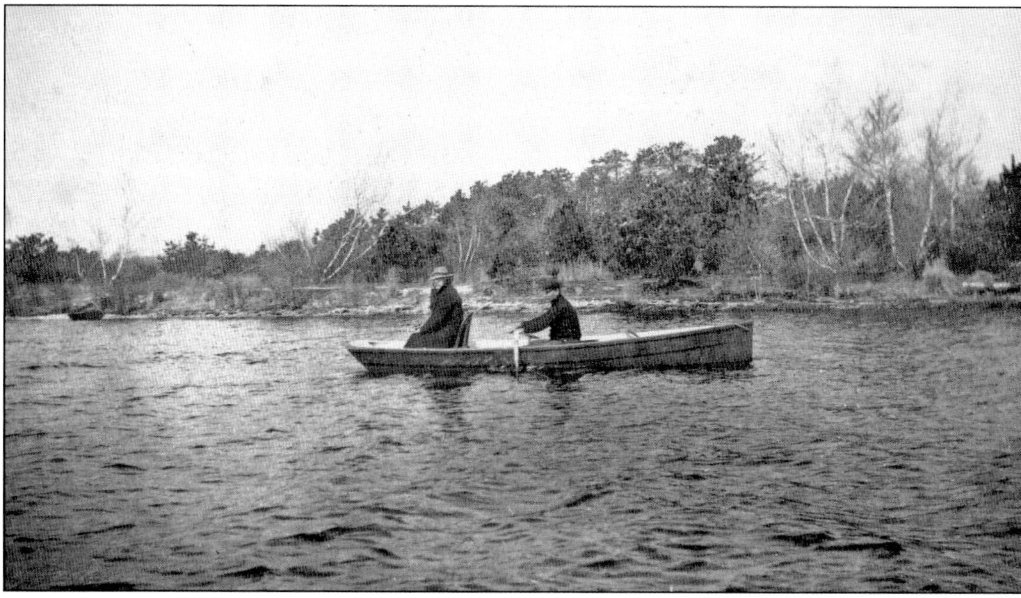

Brig. Gen. Louis Fitzgerald (left) was commander of the 7th Regiment of New York's National Guard. Col. Auguste P. Montant served with General Fitzgerald and is seen here rowing on the Connetquot River. This photograph was taken in spring 1902.

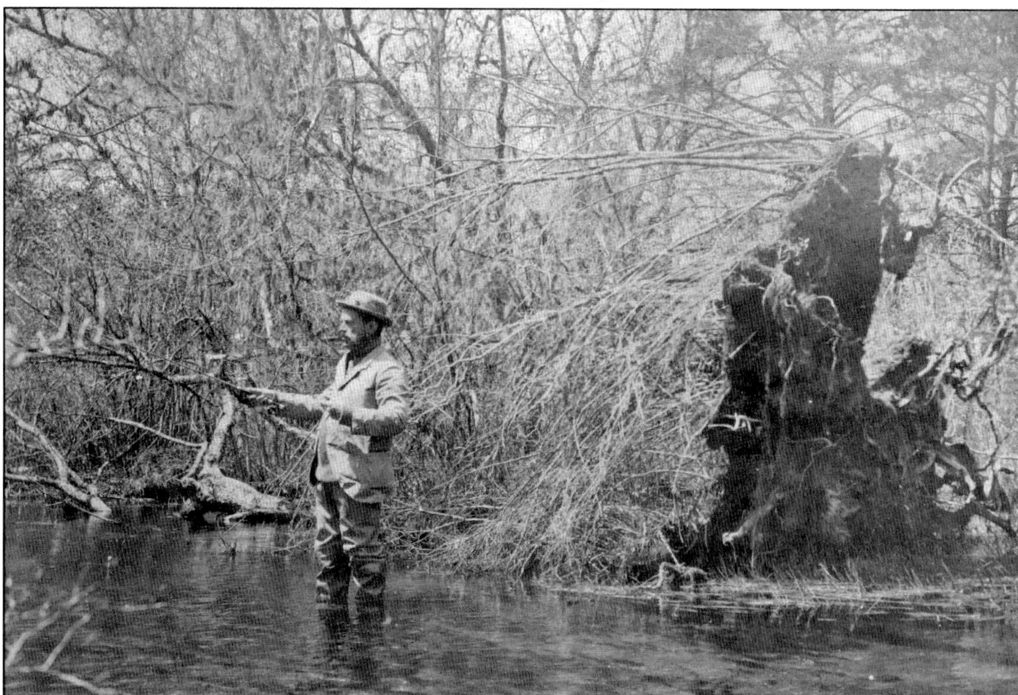

Charles R. Flint was a major industrialist who is best known for merging four companies to form the Computing-Tabulating-Recording (CTR) Company in 1911. In 1924, this company became known as the International Business Machines (IBM) Company. Charles R. Flint was an avid sportsman and is seen here fishing in the upper brook of the South Side Sportsmen's Club in May 1902.

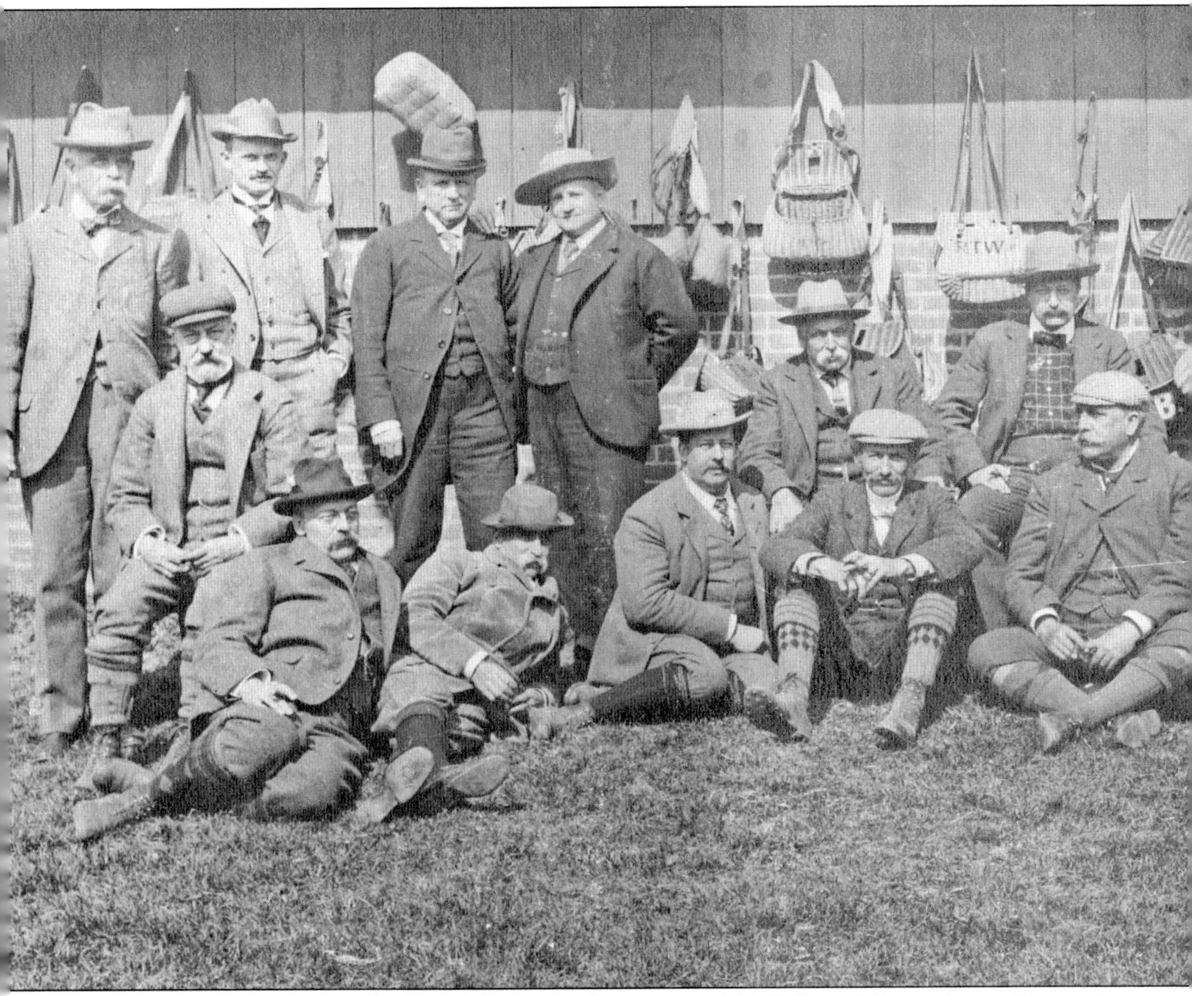

This club portrait was taken before a fishing expedition around 1902. From left to right are (first row) H. H. Hollister (banker and NYSE member), Frank L. Hall (attorney), John W. Cochrane (trustee of Bowery Savings Bank), Albert de Goicouria (member of NYSE), William E. Strong (either the Civil War general or his son), and George G. DeWitt; (second row) A. Pennington Whitehead, Fred E. Ballard, James H. Dunham, Montefiore Isaacs, H. R. Clarke, and William Robison.

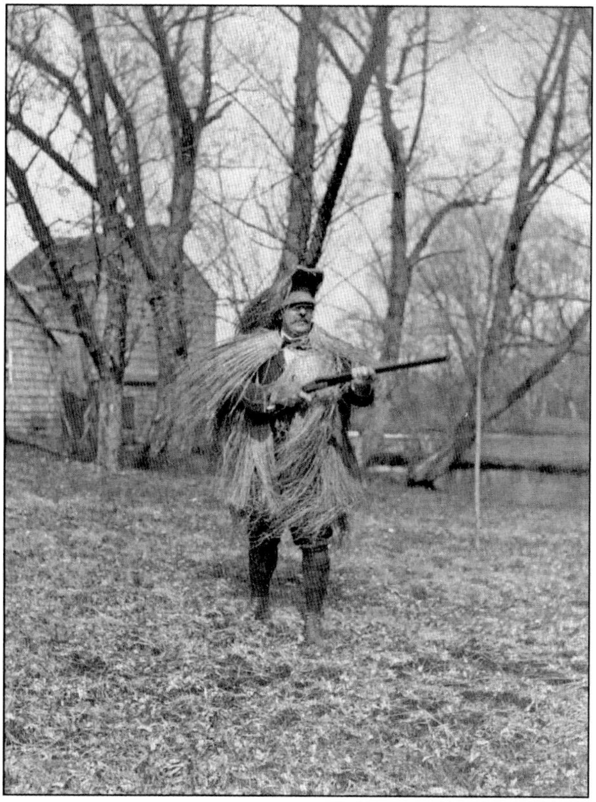

Albert de Goicouria, a member of the New York Stock Exchange, is dressed in camouflage for shooting water fowl in this 1902 photograph. Ducks, geese, swans, egrets, and osprey were all hunted on the club grounds. The old mill is clearly visible in the background.

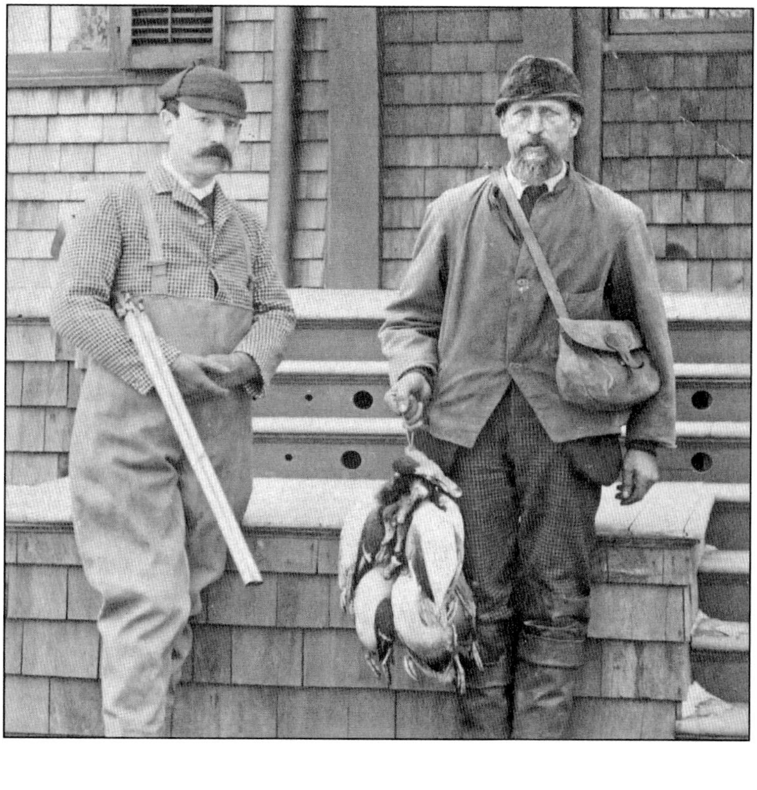

South Side Sportsmen's Club member Lucius K. Wilmerding (left) and South Side guide William Carr stand outside the main clubhouse on February 3, 1888. Carr is holding the day's kill of four broadbill and one black duck. The wildlife was plentiful in 1888, and it was not unusual to bag several birds or animals after one day's hunting.

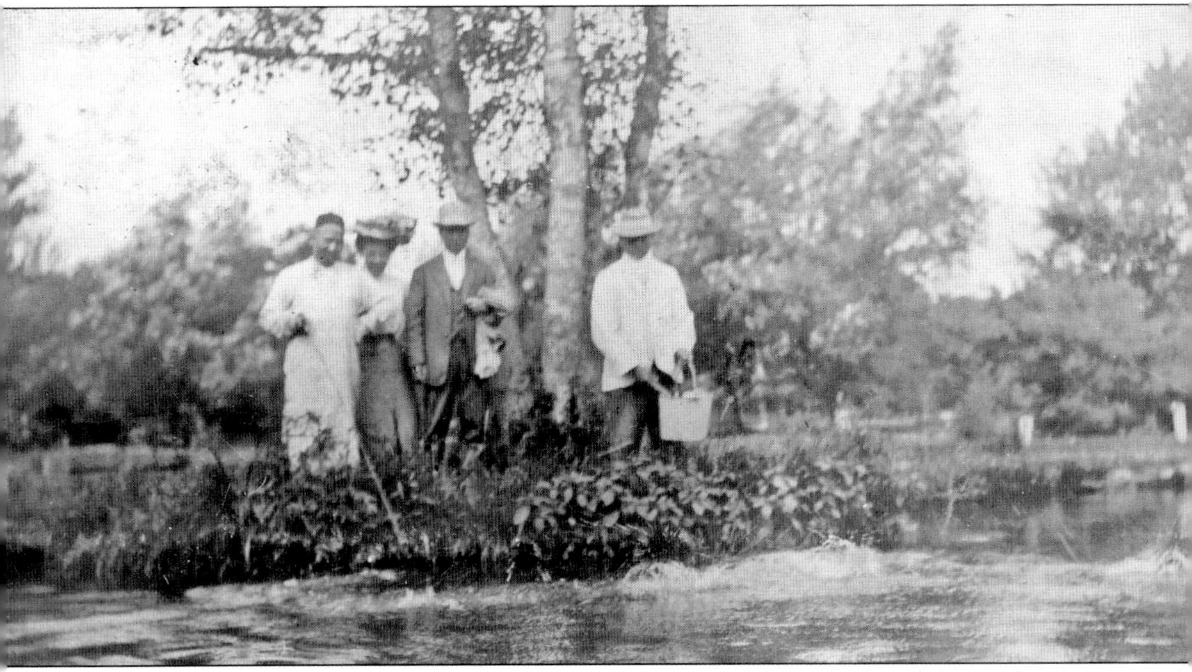

This 1906 photograph taken at the South Side Sportsmen's Club shows, from left to right, Kang Yu Wei and his party: possibly his daughter, Kang Tongbi, and her husband, Luo Chang, and an unidentified man. Kang Yu Wei was an advisor to the Guangxu Emperor, a Chinese scholar, noted calligrapher, prominent political thinker, and reformer of the late Qing Dynasty. He led movements to establish a constitutional monarchy and was an ardent Chinese nationalist. His daughter was also a reformer and early feminist in China.

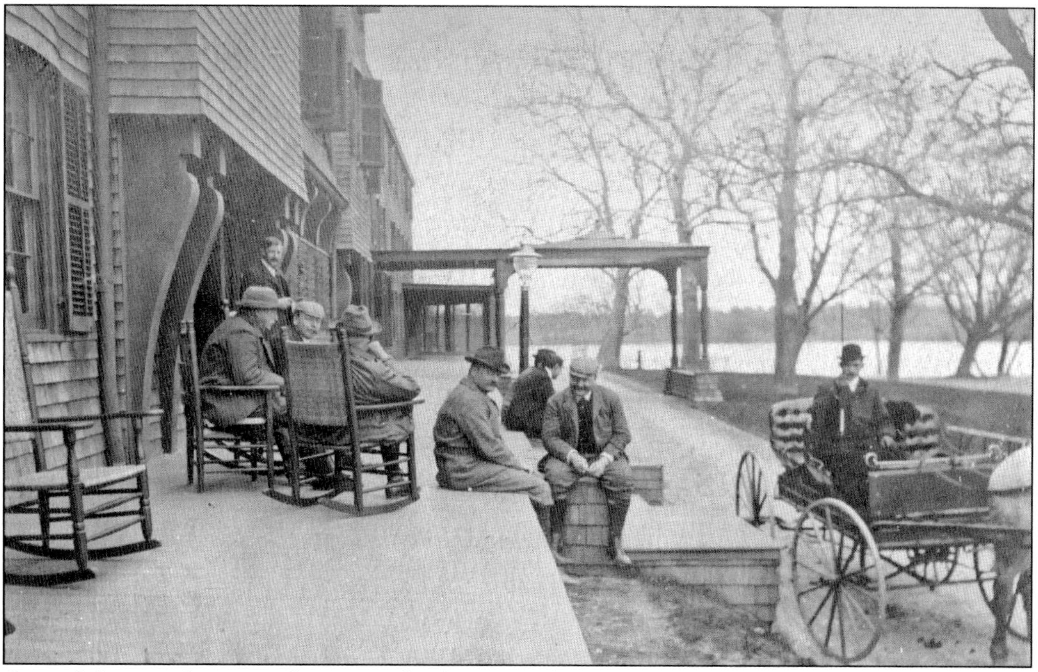

One of the members socializing on the front porch of the club in this 1902 picture is Francis O. DeLuze. He was the son of the Swiss consul, Louis Philip DeLuze, and a member of several outstanding social clubs of the day. He died suddenly in Southampton, New York, in July 1902, just a few months after this photograph was taken.

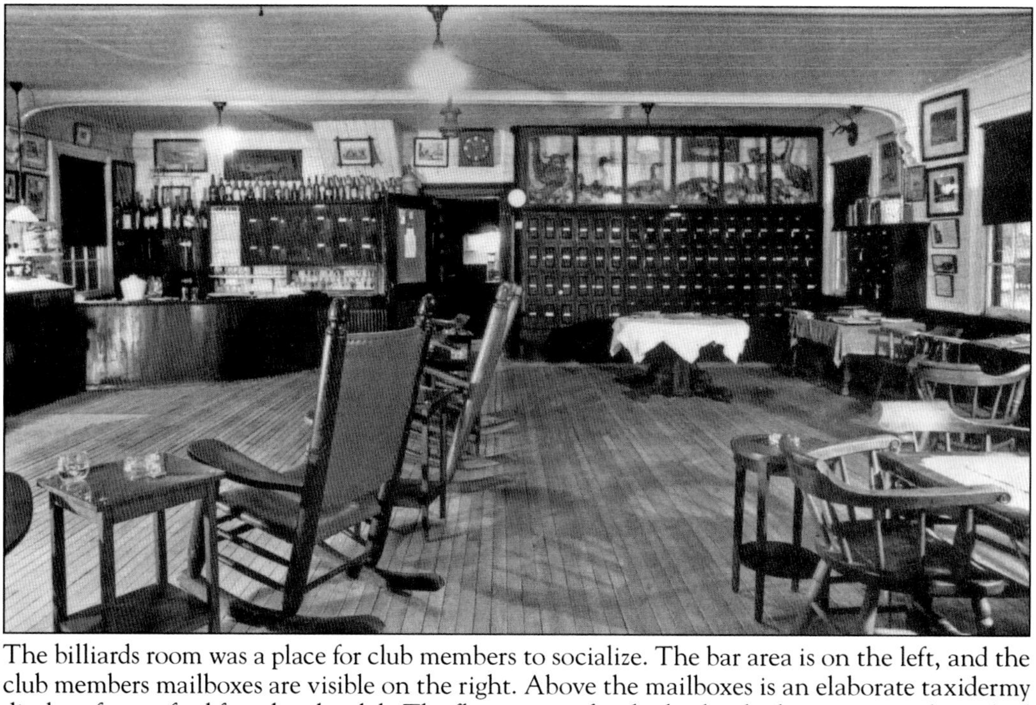

The billiards room was a place for club members to socialize. The bar area is on the left, and the club members mailboxes are visible on the right. Above the mailboxes is an elaborate taxidermy display of water fowl found at the club. The floors are unfinished oak, which were routinely washed down as members frequently came in for drinks wearing muddy boots from the day's activities.

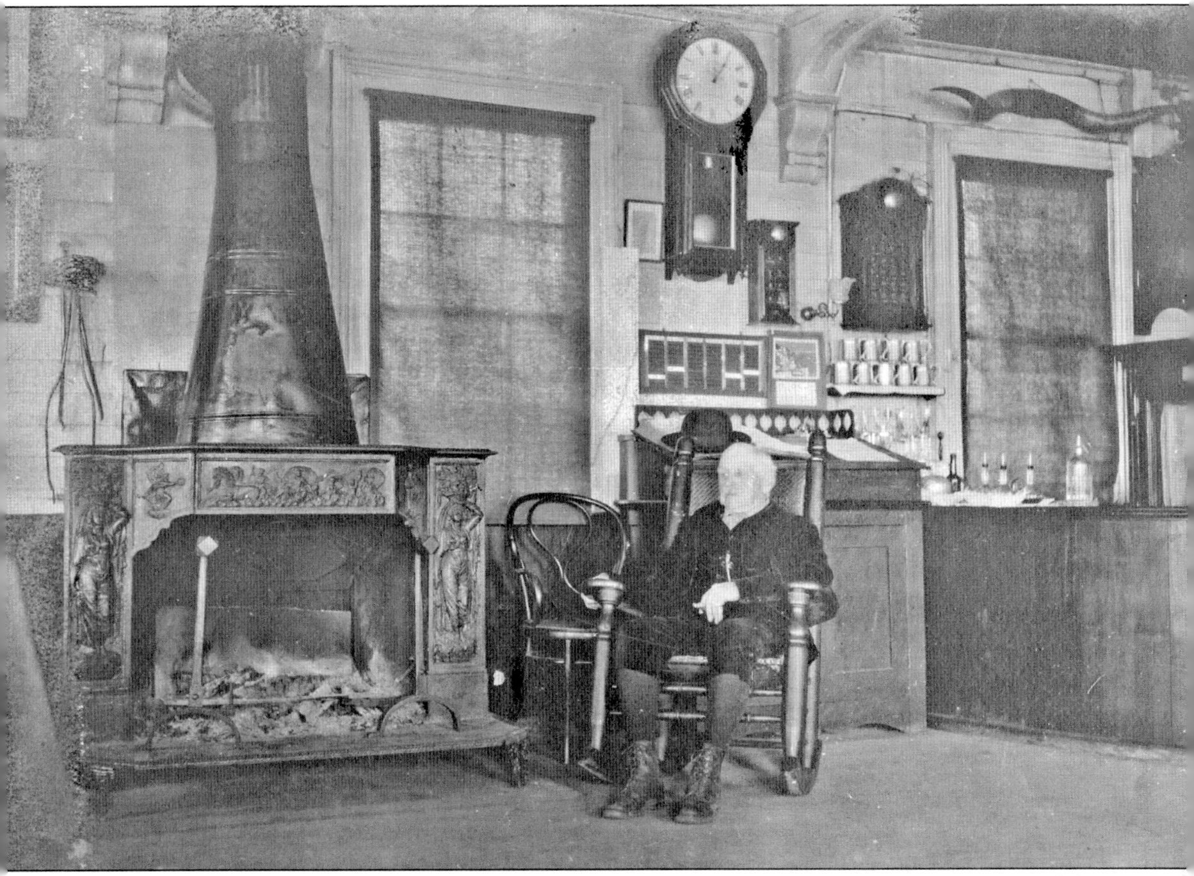

H. R. Clarke is seen here sitting by the Franklin stove inside the clubroom. Clarke wrote of this stove in 1904 as being donated to the South Side Sportsmen's Club by one of its members, Alex Stetson. Stetson owned the Astor House Hotel in New York City, where this stove was originally found in the sitting room. It was there in the sitting room, as Clarke recounts, that "many a time Daniel Webster and Henry Clay warmed their shins by its open fire before their favorite game of Boston." Boston whist is a card game.

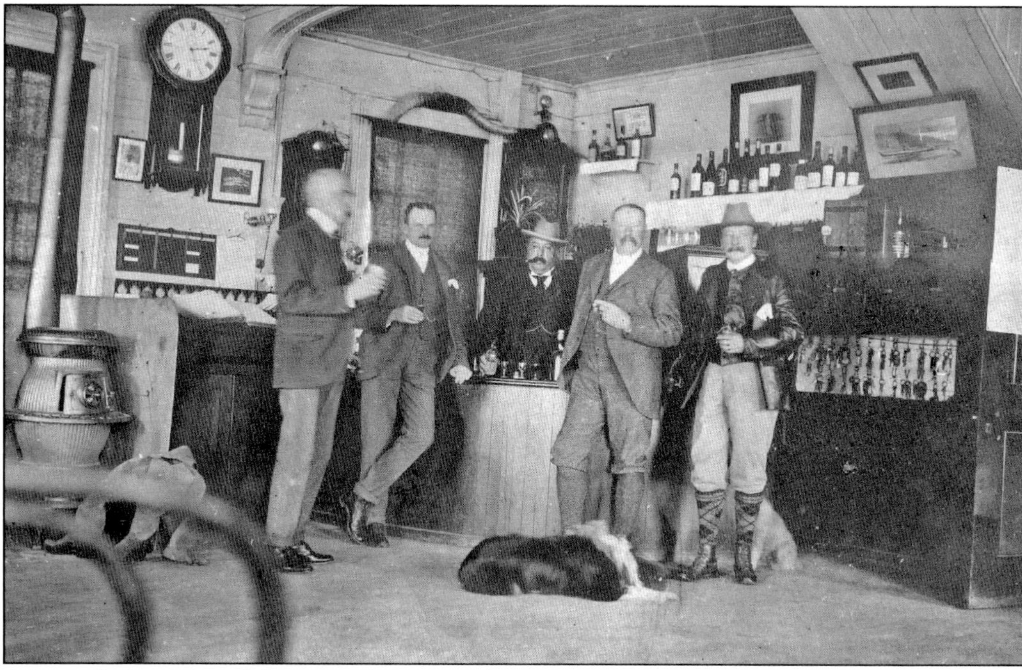

After a day's work at fishing and hunting, club members would socialize at the bar inside the clubhouse. Seen here on a February day in 1902 are, from left to right, A. Pennington Whitehead, Frederick E. Ballard (financier), Col. Auguste P. Montant, George P. Slade, and Philip H. Minis (financier/stockbroker)

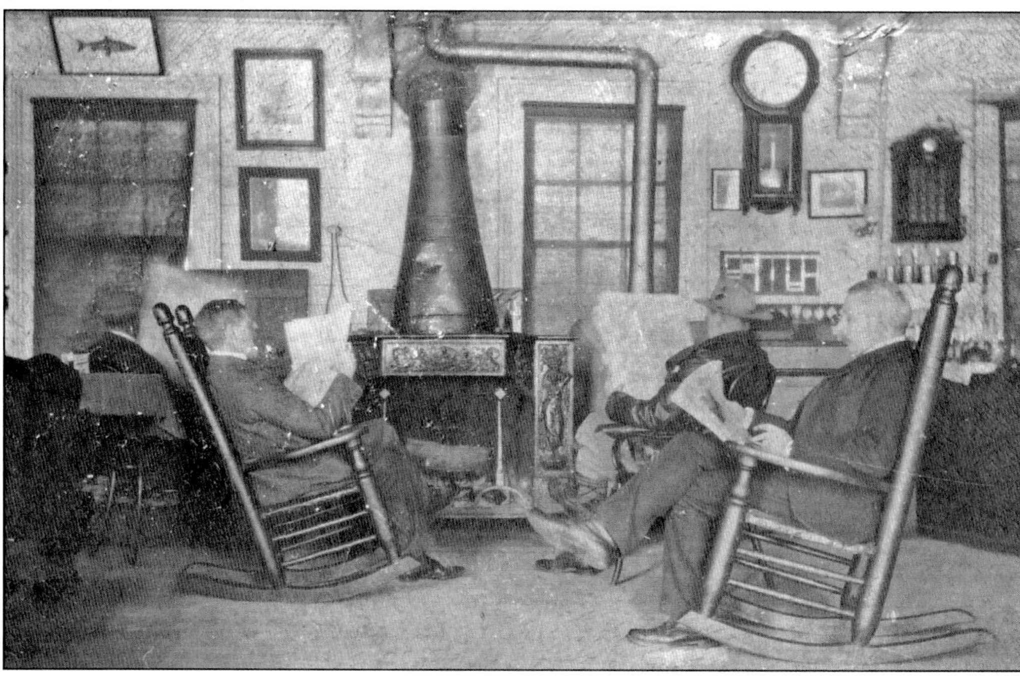

Three gentlemen are reading by the Franklin stove in this February 1902 photograph. From left to right are Bradish Johnson Jr., a member believed to be Edwin A. Johnson, and an unidentified man.

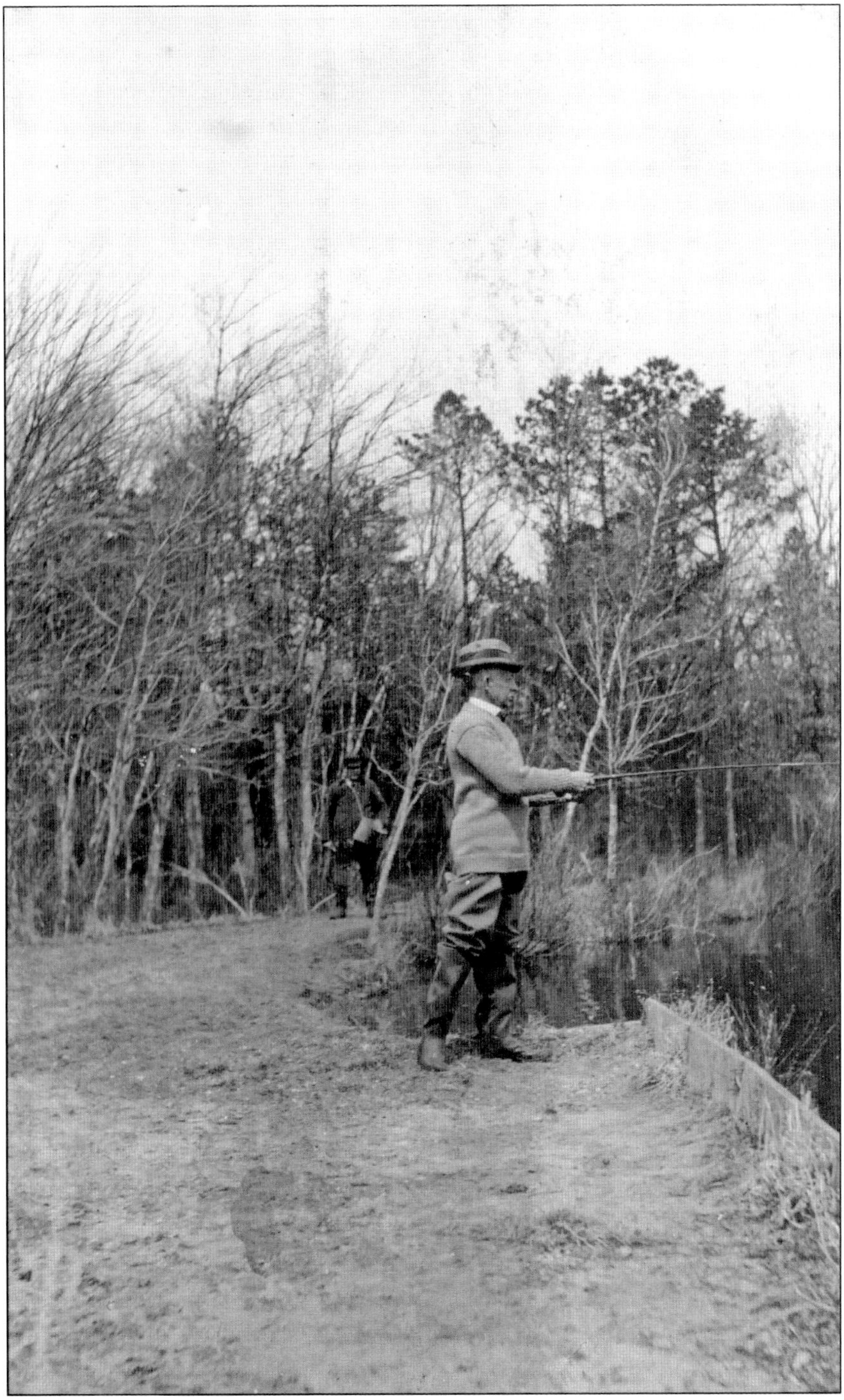

Capt. Willard H. Brownson is seen fishing at the club in this June 1904 photograph. A U.S. Navy officer, Brownson served in the Spanish-American War and was commander in chief of the Asiatic Fleet as well as superintendent of the Naval Academy. Promoted to rear admiral in 1905, Brownson resigned in 1907 following a very public disagreement with Pres. Theodore Roosevelt, who had given command of hospital ships to navy doctors.

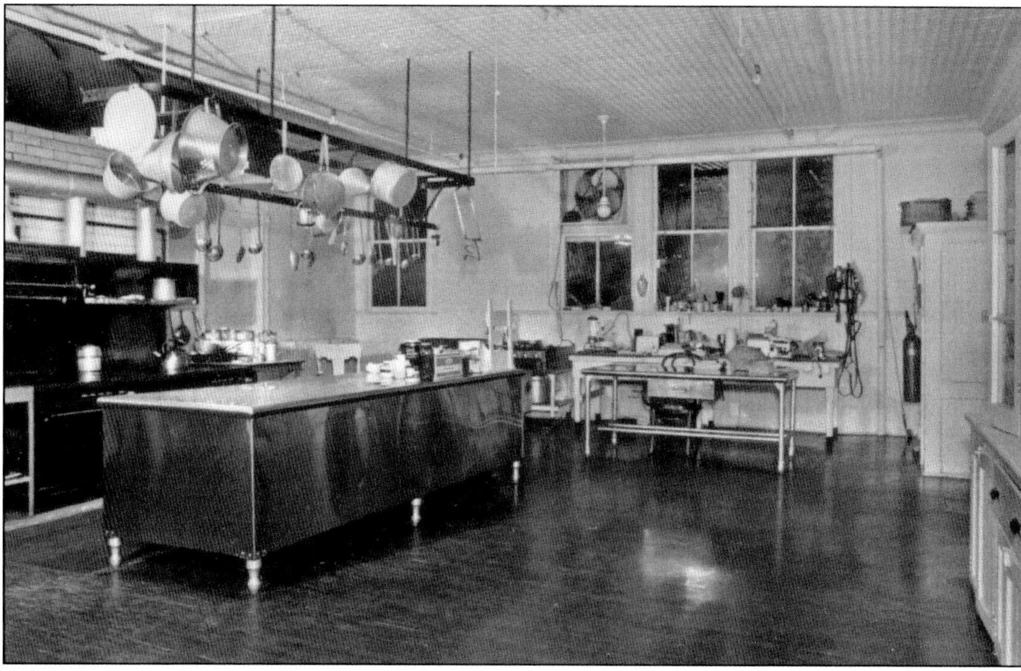

After hunting, the membership would feast on the day's catch. This is the kitchen where their meals were prepared. While it seems large in this undated picture, it was a crowded and busy place when accommodating large numbers of members and their guests.

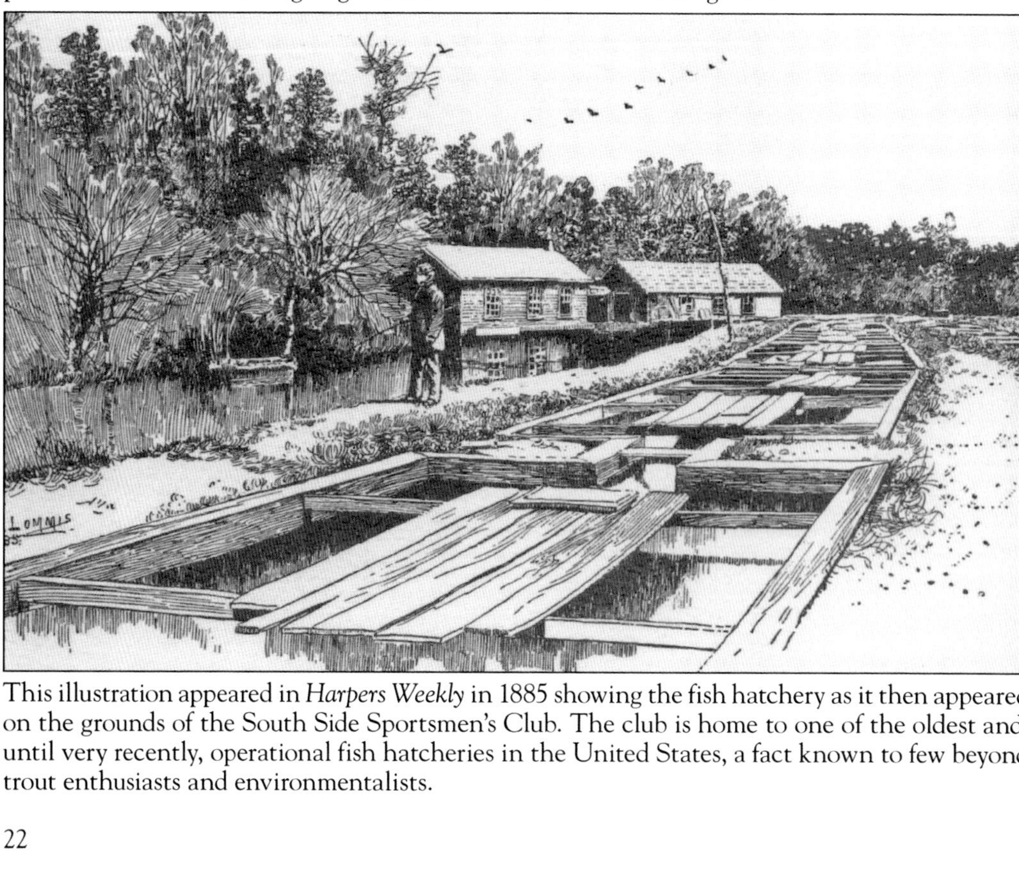

This illustration appeared in *Harpers Weekly* in 1885 showing the fish hatchery as it then appeared on the grounds of the South Side Sportsmen's Club. The club is home to one of the oldest and, until very recently, operational fish hatcheries in the United States, a fact known to few beyond trout enthusiasts and environmentalists.

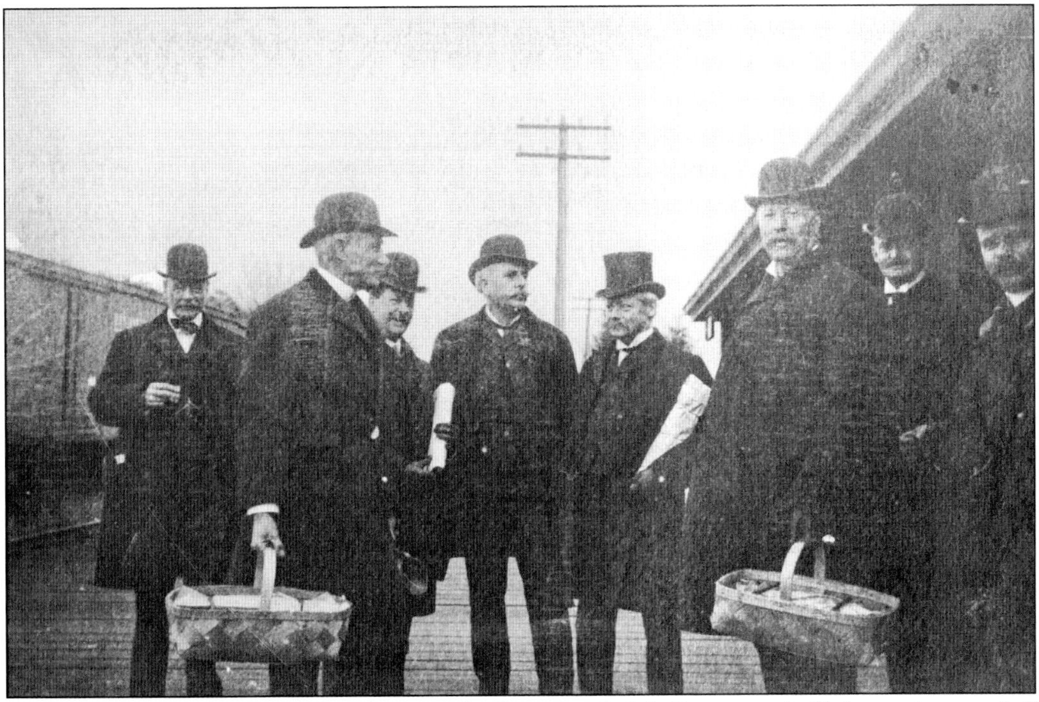

According to the caption on this photograph, these South Side Sportsmen's Club members are "off to market" in 1902. From left to right are Philip H. Minis, William E. Strong, Albert De Goicouria, George G. Dewitt, ? Wickham, ? Sherman, and an unidentified gentleman. At one point, club members did have the use of their own train station. Situated on the South Side Railroad, it was called Club Station. Although little more than a shack, it did eliminate the need to detrain at the Oakdale Station further to the east. Club Station was discontinued in the late 1800s.

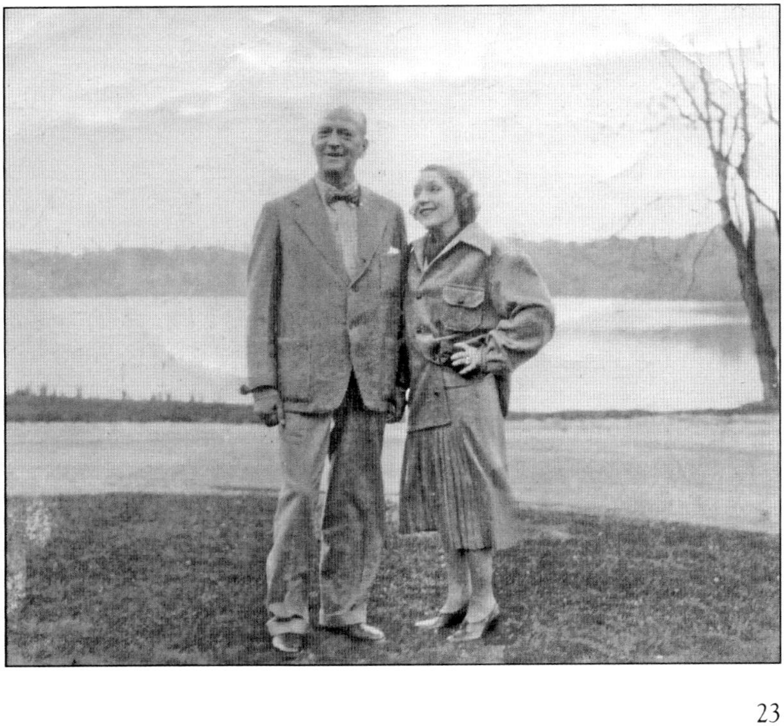

This photograph, taken around 1940, shows the actress Mary Pickford on the grounds of the South Side Sportsmen's Club posing with then president Guy Carey. Pickford, at one point, maintained a home in Centerport on Long Island.

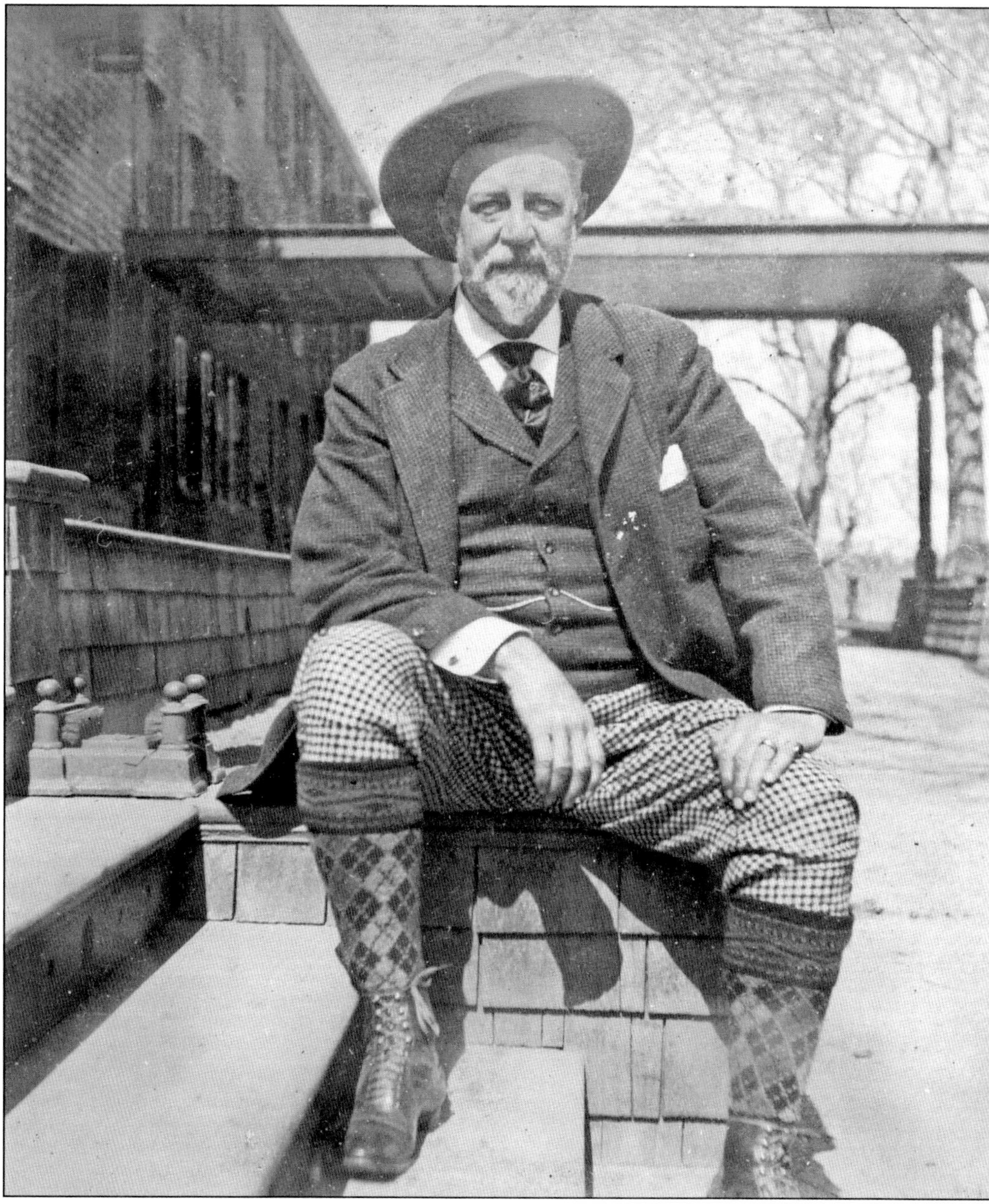

This undated photograph shows club member D. J. Warden sitting on the front porch of the South Side Sportsmen's Club. The club buildings and grounds still exist today in the Connetquot River State Park Preserve, formed in 1973 when New York State bought the property from the last members.

Two

Cutting's Westbrook Hall

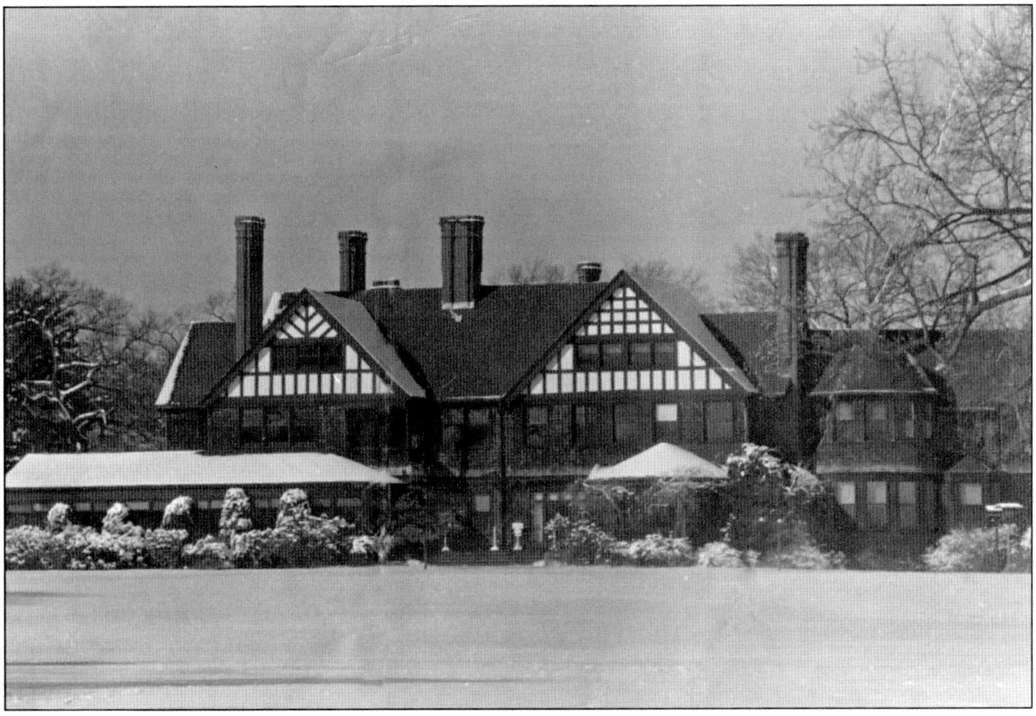

William Bayard Cutting built Westbrook in 1886. Architect Charles C. Haight designed a family home that is a mixture of Queen Anne, Tudor, and American-shingle styles. Not many photographs of Westbrook exist prior to the 1960s. To protect the Cutting family's privacy, most all of their papers and photographs were burned by their butler in the 1950s. (Courtesy of the Bayard Cutting Arboretum.)

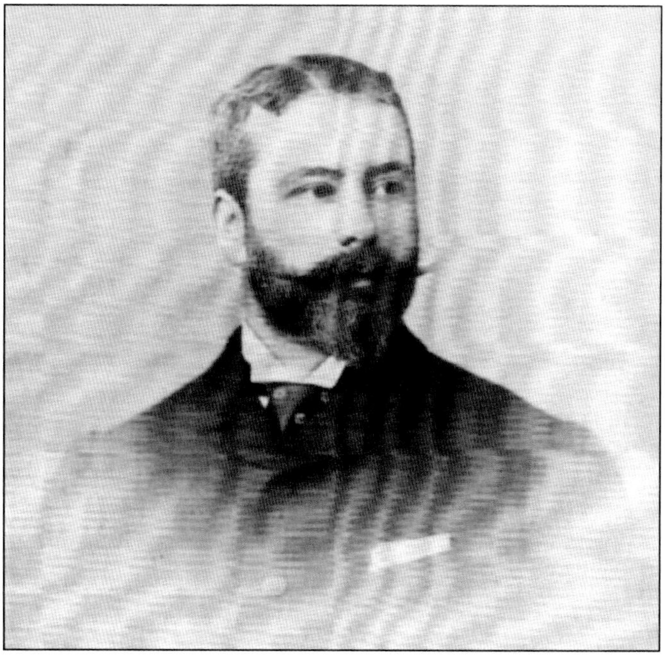

After graduating from Columbia Law School, William Bayard Cutting became president of a railroad company. Interested in land and waterfront development, Cutting developed South Brooklyn by convincing Congress to make improvements to the waterways around the port of New York. In 1886, Cutting employed the help of Frederick Law Olmsted and established a renowned arboretum on his estate in Oakdale. In 1896, he became a director of the New York Botanical Garden. (Courtesy of the Bayard Cutting Arboretum.)

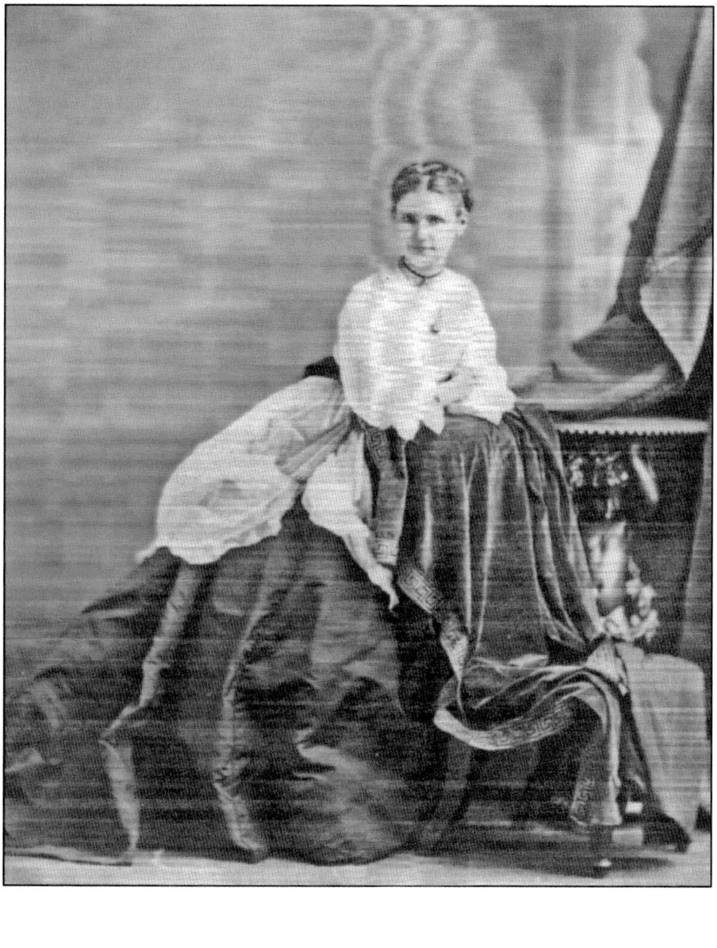

Olivia Murray had already met her future husband when this picture was taken of her in 1872. William Bayard Cutting had been courting her sister, and Olivia was underage at the time. After waiting seven years, they were married in 1877. After several lean years, the Cuttings established Westbrook in Oakdale and a house on Seventy-second Street in Manhattan. (Courtesy of the Bayard Cutting Arboretum.)

William Bayard Cutting Jr. was the eldest of the Cutting's four children. Born in 1878, he moved in to Westbrook at the age of eight and is seen here as a teenager. Later he attended Harvard University but dropped out to work for the American ambassador in London. Cutting Jr. suffered from tuberculosis and died in Egypt in 1910 when he was 31 years old. (Courtesy of the Bayard Cutting Arboretum.)

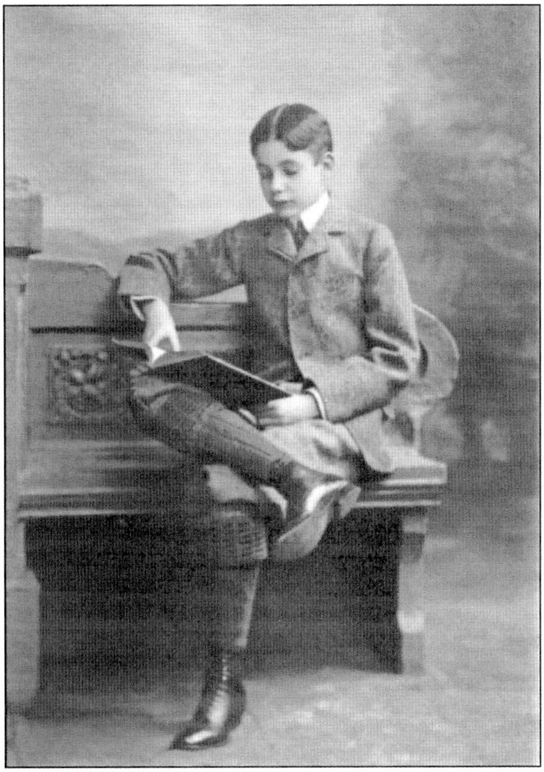

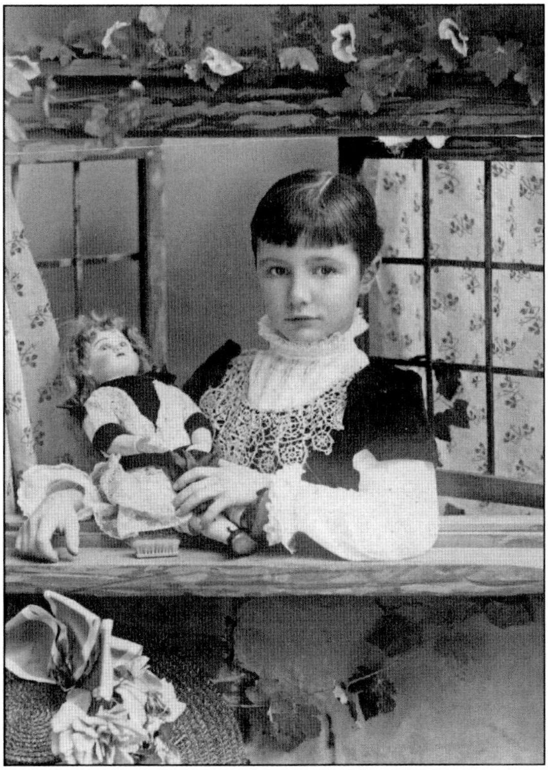

Justine Bayard Cutting was the second child of the Cuttings. Born in 1879, she became an accomplished pianist. She married George Cabot Ward and converted to Catholicism. She studied liturgical music, and in 1910, she created the Ward Method of School Music—a system of music education at Catholic University in Washington, D.C. She died in 1975. (Courtesy of the Bayard Cutting Arboretum.)

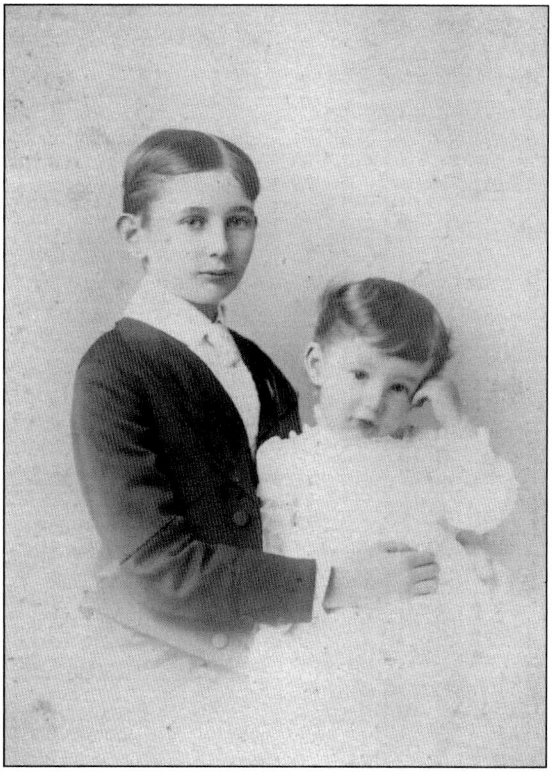

Bronson Murray Cutting is seen here with his older brother, William. Bronson, the third child of the Cuttings, was born in 1888 at Westbrook. He graduated from Harvard in 1910 and moved to New Mexico for his health. He, like William Jr., suffered from tuberculosis. (Courtesy of the Bayard Cutting Arboretum.)

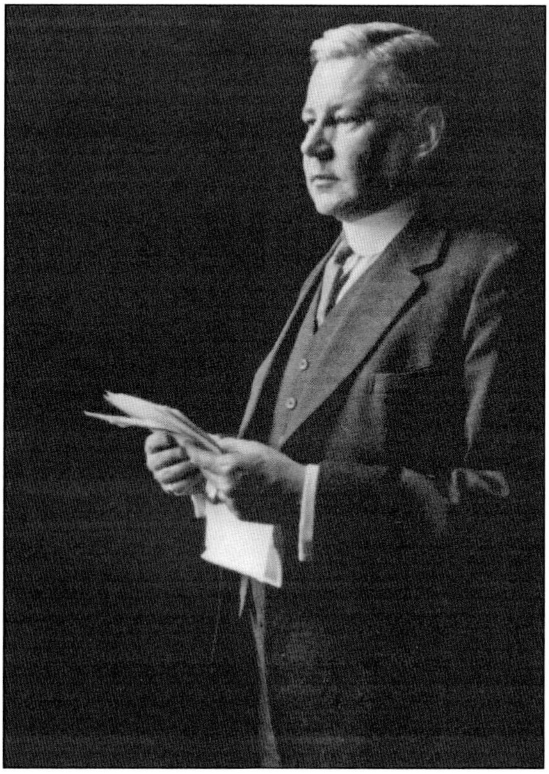

In 1912, the same year New Mexico was admitted to the United States, Bronson Murray Cutting purchased the *Santa Fe New Mexican* newspaper. After serving in World War I, he returned to New Mexico and became a U.S. senator in the late 1920s and early 1930s. This picture was taken of him while he was a senator, shortly before he died in a plane crash en route to Washington, D.C. (Courtesy of the Bayard Cutting Arboretum.)

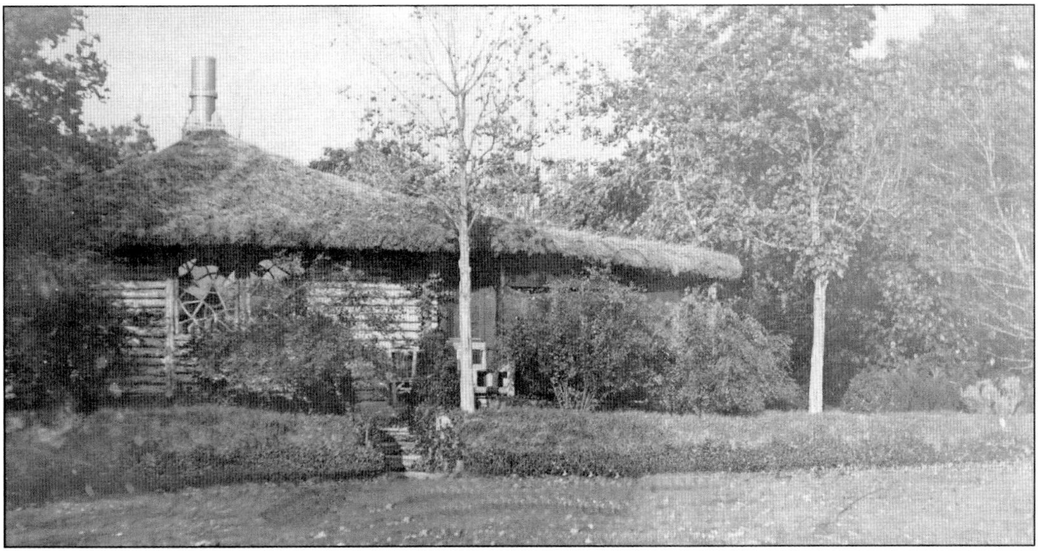

Six cabins, like the one pictured here, were constructed on the Westbrook property for workers to live in. The one in this undated postcard is referred to as Miss Olivia Cutting Cabins. Olivia Cutting was the fourth child of William Bayard Cutting. (Courtesy of the Bayard Cutting Arboretum.)

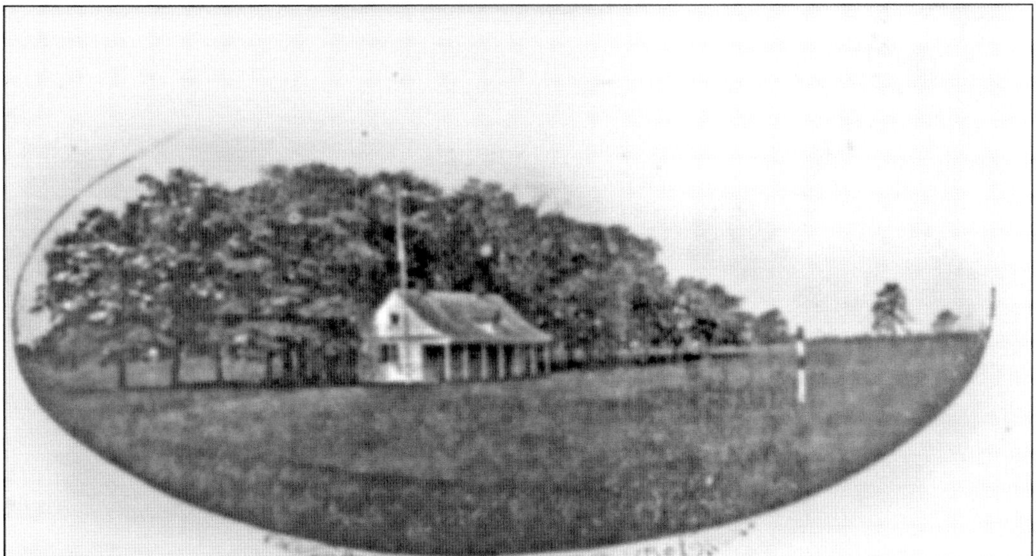

Built by William Bayard Cutting in 1895, the Westbrook Golf Links was one of the earliest golf courses on Long Island. It was designed by William Dunn Jr., who had designed Shinnecock Hills Golf Links in 1891. This postcard shows the caddy shack around 1910. (Courtesy of the Bayard Cutting Arboretum.)

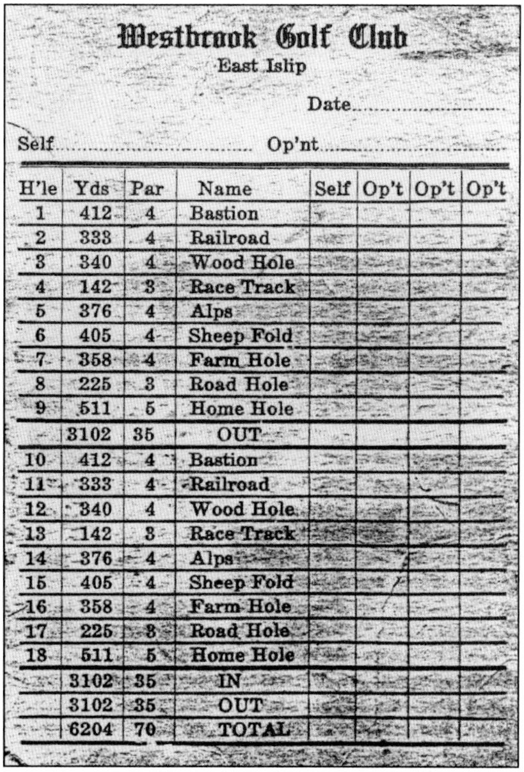

Westbrook Golf Club
East Islip

Date...........................

Self..................... Op'nt..........................

H'le	Yds	Par	Name	Self	Op't	Op't	Op't
1	412	4	Bastion				
2	333	4	Railroad				
3	340	4	Wood Hole				
4	142	3	Race Track				
5	376	4	Alps				
6	405	4	Sheep Fold				
7	358	4	Farm Hole				
8	225	3	Road Hole				
9	511	5	Home Hole				
	3102	35	OUT				
10	412	4	Bastion				
11	333	4	Railroad				
12	340	4	Wood Hole				
13	142	3	Race Track				
14	376	4	Alps				
15	405	4	Sheep Fold				
16	358	4	Farm Hole				
17	225	3	Road Hole				
18	511	5	Home Hole				
	3102	35	IN				
	3102	35	OUT				
	6204	70	TOTAL				

Westbrook Links was a nine-hole reversible course, meaning one played each hole twice to get 18 holes. It was located on the Westbrook estate property, adjoining the South Side Sportsmen's Club and, like that club, had an exclusive membership that included John E. Roosevelt, Horace O. Havemeyer, and William K. Vanderbilt. (Courtesy of the Bayard Cutting Arboretum.)

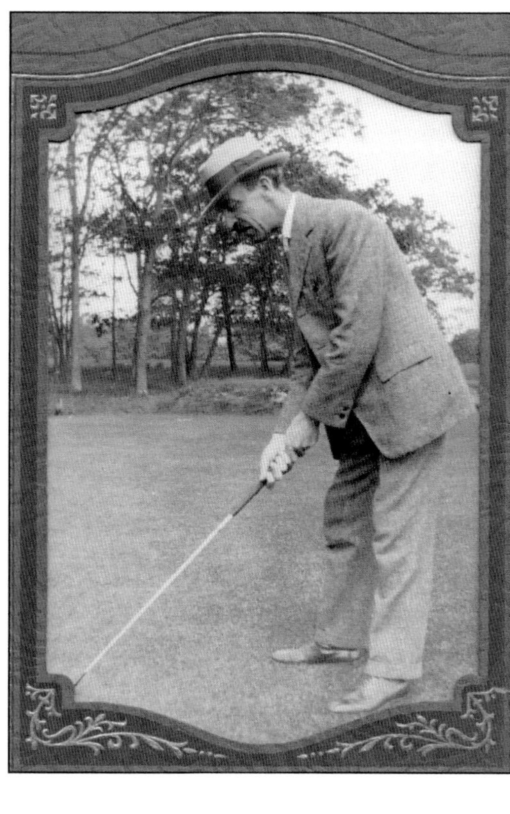

In 1897, Arthur George "Griffs" Griffiths became the golf professional at the Westbrook course, serving in that capacity until the course was closed in the early 1940s. Griffs became well known for his golf club–making ability and became one of the best club makers in America during the early 1900s. (Courtesy of the Bayard Cutting Arboretum)

Arthur George "Griffs" Griffiths is seen here teeing off at the Westbrook Links in the early 1900s. Behind him the geography of the Westbrook Golf Links can clearly be seen. Westbrook Golf was truly a "links," which is a Scottish term for "strips of treeless, coastal land with poor sandy soil and dunes buffeted by winds." (Courtesy of the Bayard Cutting Arboretum.)

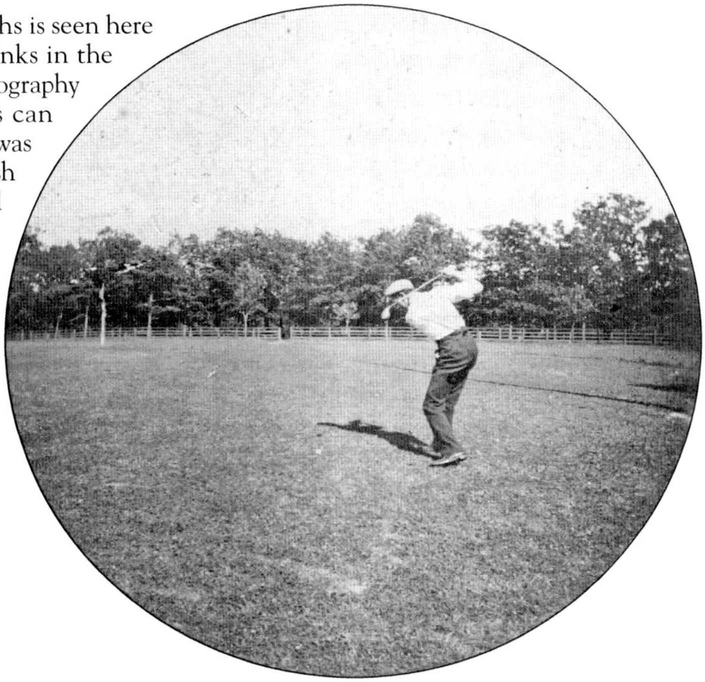

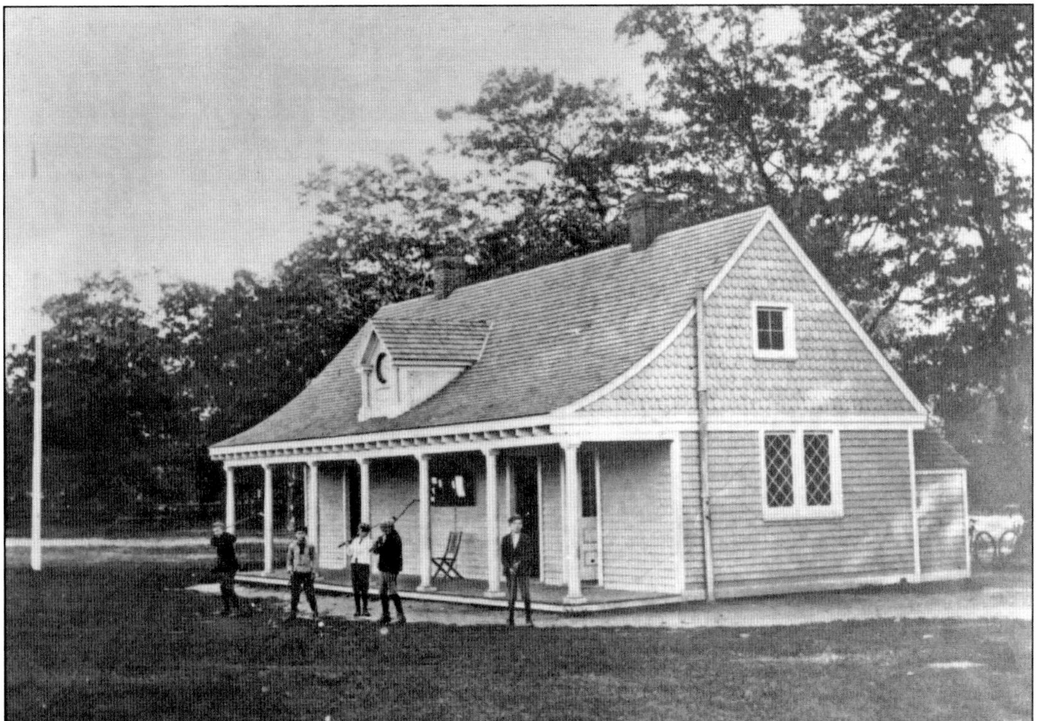

Golfers and caddies stand in front of the caddy shack in 1925. The caddy shack was moved from Westbrook Links in the 1940s two miles east on Montauk Highway, to the center of Oakdale. It has been used through the years as various restaurants and pubs. It still stands today after undergoing a major renovation in 2008. (Courtesy of the Bayard Cutting Arboretum.)

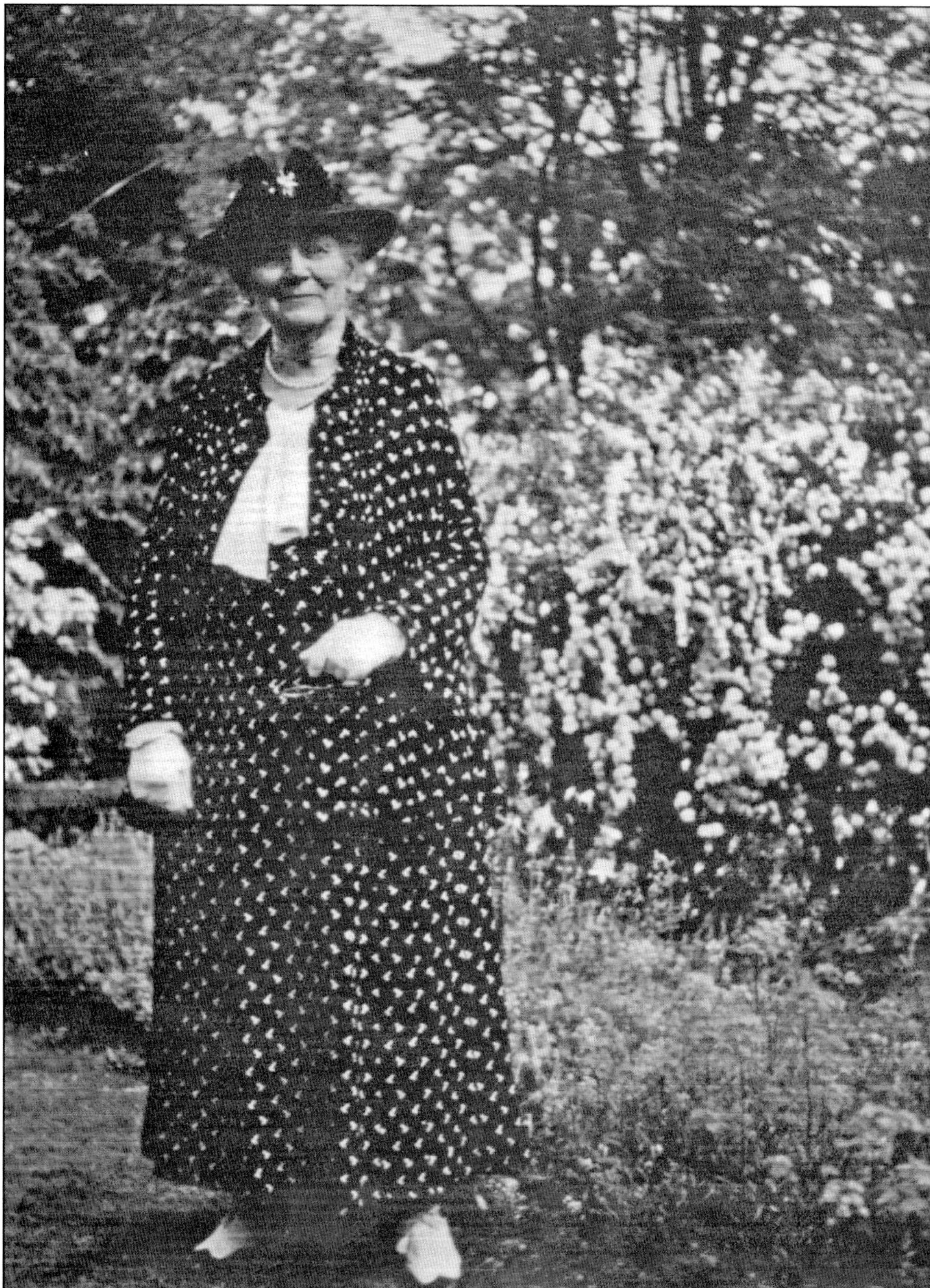

Olivia Cutting James is seen here in 1964. She was the fourth and last surviving child of William Bayard and Olivia Cutting. She and her mother were instrumental in establishing the Bayard Cutting Arboretum. They donated the grounds to New York State "to provide an oasis of beauty and quiet for the pleasure, rest and refreshment of those who delight in outdoor beauty; and to bring about a greater appreciation and understanding of the value and importance of informal planting." (Courtesy of the Bayard Cutting Arboretum.)

Three

Robert's Pepperridge Hall

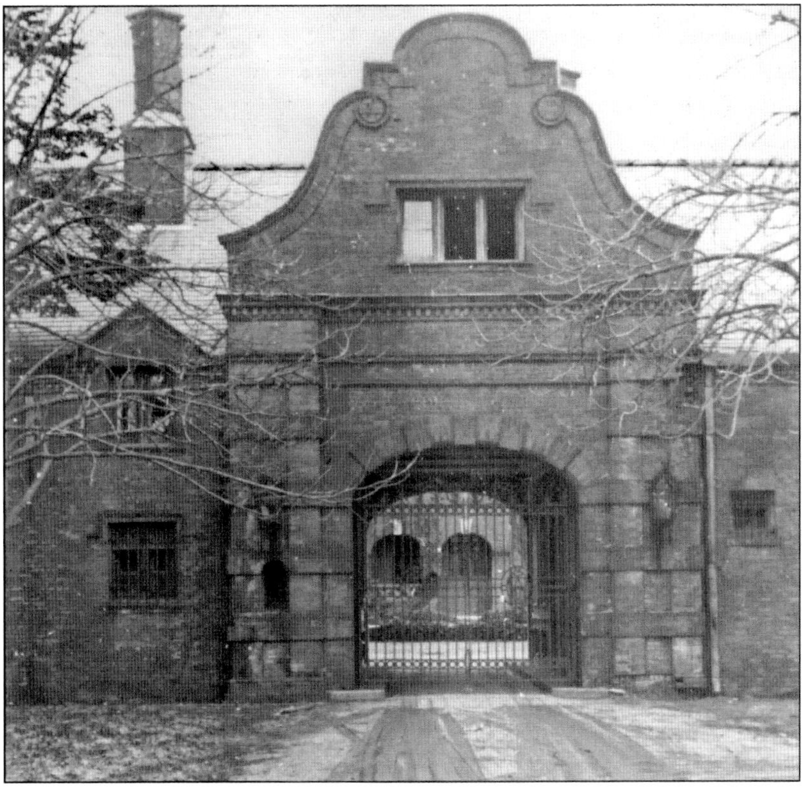

This undated photograph shows the entrance to Pepperidge Hall looking south from the driveway leading up to the house. The stables are on the right of the archway, and the coach house is on the left. The center courtyard and fountain swimming pool are visible behind the iron work. The area of Pepperidge Hall was just southwest of Blue Pont Road and Anisko Landing.

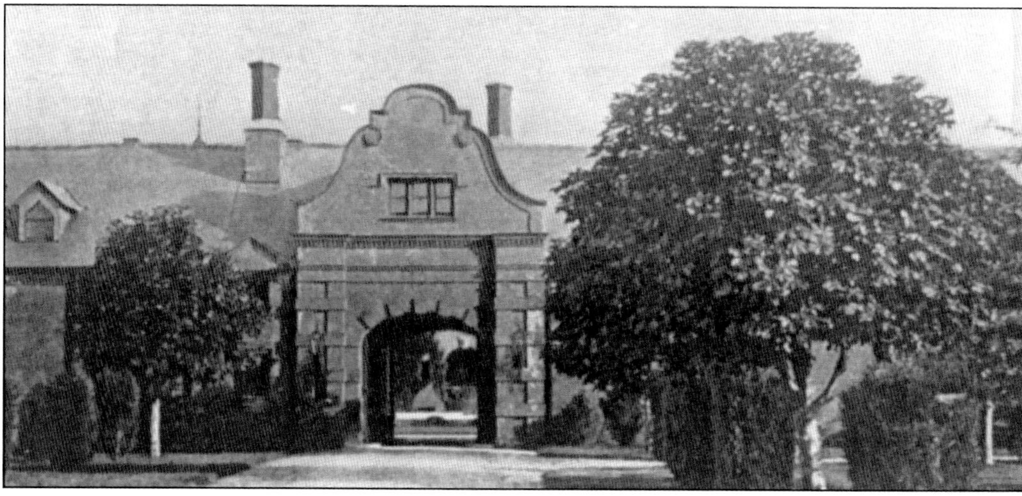

Christopher Rhinelander Robert Jr. was born in 1830 to a local family made prosperous by trade with the West Indies and real estate investments. A member of the South Side Sportsmen's Club since 1873, Robert chose a marshy area to build a country estate for his second wife, Julia Remington Morgan, whom he had married in 1875. He employed the architect H. Edward Ficken in 1889 to design a massive English-style house facing the Great South Bay. It took seven years to complete. Robert abruptly sold the property, presumably at the insistence of his wife. New York lawyer W. K. Aston bought the property in 1896. Robert died in 1899, an apparent suicide.

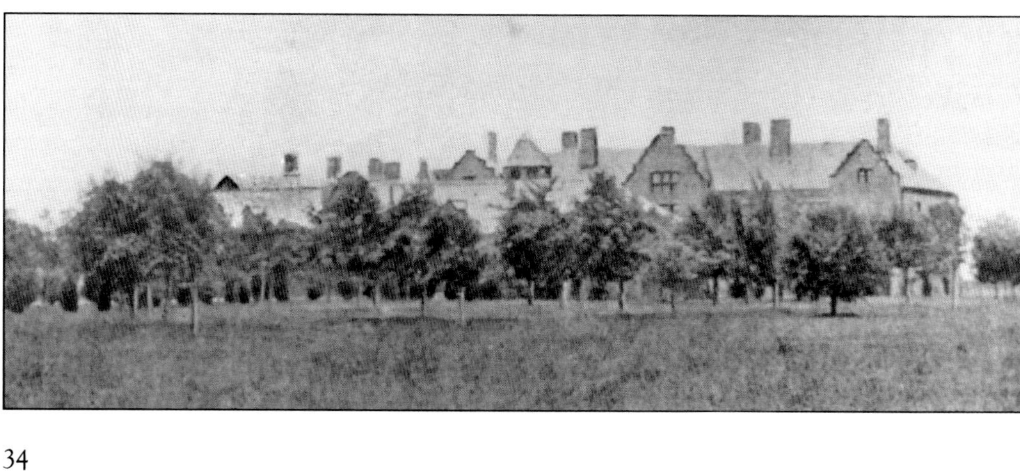

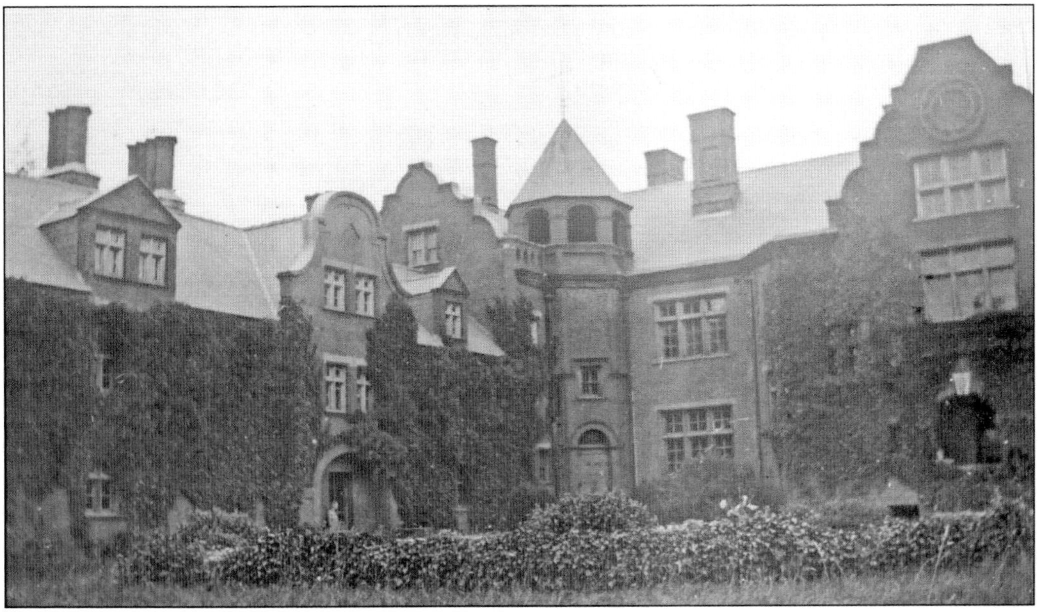

The house was used sparingly by W. K. Aston, who had another summer estate in New Hampshire, and mostly remained empty and unused until its demolition in the late 1930s. The house was not called Pepperidge Hall until Aston purchased it. Named for the colorful trees planted around it, the house itself had a rectangular shape centered around a large courtyard and incorporated unusual features such as the stables, a coach house, and a 109-foot-long greenhouse into its plan.

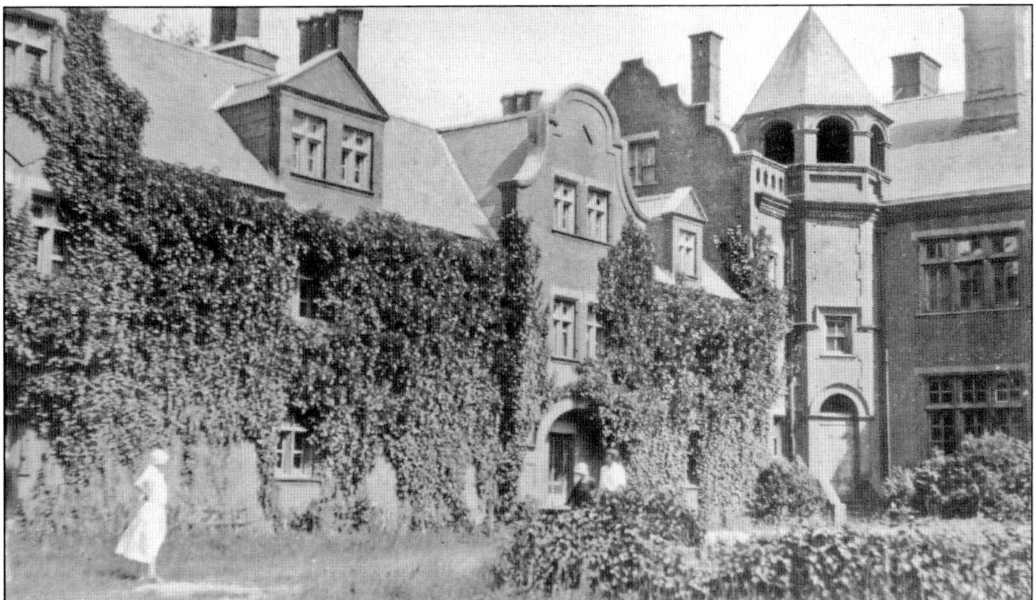

Robert did not call his estate Pepperidge Hall, although there is some speculation that he referred to it as La Rochelle. This is perhaps a nod to his ancestors who were French Huguenots from the town of La Rochelle. This photograph from a later date, roughly the late 1930s, shows the inner courtyard overgrown and uncared for.

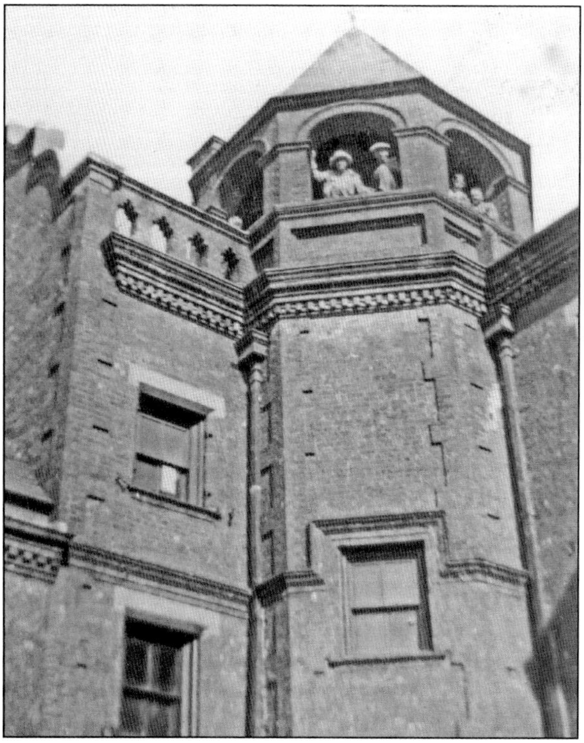

Drawn to the unique atmosphere, Vitagraph Pictures, located in nearby Bayshore to the west, filmed a number of silent movies on the estate with Pepperidge Hall serving as the atmospheric backdrop for such films as *My Ladies' Slipper* (1916), *To Hell With the Kaiser* (1918), and *Dead Men Tell No Tales* (1920).

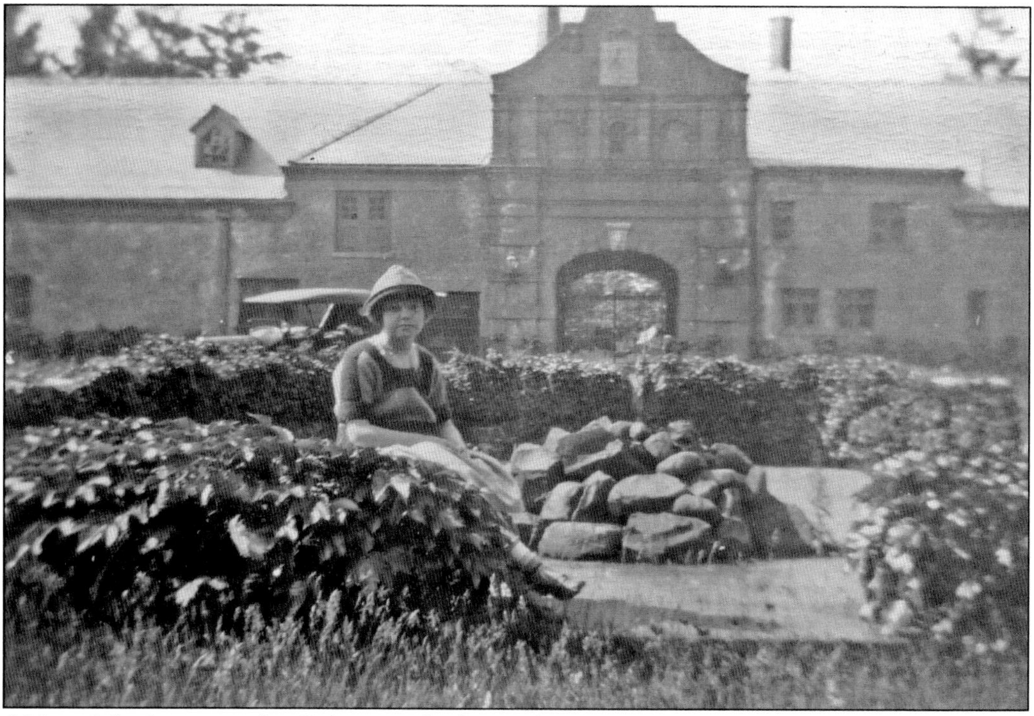

Although built to appeal to Robert's wife, the pool was never used by her. This photograph, shot from within the now empty and overgrown swimming pool looking north, dates from around the late 1920s.

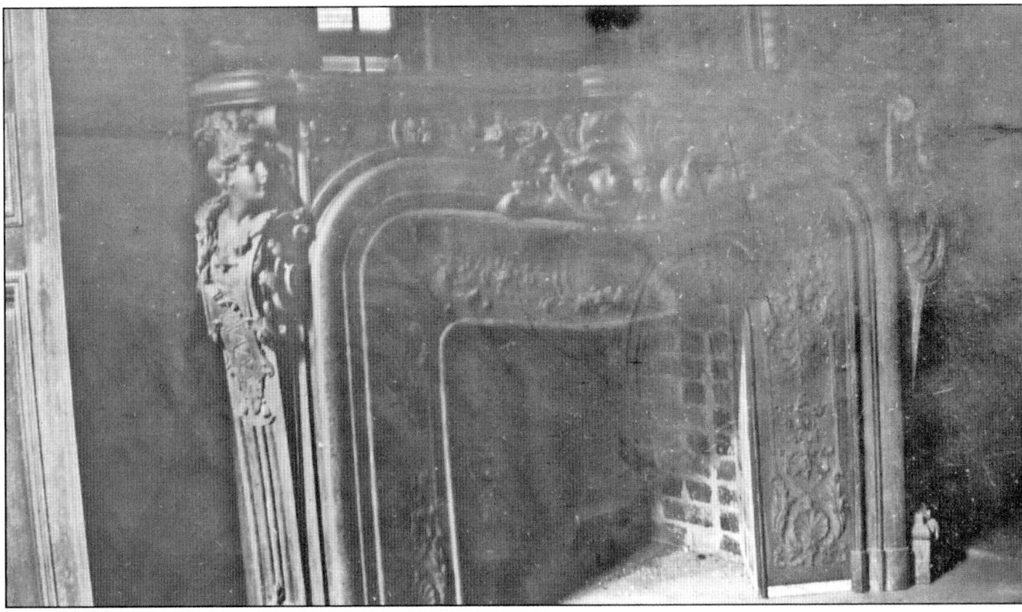

While the exterior of Pepperidge Hall was Jacobean in style, the interiors of Pepperidge Hall were taken directly from a French chateau in Normandy and shipped to Oakdale. It was architect H. Edward Ficken's job to make the interiors fit seamlessly into the new building. The fireplace photograph is thought to be from one of the bedrooms. The intricately detailed woodwork is thought to be from the dining room.

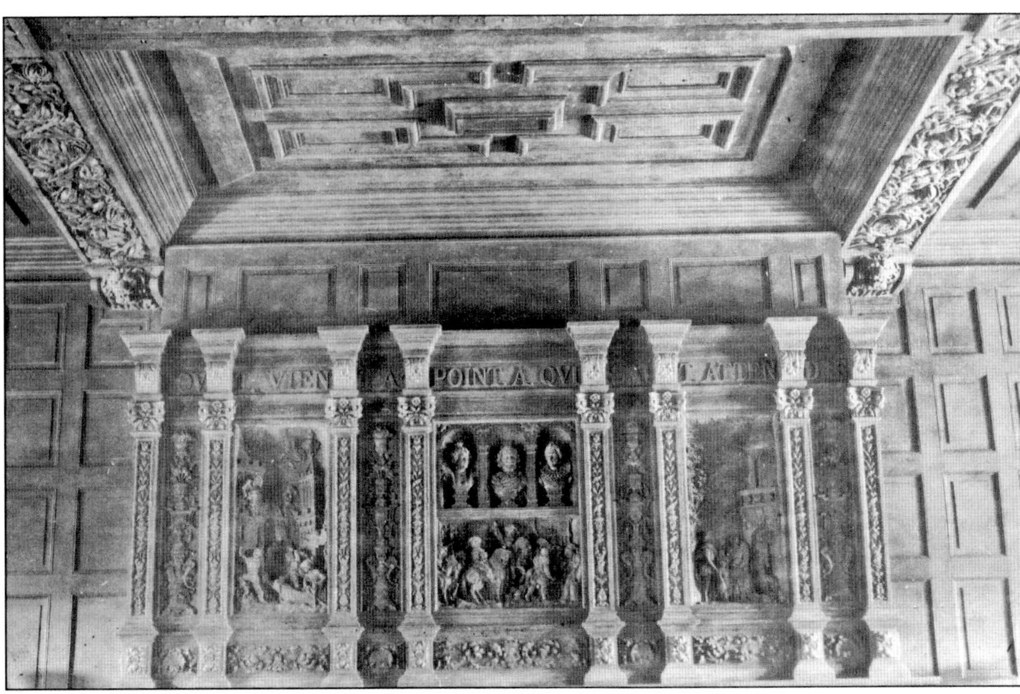

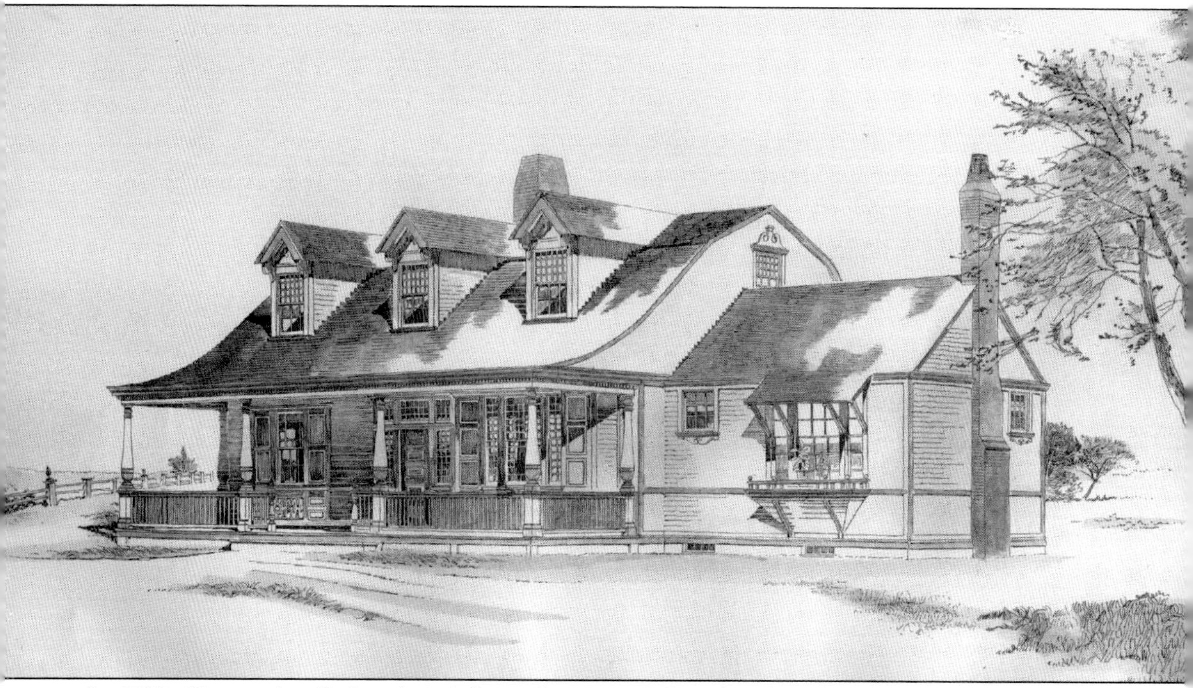

In 1882, Christopher Robert hired the architect H. Edward Ficken to design this hunting lodge in Oakdale. Although it was not thought of as a "proper" home for his wife, the Roberts stayed in this lodge for seven years before the building of Pepperidge Hall on the same property. This rendering of the hunting lodge appeared in the November 5, 1887, issue of the *American Architect and Building News*. The lodge mysteriously burned in 1889.

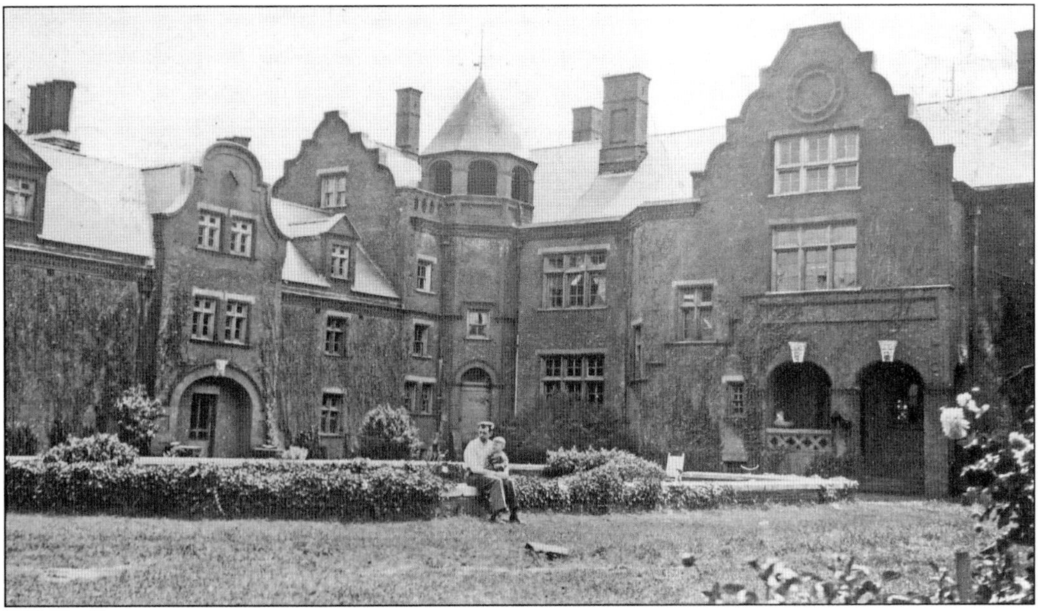

This picture shows the main living area of Pepperidge Hall to the right of the tower and the kitchen and servants' wing to the left of the tower. It was taken from inside the courtyard in the late 1930s, shortly before its demolition. The man is believed to be Jack Davies, last caretaker of the estate, and his son.

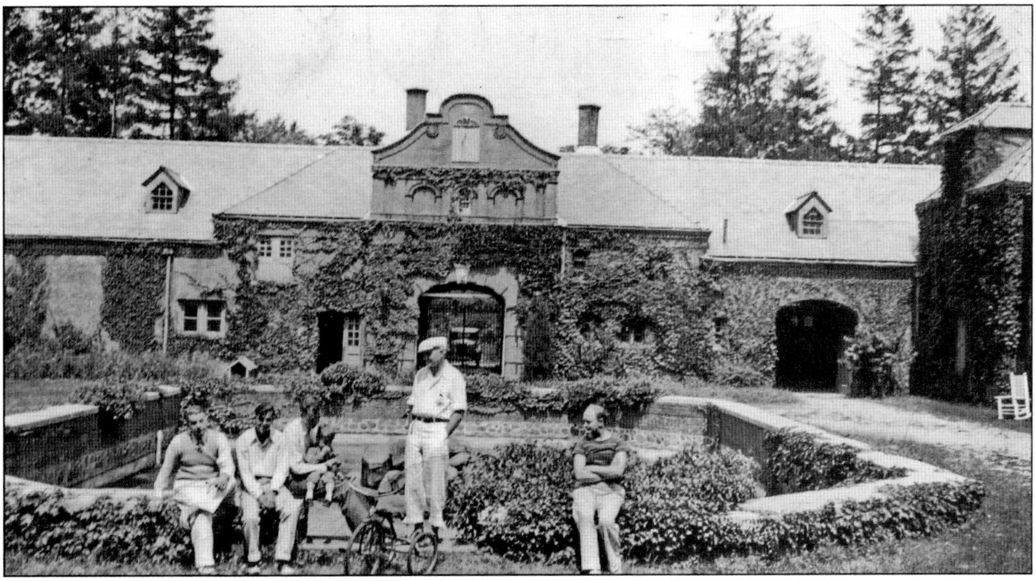

The unidentified people in this photograph are enjoying the courtyard at Pepperidge Hall. In the background, the entrance archway to the courtyard is visible. The coach house is to the right of the archway, and the stables are to the left. The pool behind them measured 30 by 50 feet, which gives an indication of the grand scale of this estate.

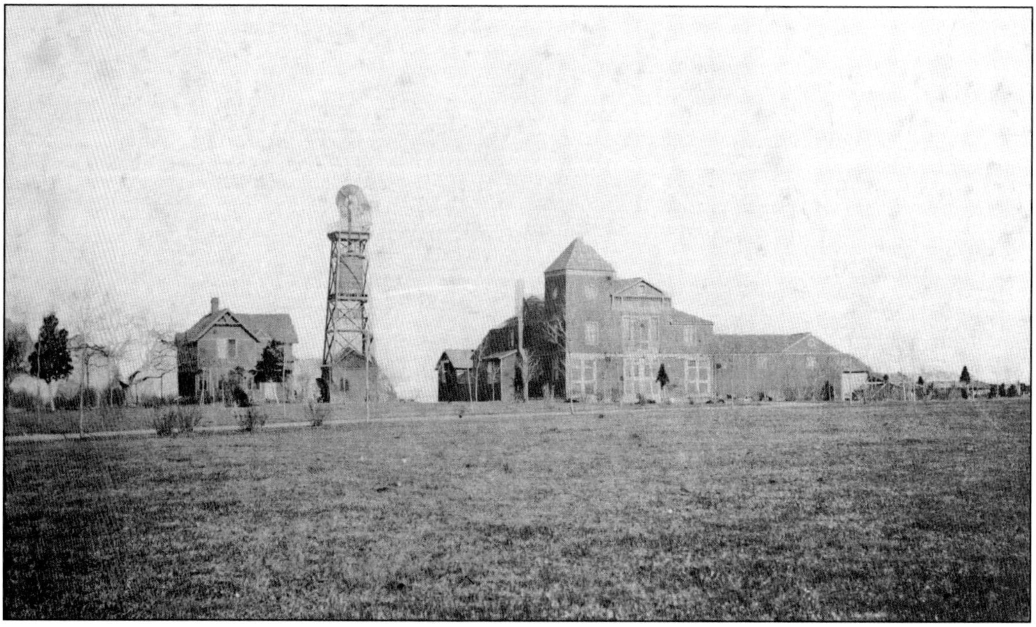

These photographs, dating to around 1915, show the cow barn and poultry house erected by Christopher Robert on his Pepperidge Hall estate. Bason and Son of Sayville provided the brickwork. Built in 1882, these buildings, along with the large piggery, were praised by the local paper. All of the estate owners along the south shore in Oakdale sought to outdo each other in their farming activities, and the ornateness and extravagance of their farm buildings were often commented on approvingly.

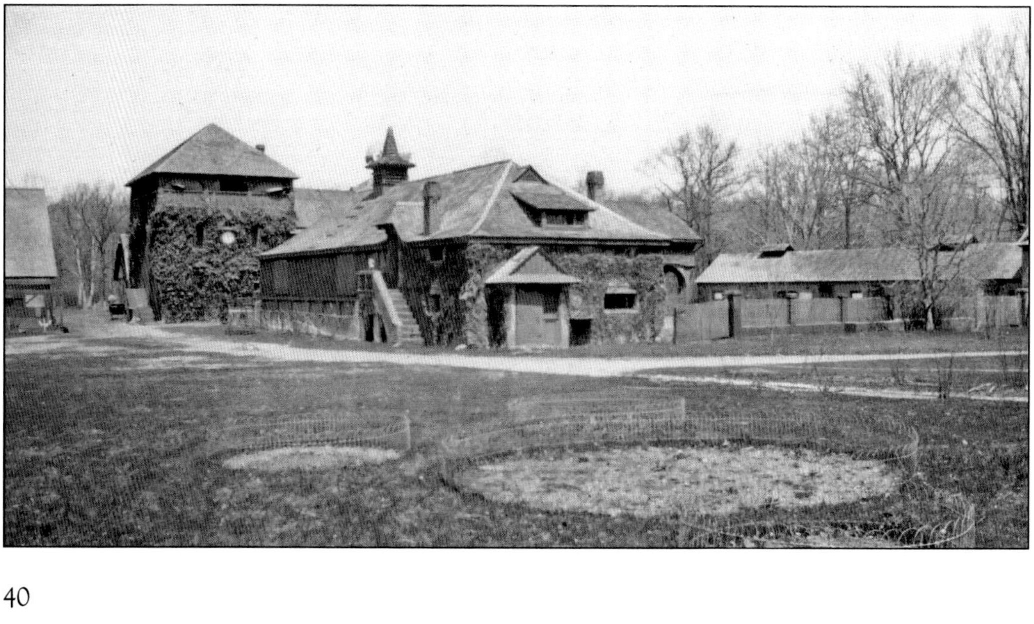

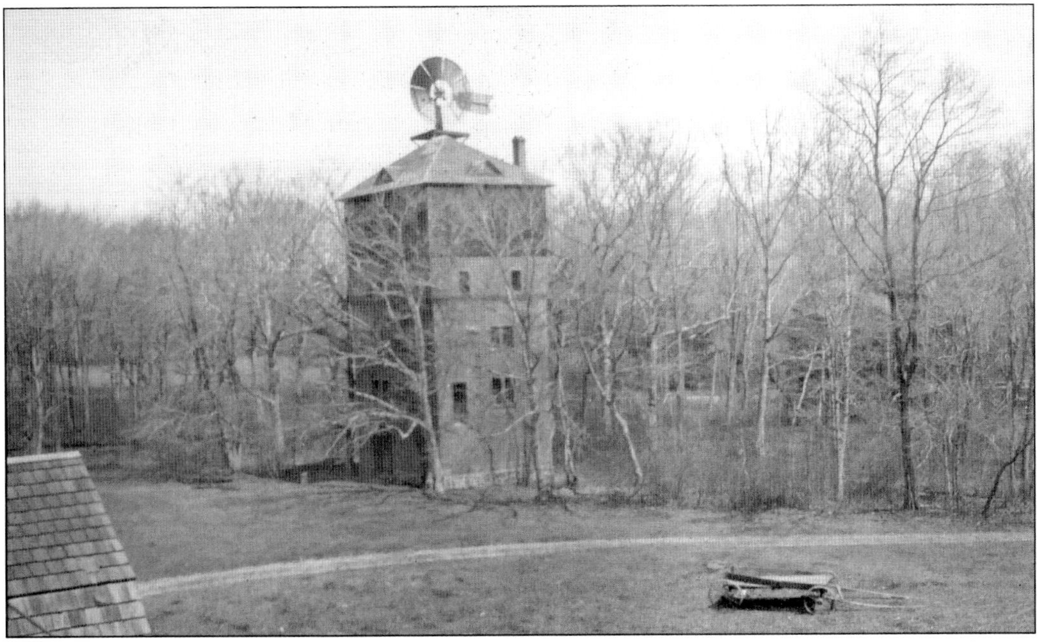

This undated photograph shows the water tower and windmill in the farm complex of the former Pepperidge Hall estate. The odd structure would eventually be converted into apartments before it burned to the ground by the early 1980s.

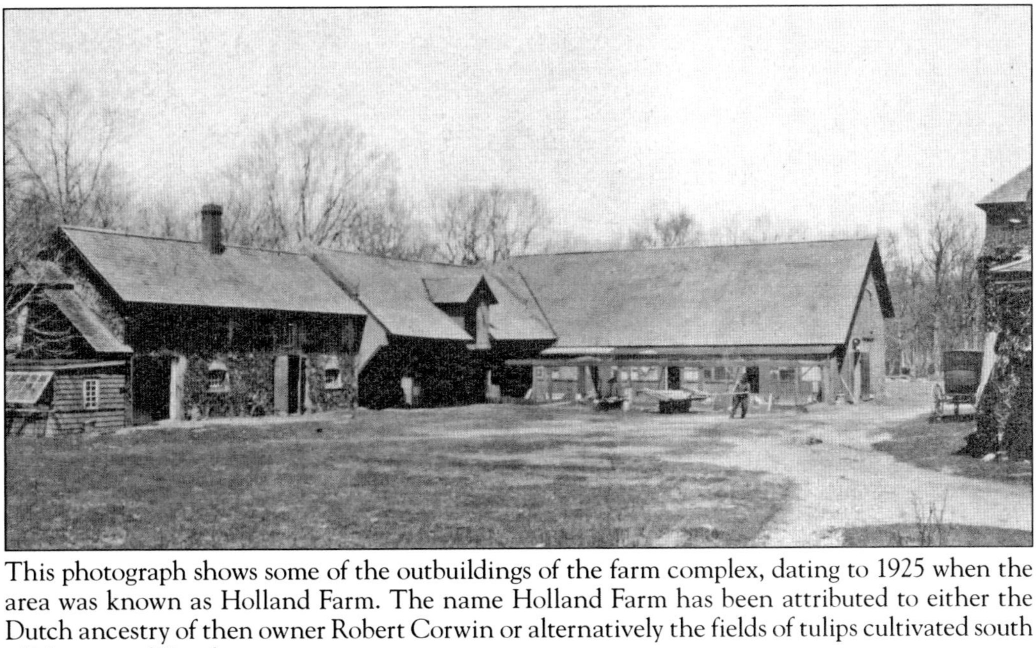

This photograph shows some of the outbuildings of the farm complex, dating to 1925 when the area was known as Holland Farm. The name Holland Farm has been attributed to either the Dutch ancestry of then owner Robert Corwin or alternatively the fields of tulips cultivated south of Homestead Road.

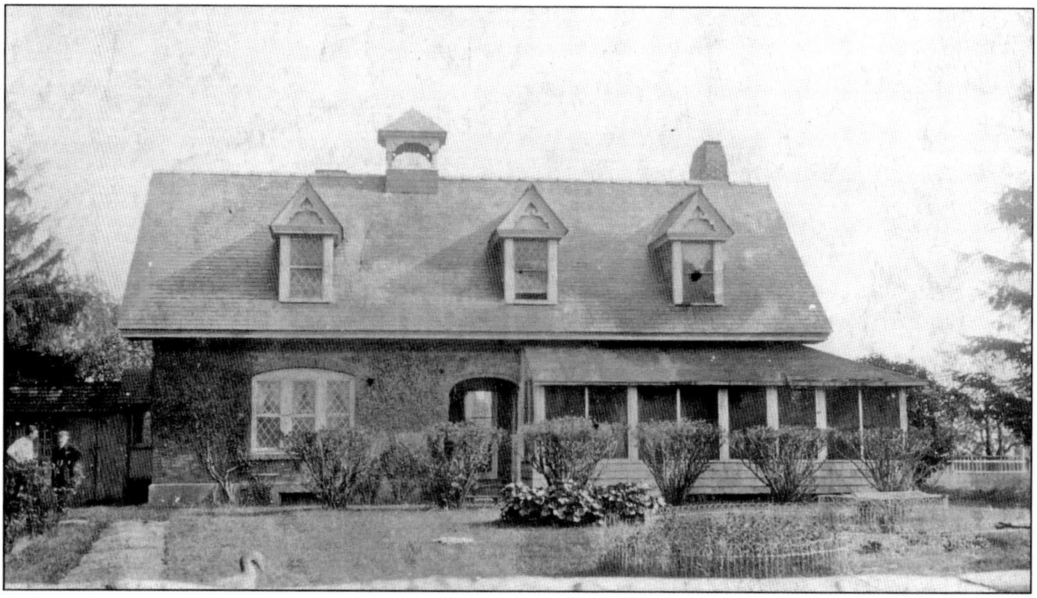

Robert Corwin of New York City bought the Pepperidge Hall farm complex and surrounding land from W. K. Aston prior to 1915. Corwin (right) is seen standing next to the manager's cottage of the estate. The design of this 1888 building is similar to that of the hunting lodge also built by H. Edward Ficken for Christopher Robert in 1882. The manager's cottage has been modified over the years but still exists as a private residence on Homestead Road.

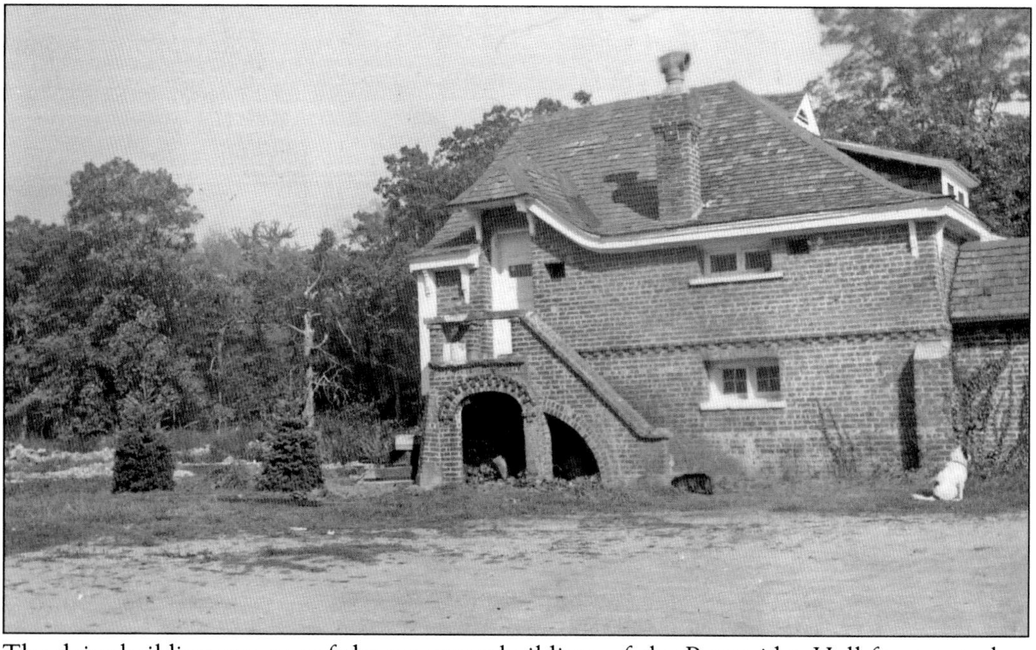

The dairy building was one of the accessory buildings of the Pepperidge Hall farm complex, pictured above around 1930 when it was known as Holland Farm. This building is today a private residence on Homestead Road.

Four

Bourne's Indian Neck Hall

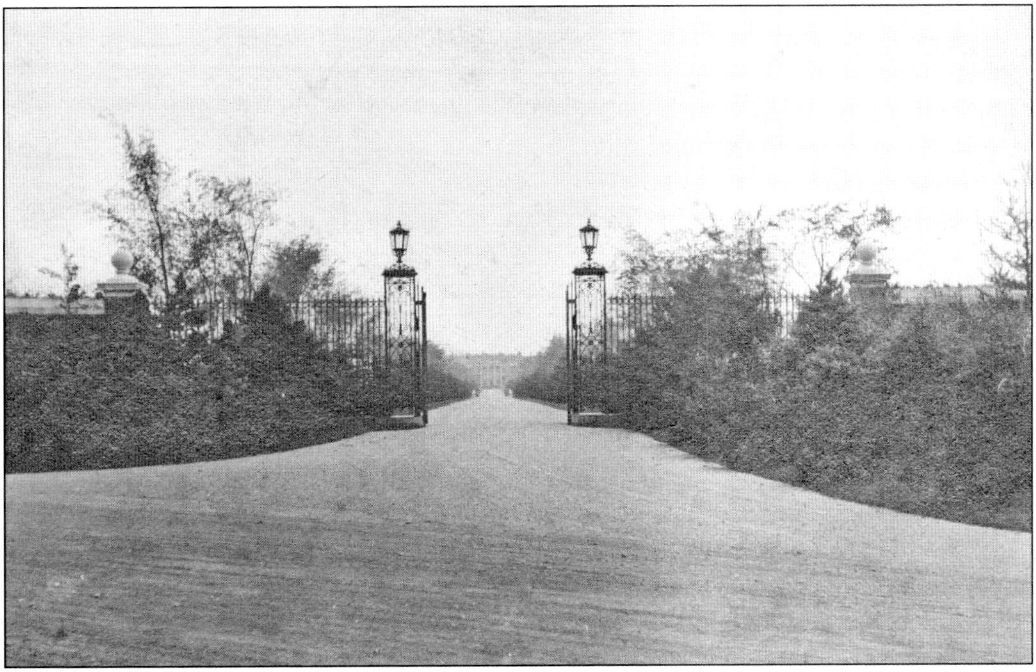

Although designed with the bay as its front door, the main land-based entrance to Indian Neck Hall was down a long straight road off Montauk Highway. The dust and mud that went with the dirt roads of the time eventually led Bourne to pay to have the stretch of Montauk fronting his estate macadamized. (Courtesy of the Long Island Maritime Museum.)

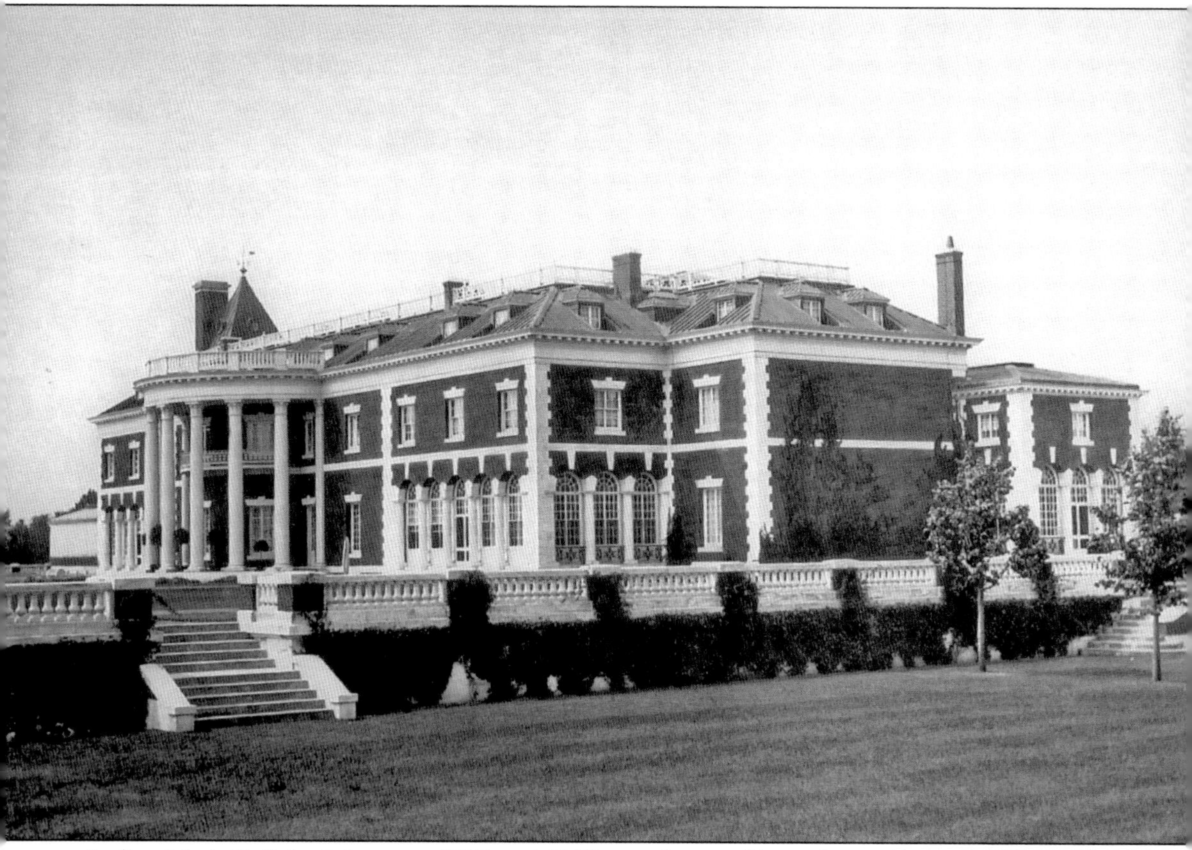

Indian Neck Hall, built between 1897 and 1900, was designed by architect Ernest M. Flagg. The marble-trimmed brick structure in the Colonial Revival style was the largest mansion on Long Island when completed. Flagg studied at the Ecole des Beaux-Arts in Paris. His other notable commissions included New York's Singer Building, once the tallest building in the world, and The Towers, a castle Bourne had constructed on Dark Island in the St. Lawrence Seaway beginning in 1902. Indian Neck Hall contained over 100 rooms and featured, among other amenities, a Turkish bath and swimming pool. (Courtesy of the Long Island Maritime Museum.)

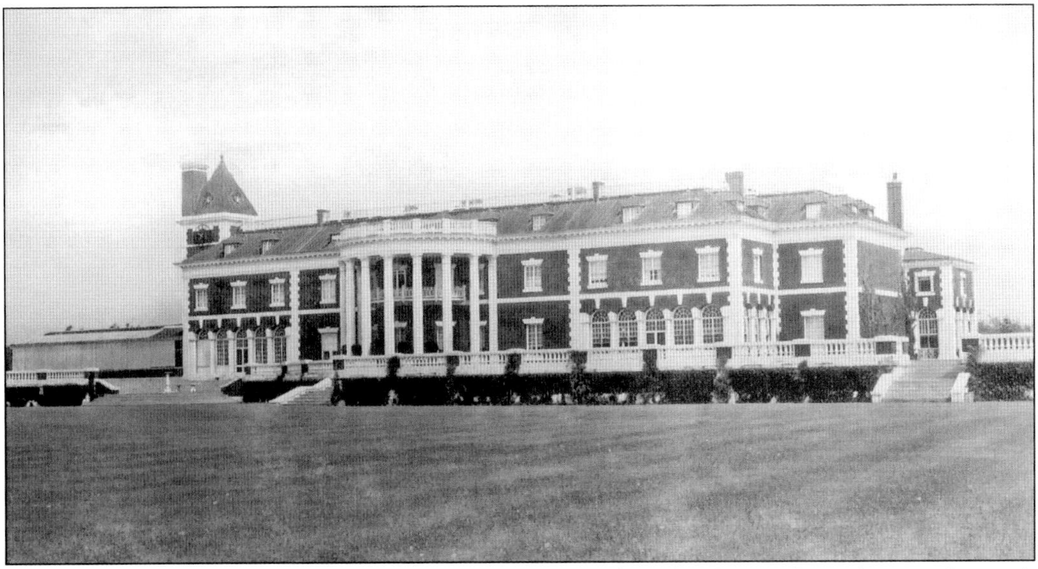

Like the Christopher Robert estate just across Ludlow's and Brick Kiln Creeks to the west, Bourne's Indian Neck Hall was on very low-lying land near the bay. The 100-yard lawn that became such a commanding feature of Bourne's estate was achieved by a considerable amount of backfill added to the marshland between the bay and Indian Neck Hall's front porch. (Courtesy of the Long Island Maritime Museum.)

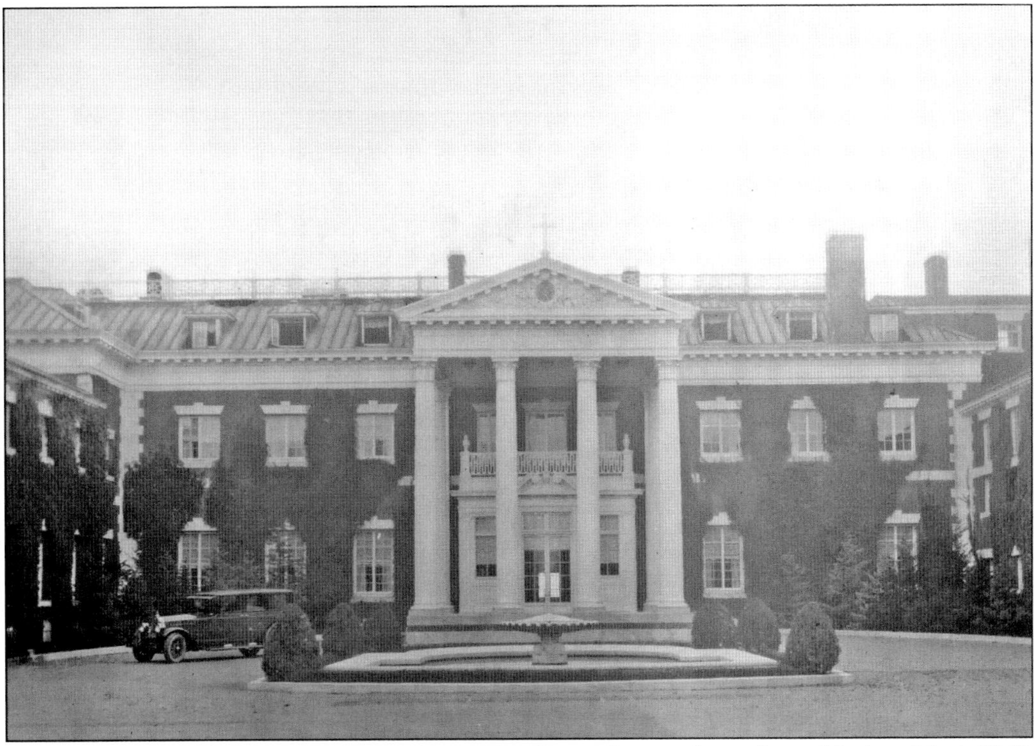

This photograph, from sometime in the 1920s, shows the northern face of Indian Neck Hall. (Courtesy of LN509—La Salle Military Academy. De La Salle Christian Brothers Archives of the Long Island-New England District. Manhattan College.)

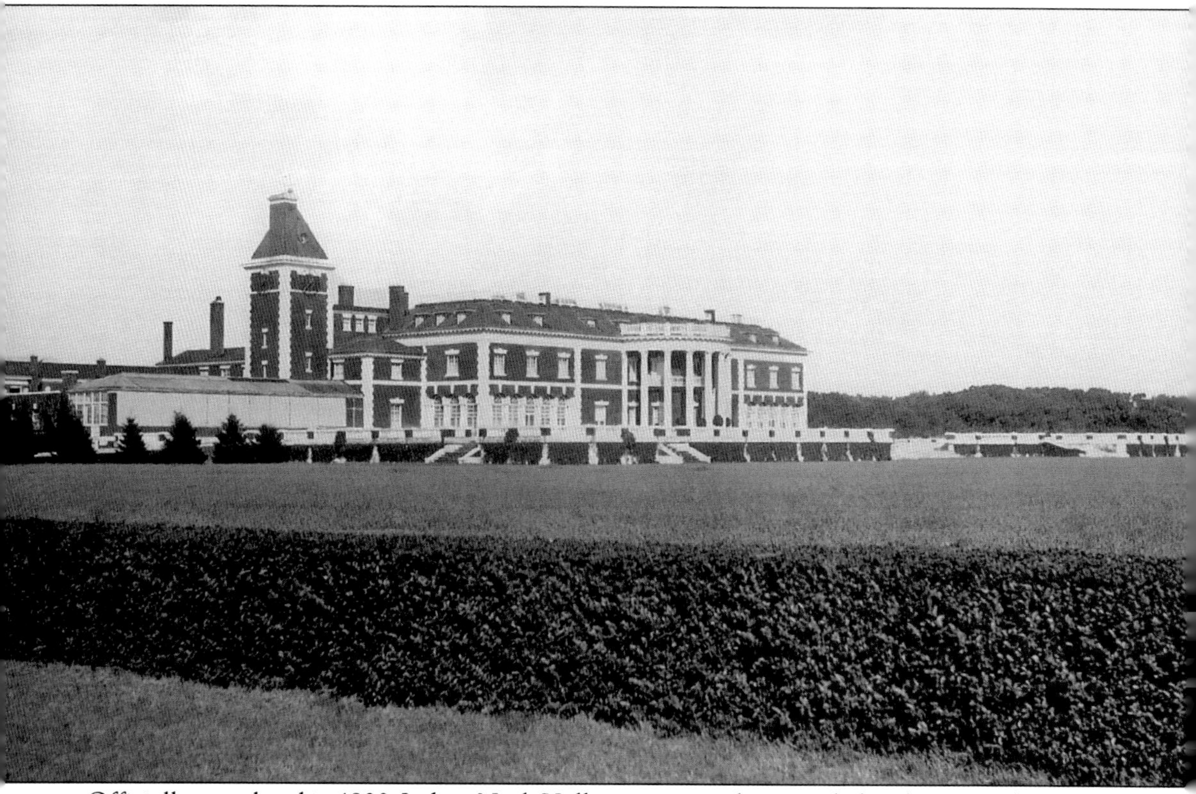

Officially completed in 1900, Indian Neck Hall was constantly expanded and improved. In 1903, Bourne added greenhouses and conservatories as well as a windmill. Beyond a major renovation overseen by Ernest Flagg in 1907, Bourne constructed a clock tower in 1912. Seen in this picture on the west side of the mansion, the tower still stands although the conservatory visible here at its base does not. (Courtesy of the Long Island Maritime Museum.)

This photograph from around 1929 gives a sense of the tranquil and secluded grounds of the Indian Neck Hall estate. When creating the property, Bourne hired the same landscapers who had worked on the Chicago Exposition in 1893. (Courtesy of LN509—La Salle Military Academy. De La Salle Christian Brothers Archives of the Long Island-New England District. Manhattan College.)

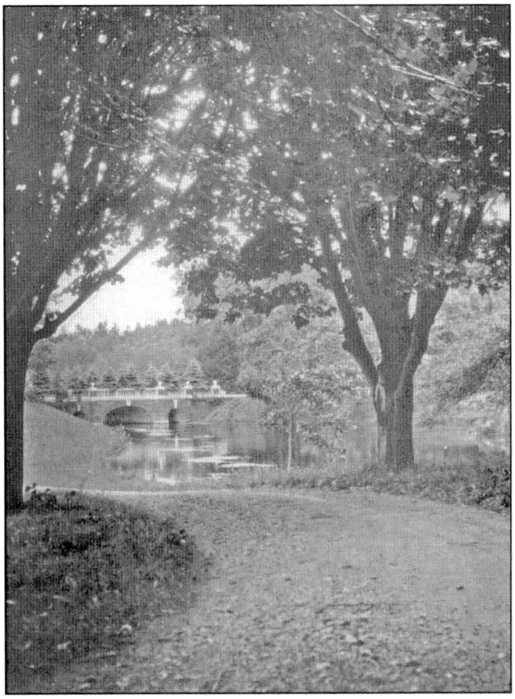

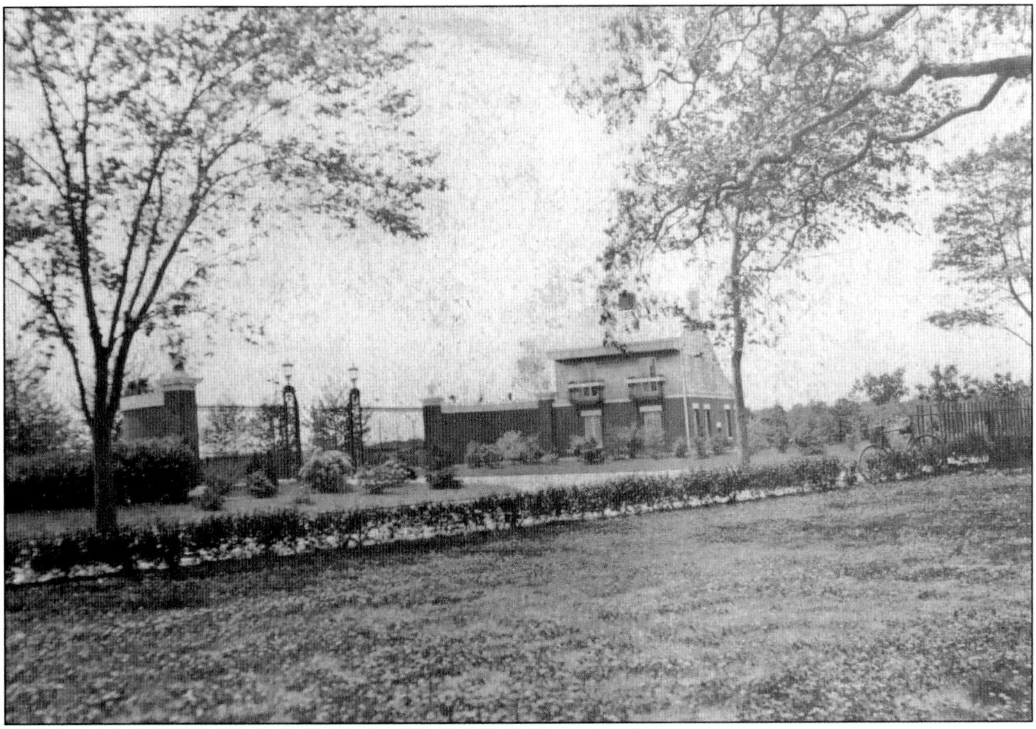

This photograph from around 1900 shows the gate lodge along Montauk Highway shortly after the completion of Indian Neck Hall. The *Suffolk County News* reported unrest among the laborers working to complete the lodge. According to accounts, the bricklayers sought a nickel raise in their hourly rate. They walked off the job when their request was denied, but the work continued apace.

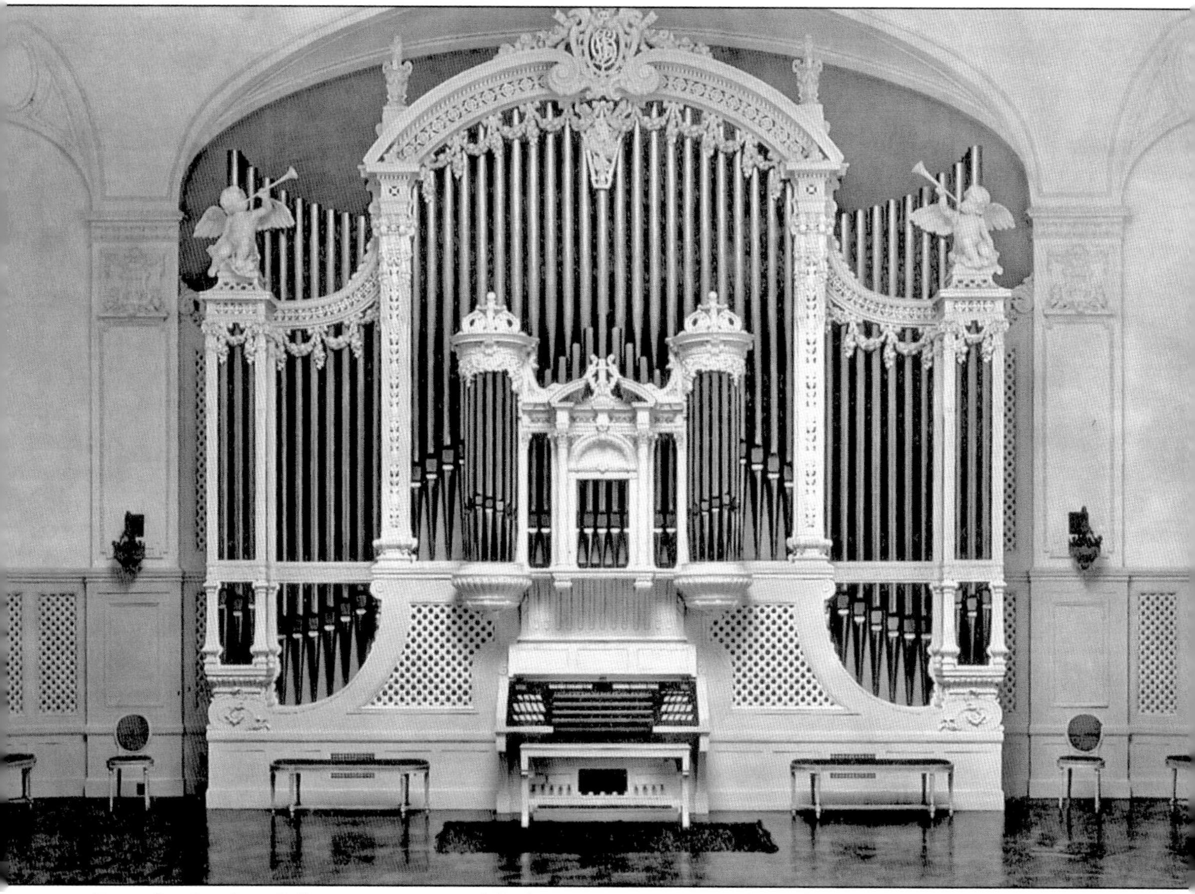

Since his boyhood, Bourne was noted for his singing voice. When the time came for Indian Neck Hall to be built, he had an elaborate pipe organ installed by the Aeolian Company. He took advantage of his 1907 renovations to expand the music room to include the organ pictured above, installed in 1908. A company brochure of the period proclaimed it "the Largest and Most Complete House Organ in the World." The organ was in use for Bourne's funeral in 1919 to accompany the choir from the Catholic Church of St. John the Divine in New York City. (Courtesy of the Long Island Maritime Museum.)

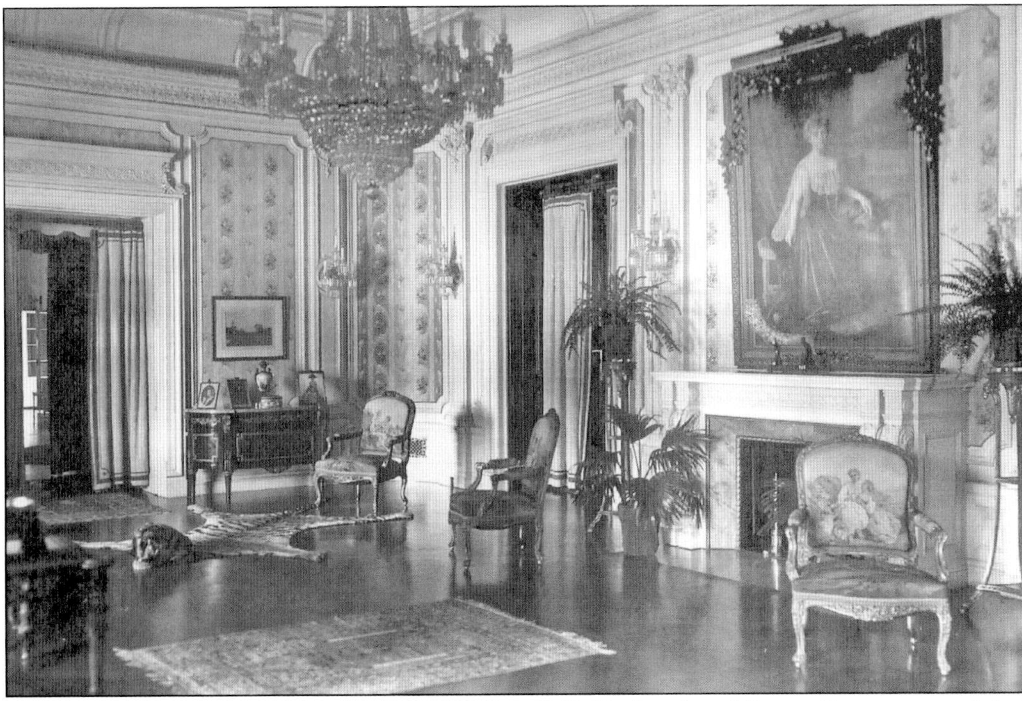

At the opening reception for Indian Neck Hall in 1900, Frederick and Emma Bourne greeted their guests from the main hall, shown below. Over a hundred guests came, including Admiral Dewey, hero of Manila Bay in the Spanish-American War just two years previously. For the occasion, Indian Neck Hall was decorated with white roses, lilies, and azaleas. The drawing room, above, was cleared for dancing as an orchestra played behind a wall of palms. The upstairs rooms for the family featured polished wood wainscoting in mahogany trim while downstairs there was a skating rink under the veranda and a bowling alley under the conservatory. (Both, courtesy of the Long Island Maritime Museum.)

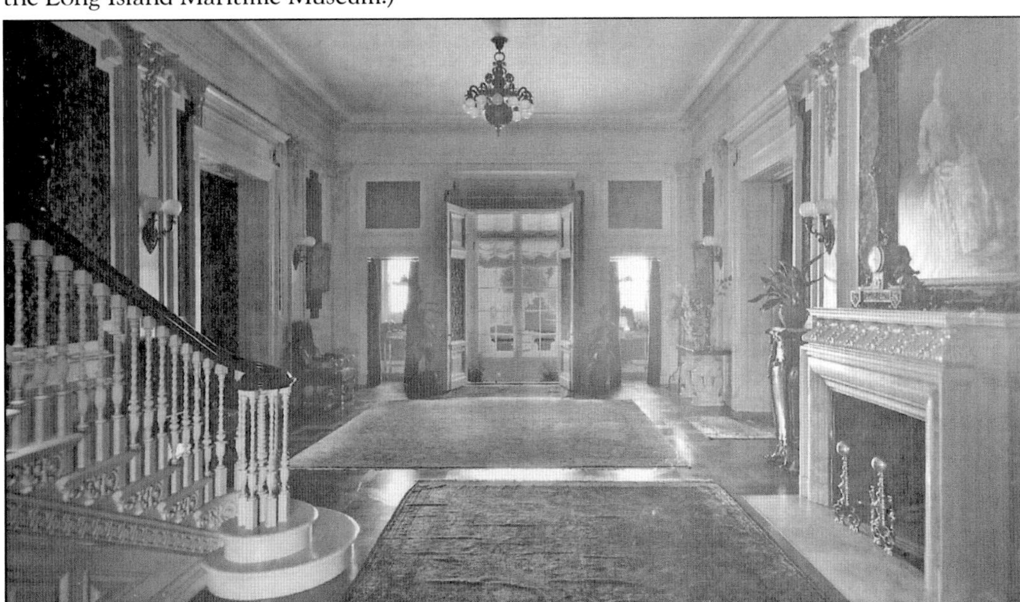

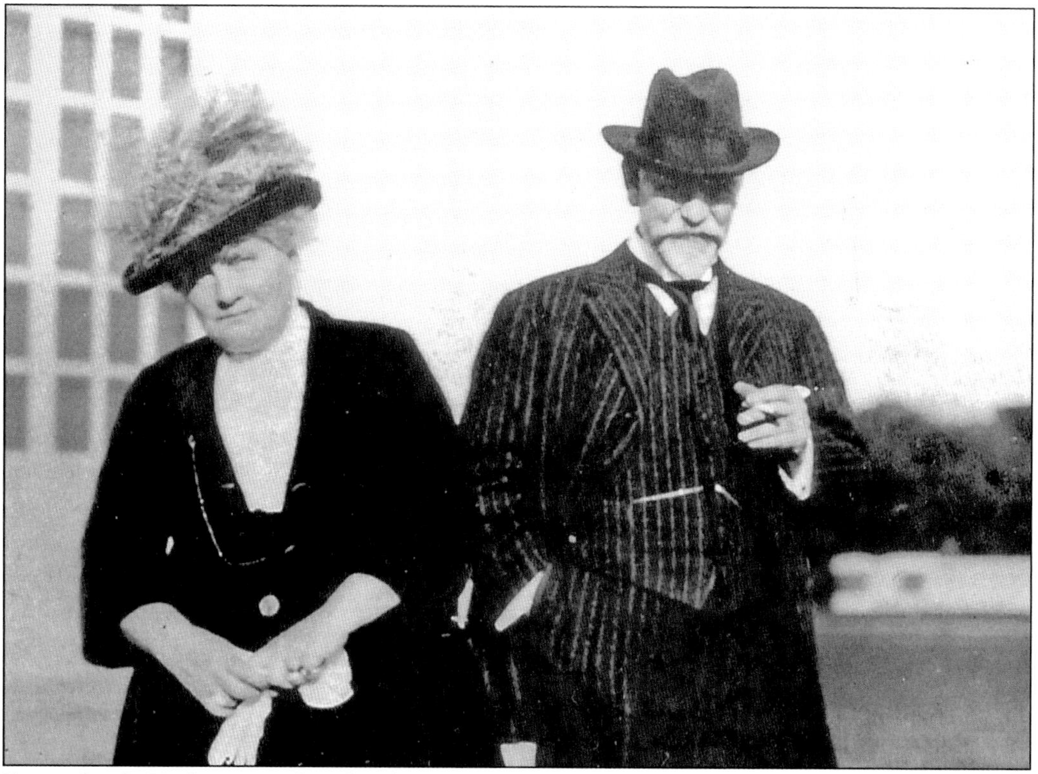

Emma Sparks Keeler married Frederick Bourne on February 9, 1875. The Bournes' 25th anniversary served as the official opening day celebration of Indian Neck Hall, attended by a lavish party. Indian Neck continued to be a home for the Bourne family. Frederick retired there by 1905. Emma died on the estate on August 31, 1916, at the age of 62. Bourne also died at Indian Neck on March 9, 1919. (Courtesy of the Long Island Maritime Museum.)

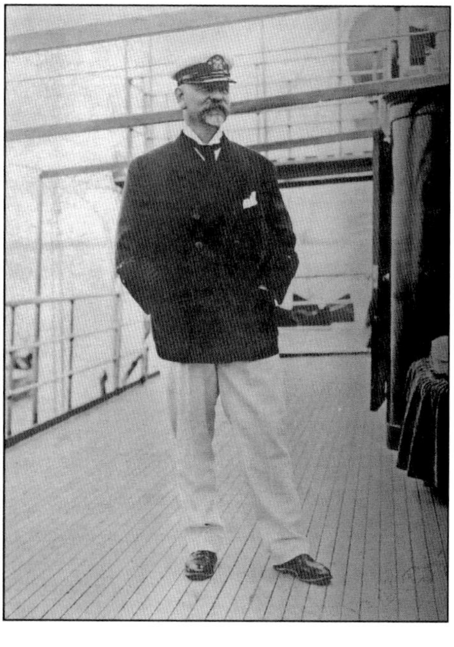

One of Frederick Bourne's passions was sailing. He was a member of the New York Yacht Club, serving as commodore in 1903 with two of his many yachts, the *Delaware* and the *Colonia*, servings as his flagships. He helped sponsor American entrants in the America's Cup and also developed a friendship with Sir Thomas Lipton, avid Scottish yachtsman and longtime rival for the Cup. (Courtesy of the Long Island Maritime Museum.)

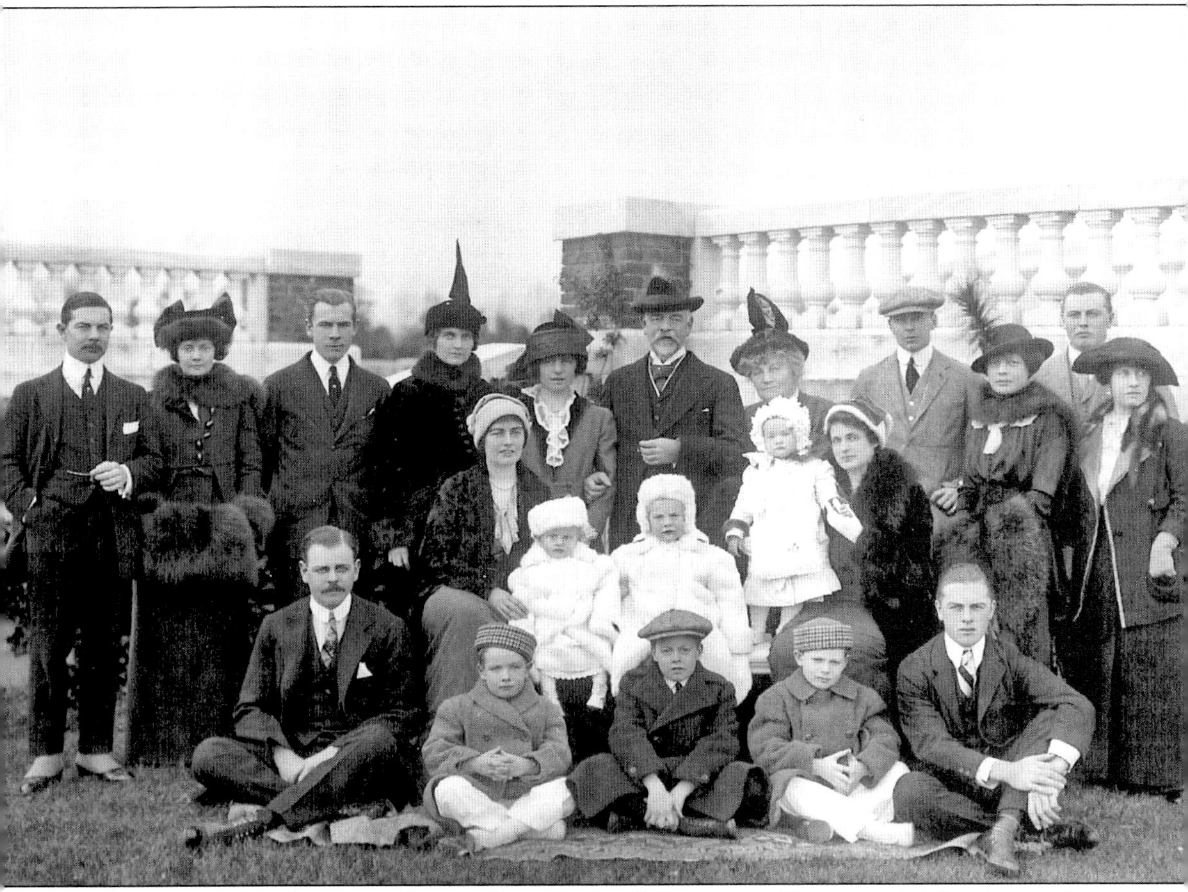

This photograph, taken around 1913, shows Frederick Bourne and his extended family posed on the lawn of his Indian Neck Hall estate. From left to right are (first row) Anson Hard, Kenneth Bourne, Arthur K. Bourne Jr., Alfred S. Bourne Jr., and Howard D. Bourne; (second row) Florence Bourne Hard, possibly George Hard, Frederick Gilbert Bourne Hard, Barbara Bourne, and Hattie Louise Bourne; (third row) Arthur K. Bourne Sr., Ethel Hollins Bourne, George C. Bourne, Helen Cole Whitney, Marjorie Bourne, Frederick G. Bourne, Emma Keeler Bourne, Ralph B. Strassburger, May Bourne Strassburger, Alfred S. Bourne Sr., and Marion C. Bourne. (Courtesy of the Long Island Maritime Museum.)

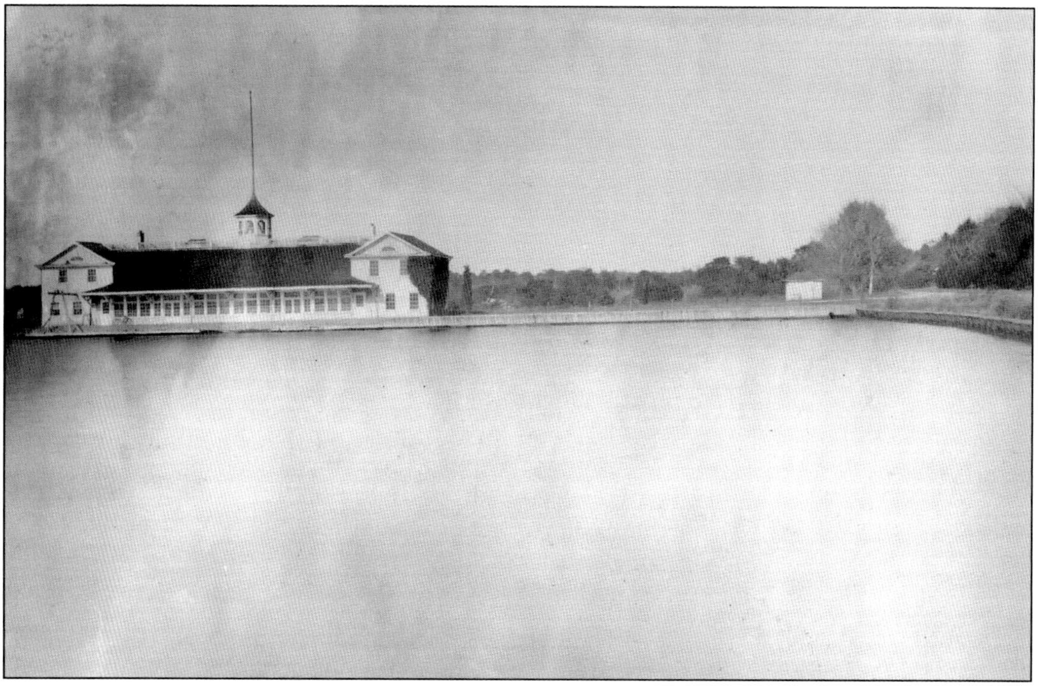

This undated photograph shows the boathouse and basin at Indian Neck Hall. This is actually the second boathouse Frederick Bourne had constructed on this site. He sold the first boathouse to local oysterman Jacob Ockers, who floated it down the bay and used it in his new oystering operations in West Sayville. (Courtesy of LN509—La Salle Military Academy. De La Salle Christian Brothers Archives of the Long Island-New England District. Manhattan College.)

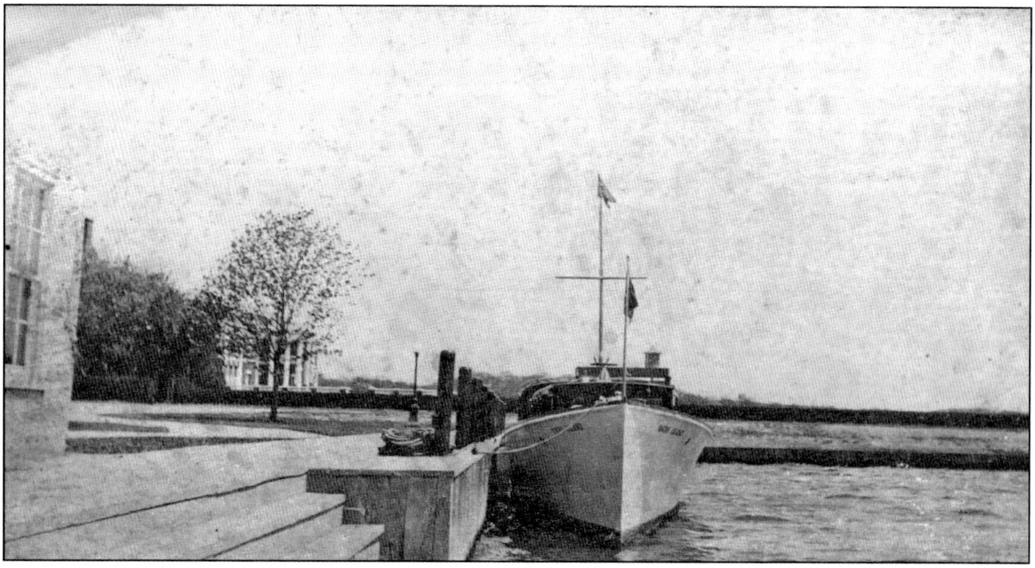

Bourne owned many boats during his lifetime. Pictured above is the powerboat *Dark Island*, named after his property in the St. Lawrence, placing this picture as sometime around 1903. A very limited list of the ships in Bourne's fleet would include the steam yachts *Alberta*, *Colonia*, and *Delaware* (his largest at some 300 feet), along with *Reverie* and the sloop *Ginty*. (Courtesy of the Long Island Maritime Museum.)

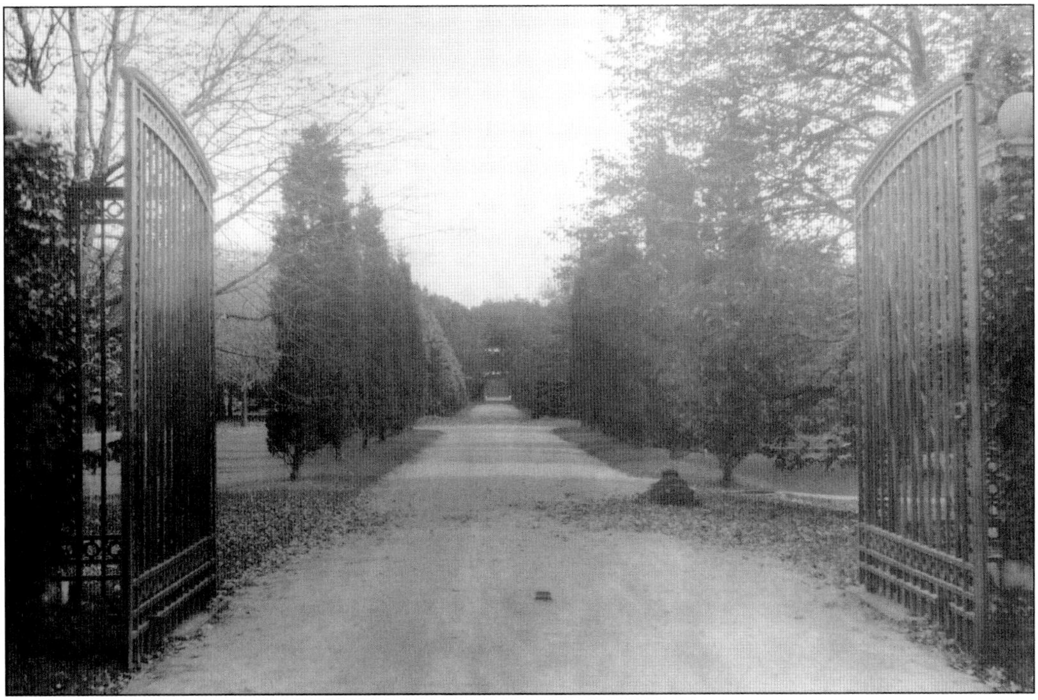

Bourne was keenly interested in automobiles in the early 1900s. Not only did he own a number of his own cars but he was an early backer of the Long Island Motor Parkway. He built a six-car garage to accommodate his Mercedes and other vehicles in 1901. The picture above, taken around 1930, shows the road to the garage leading south off Montauk Highway. Below, dated to about the same period, is a photograph of the stables adjoining the garage. (Both, courtesy of LN509—La Salle Military Academy. De La Salle Christian Brothers Archives of the Long Island-New England District. Manhattan College.)

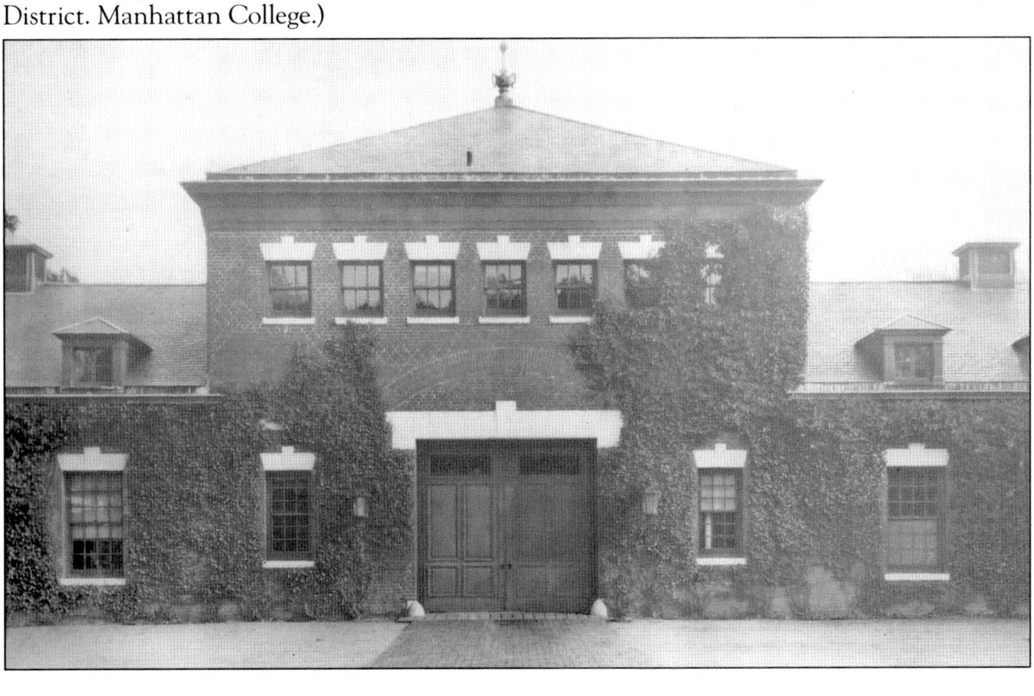

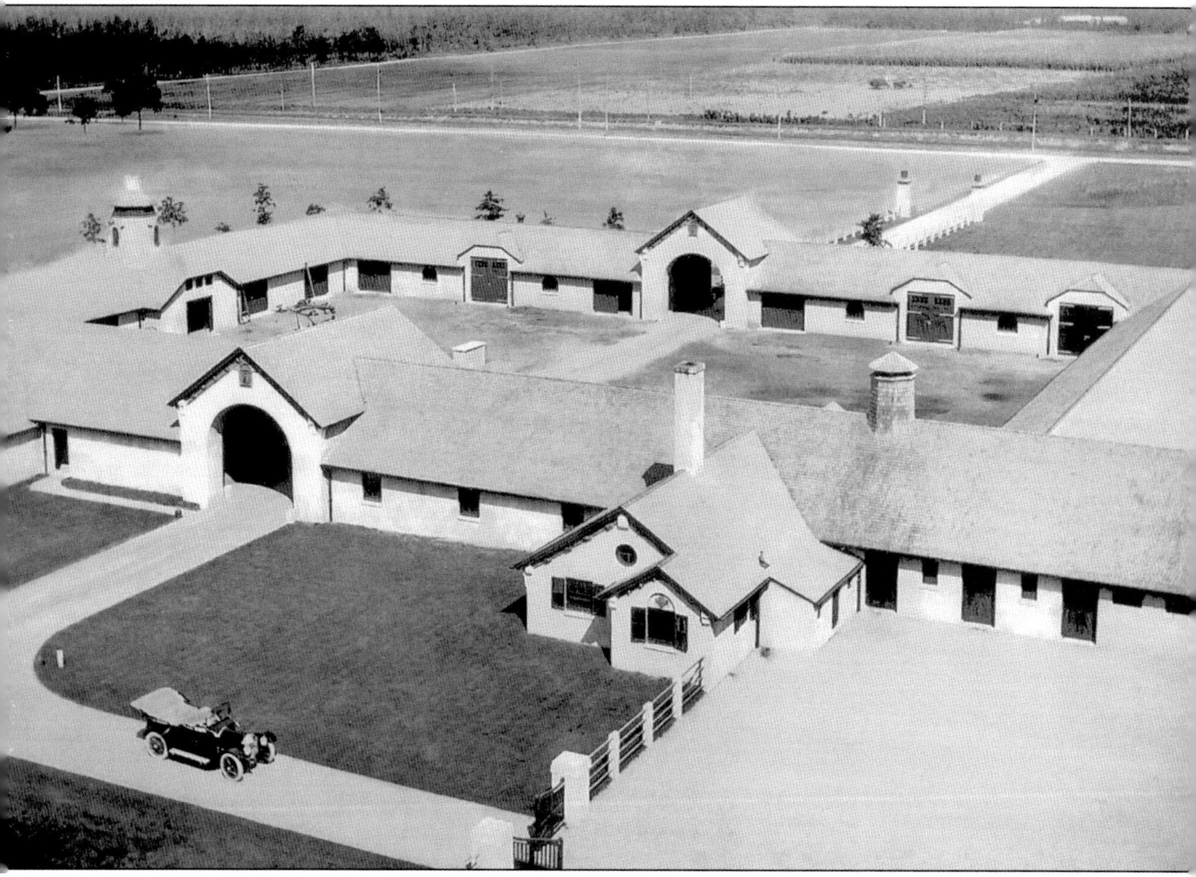

Over the years, Bourne expand his initial Oakdale estate of the Ludlow farm property by purchasing more land from the Ludlow family. It was on such a tract lying north of Montauk Highway that he began to develop a comprehensive farm complex in 1910. His previous farming efforts had been concentrated to the east of Indian Neck Hall south of Montauk Highway where William Ludlow had once farmed. That land is now owned by the West Oak Recreational Club. (Courtesy of the Long Island Maritime Museum.)

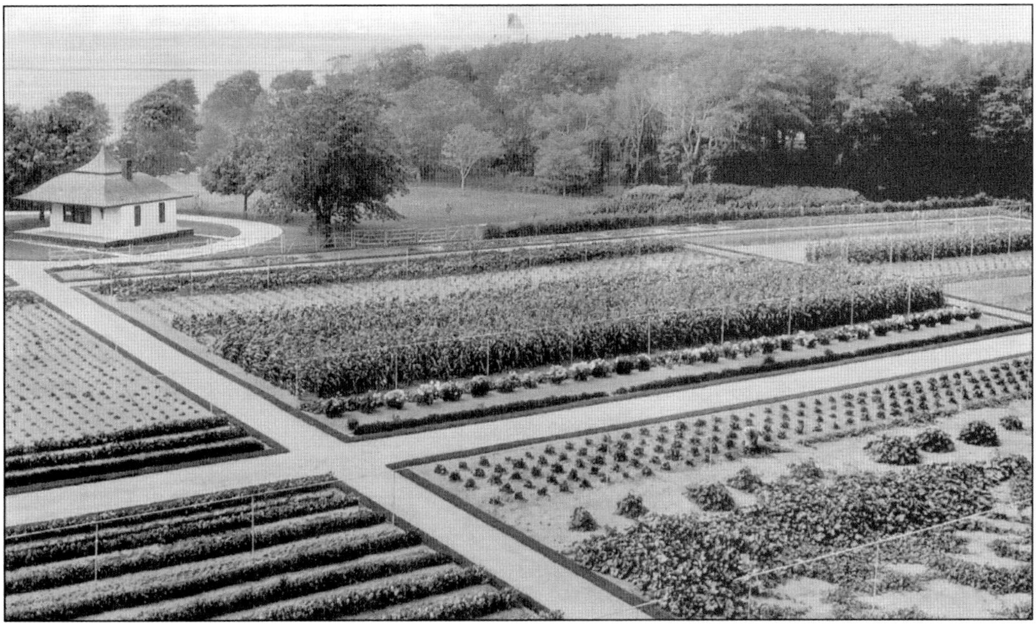

Stuccoed concrete farm buildings designed by noted farm architect Alfred Hopkins helped create what the *Suffolk County News* predicted would become known as "one of the show places of America." Frederick Bourne's new farm ended along the Long Island Rail Road tracks to the north, providing a convenient staging ground for loading and unloading material and produce. The farm buildings were destroyed in 1976, but the distinctive windmill-shaped water tower survived until 2005 when it was torn down. The farm was entered via Chicken Street. This road, today's Dale Drive, also contained the homes of many of the workers on Bourne's farm. (Both, courtesy of the Long Island Maritime Museum.)

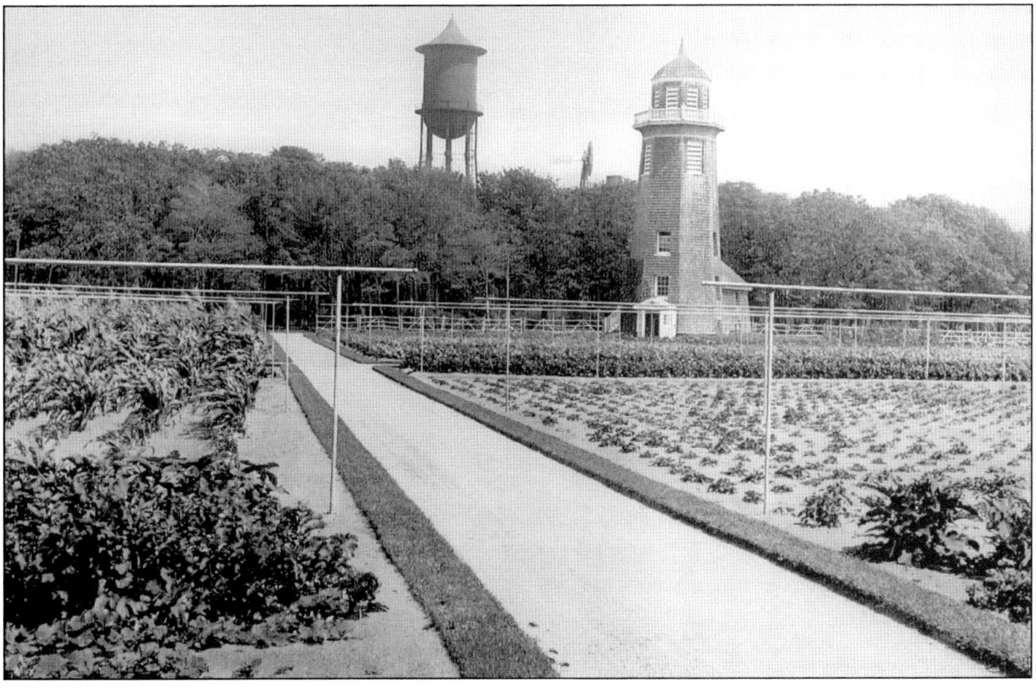

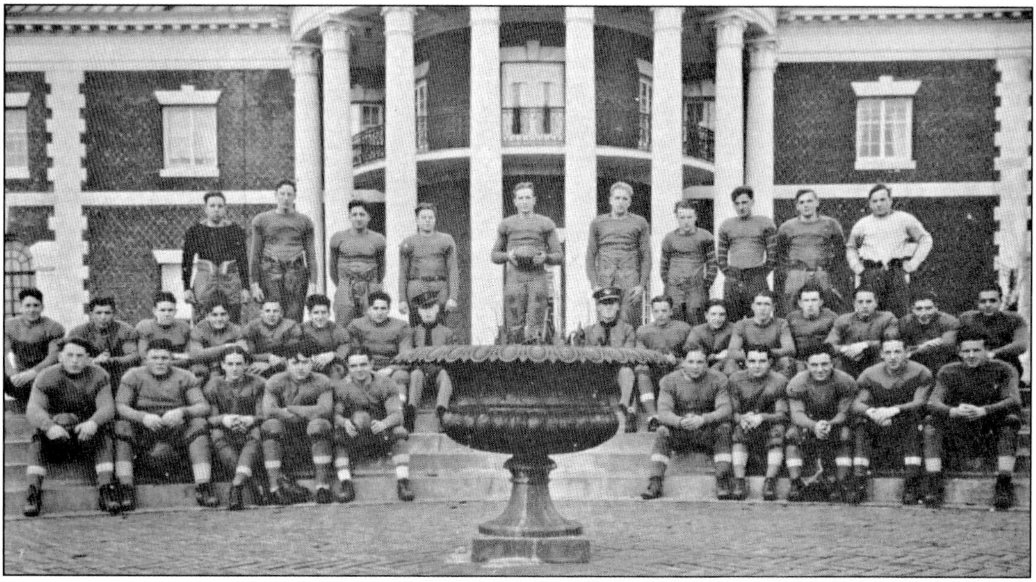

In 1926, Indian Neck Hall was sold to the Institute of the Brothers of the Christian Schools who moved their Clason Point Military Academy from the Bronx to Oakdale. They also changed their name to the La Salle Military Academy. As a result of the relocation, the football team seen in this 1928 photograph, got off to a late start and were not able to schedule any regular games. (Courtesy of LN509—La Salle Military Academy. De La Salle Christian Brothers Archives of the Long Island-New England District. Manhattan College.)

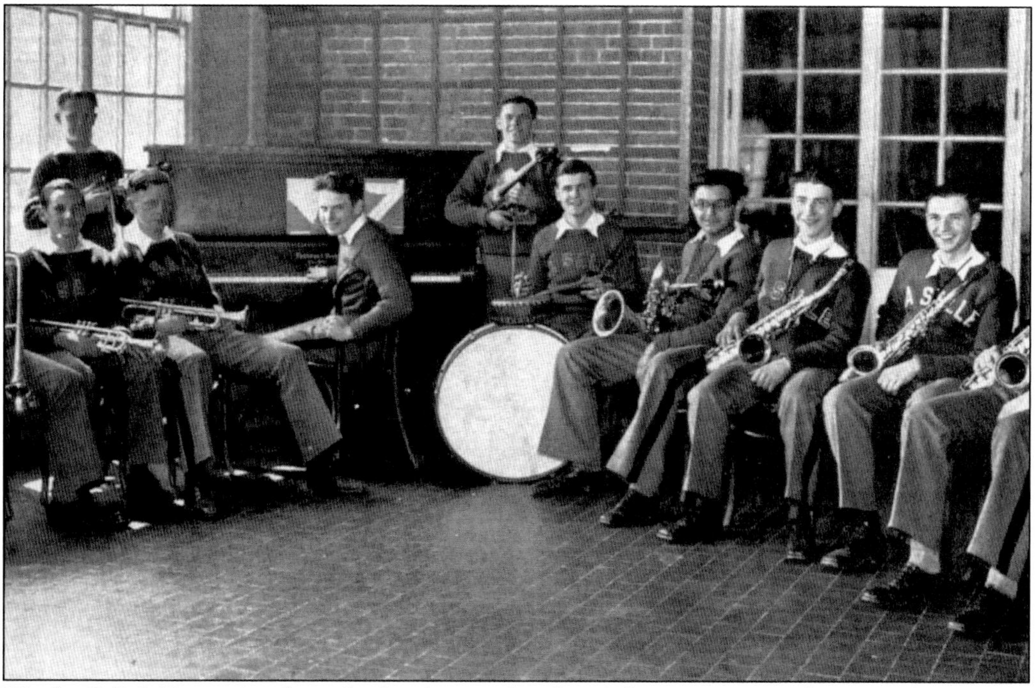

The La Salle Military Academy rhythm kings take a break from practice in this 1930 photograph. (Courtesy of LN509—La Salle Military Academy. De La Salle Christian Brothers Archives of the Long Island-New England District. Manhattan College.)

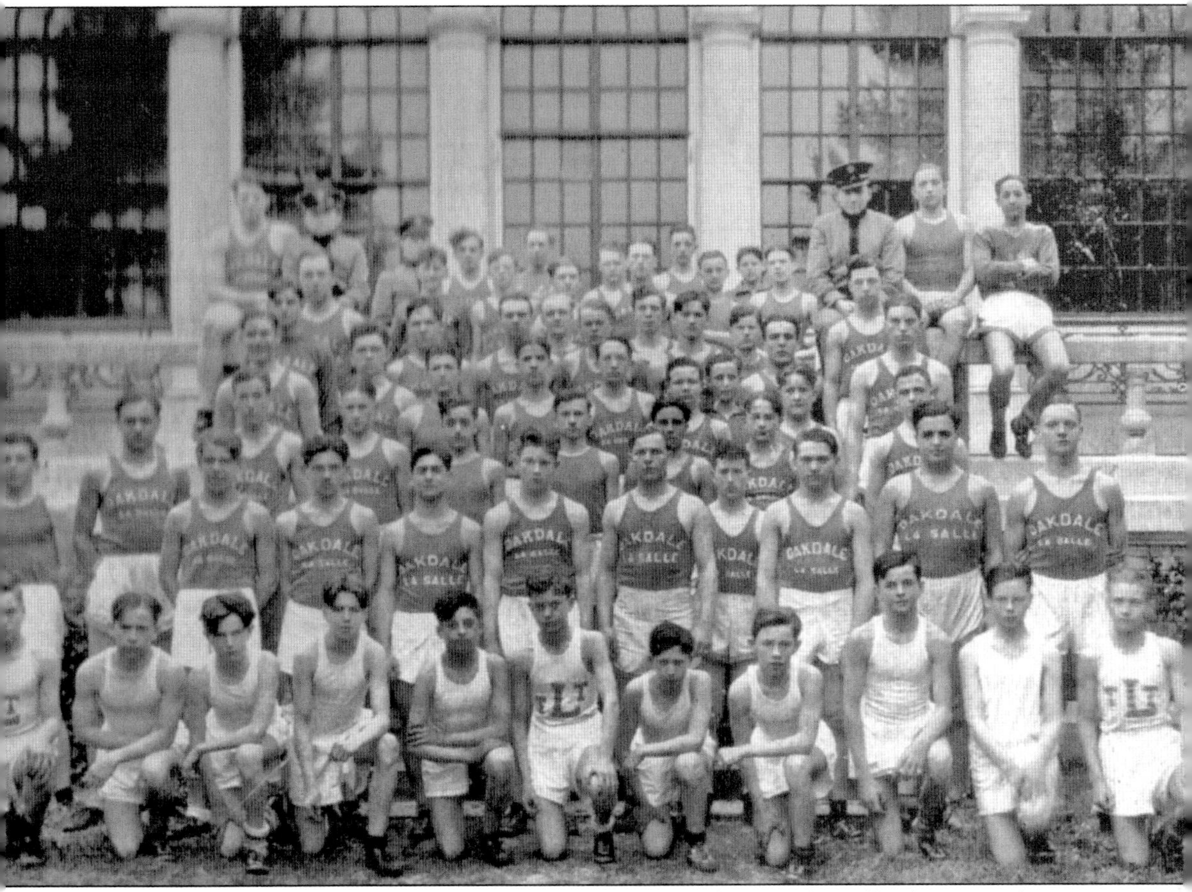

The La Salle track team for 1928–1929 poses in front of Indian Neck Hall. That year, the team came in third in the Catholic High School indoor track championships, making it their most successful year to date. (Courtesy of LN509—La Salle Military Academy. De La Salle Christian Brothers Archives of the Long Island-New England District. Manhattan College.)

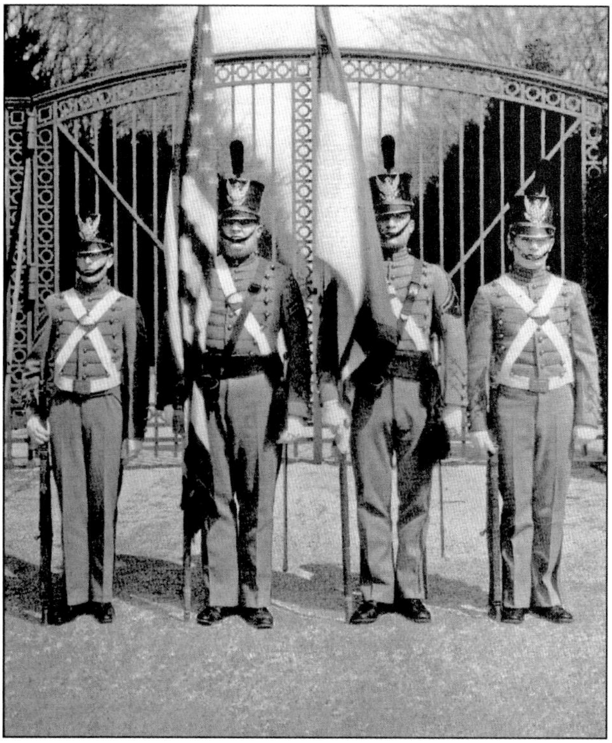

The 1930 La Salle color guard included, from left to right, George Stupalsky, 1930 color sergeant; William Stephani, 1930 color sargeant; John Manning, 1932 color corporal; and John Murphy, 1932 color corporal. (Courtesy of LN509—La Salle Military Academy. De La Salle Christian Brothers Archives of the Long Island-New England District. Manhattan College.)

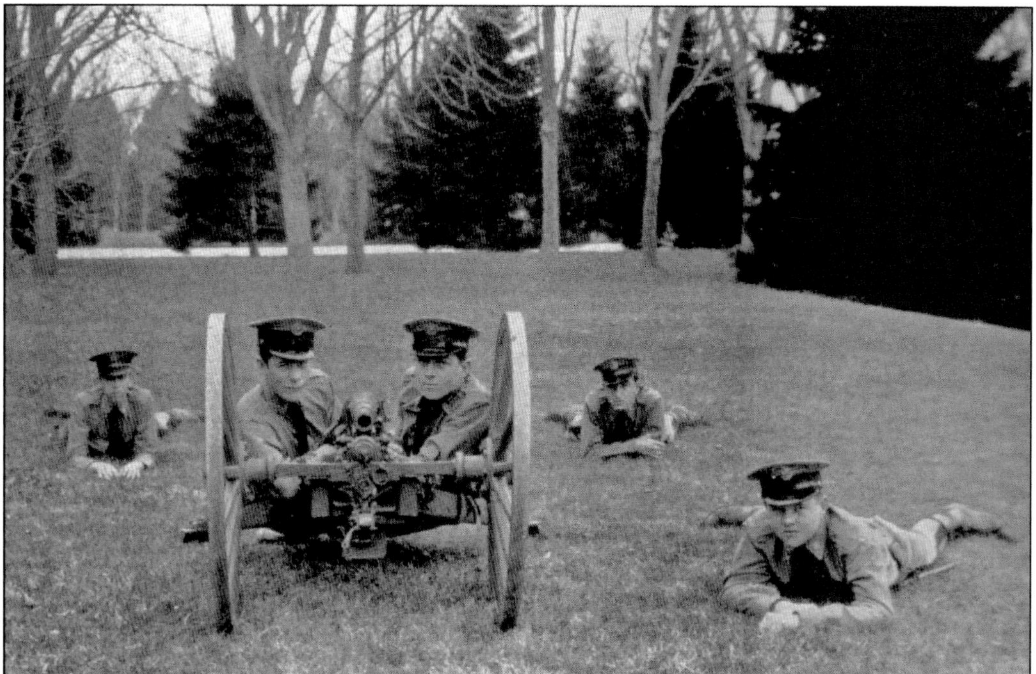

This photograph from the 1928 yearbook shows a machine gun crew of cadets posing on the grounds of the La Salle Military Academy. (Courtesy of LN509—La Salle Military Academy. De La Salle Christian Brothers Archives of the Long Island-New England District. Manhattan College.)

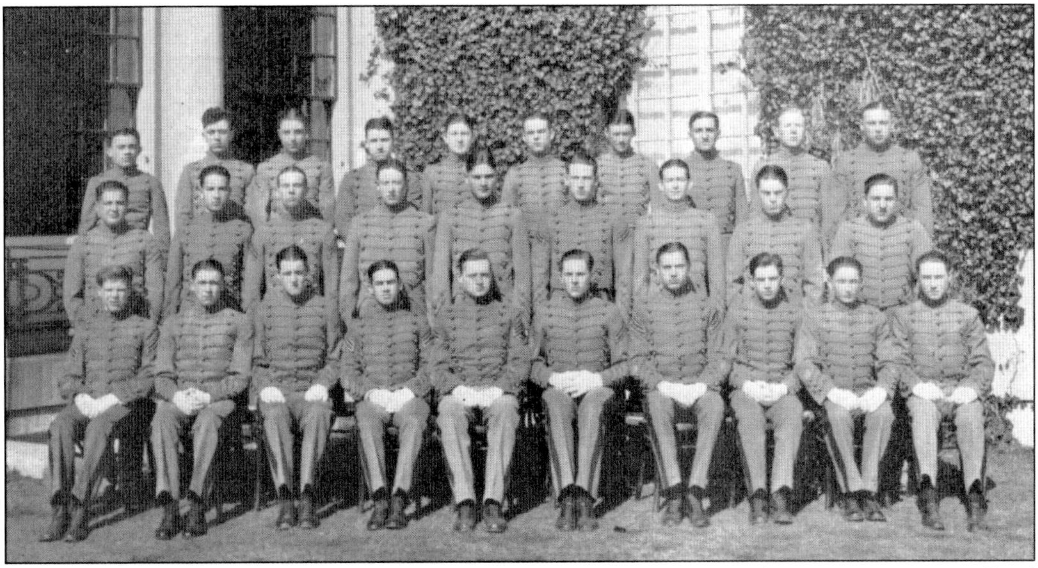

The La Salle Military Academy remained an all-male boarding school into the 1990s. In 1993, it offered a nonmilitary option as well as kindergarten through eighth grade. In 1995, they became coeducational. This photograph from 1928 shows the third year A class, part of the first group to make the move from the Bronx to Oakdale. (Courtesy of LN509—La Salle Military Academy. De La Salle Christian Brothers Archives of the Long Island-New England District. Manhattan College.)

This 1928 photograph shows the La Salle Military Academy battalion staff. From left to right are Maj. John H. Schaefer, Capt. Harold R. Morton, and Sgt. Maj. Jerome P. Knight. Some prominent La Salle alumni include White House chief of staff John Sununu and Los Angeles Dodgers owner Peter O'Malley. (Courtesy of LN509—La Salle Military Academy. De La Salle Christian Brothers Archives of the Long Island-New England District. Manhattan College.)

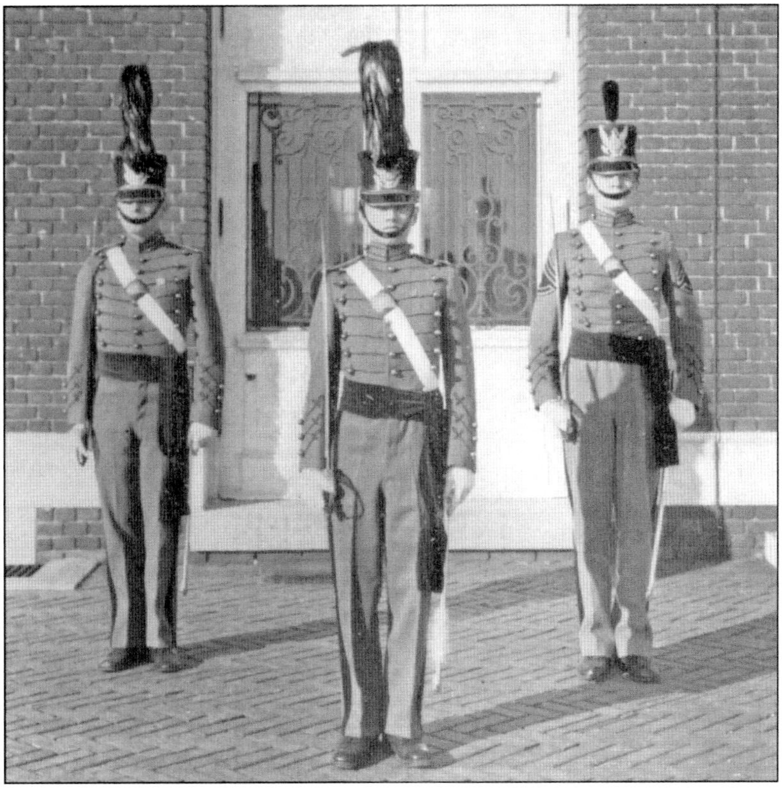

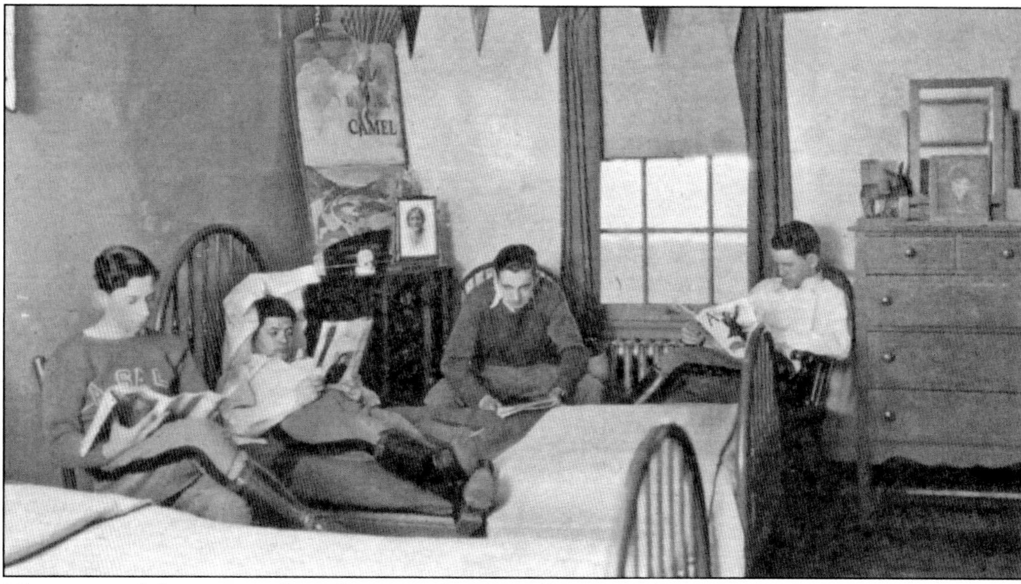

This postcard shows a number of unnamed cadets relaxing in their quarters at the La Salle Military Academy. The school drew its student body from the five boroughs of Manhattan as well as the Long Island area, but it also contained a noticeable amount of foreign students, particularly from South America.

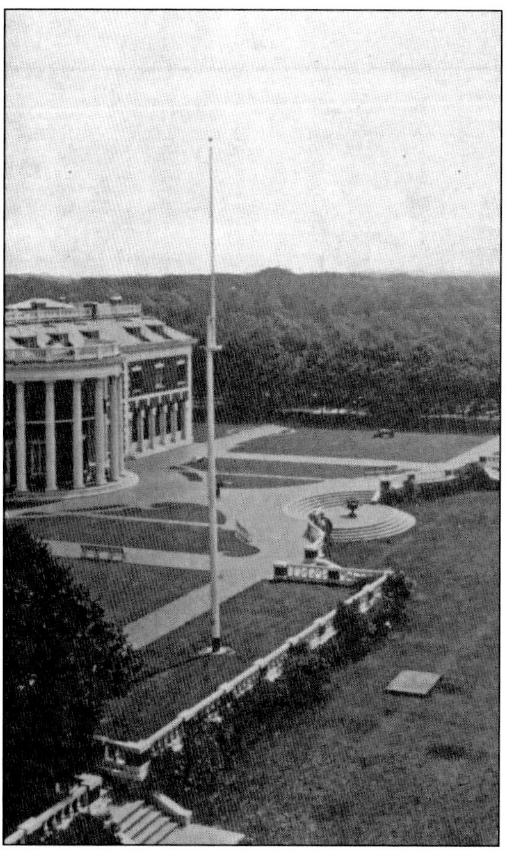

This postcard, dating from around the 1940s, shows the esplanade that overlooks the bay to the south. La Salle closed in 2001, and the property is now owned and run by St. John's University as their Oakdale campus.

Five

Vanderbilt's First and Second Idle Hour Mansions

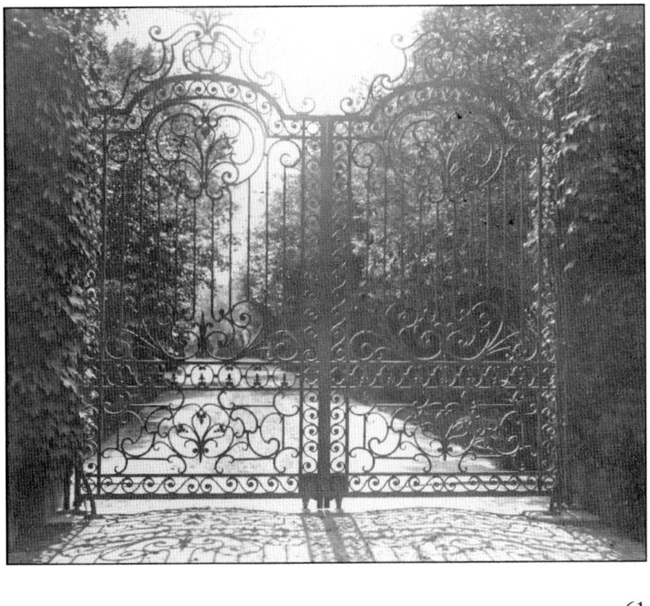

This undated photograph shows the west gate entrance to William K. Vanderbilt's Idle Hour estate in Oakdale. Vanderbilt was the grandson of Commodore Cornelius Vanderbilt and the son of William H. Vanderbilt. He would eventually line the entire north face of his estate fronting Montauk Highway with an iron fence. He would own two mansions on this property. (Courtesy of the Milstein Division of U.S. History, Local History, and Genealogy, the New York Public Library, Astor, Lenox, and Tilden Foundations.)

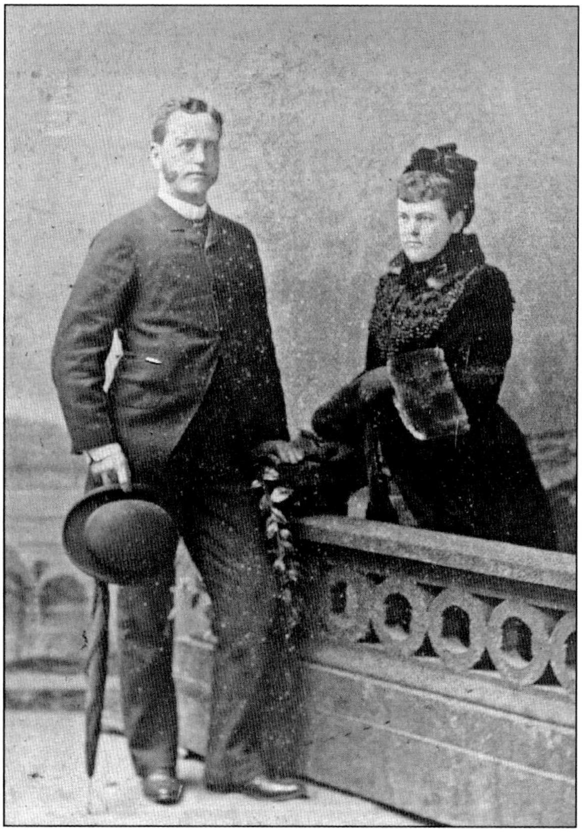

On April 20, 1875, around the time this photograph was taken, Vanderbilt married Alva Erskine, his first wife. The daughter of an Alabaman merchant, she was intent on establishing her family among New York's social elite. She had three children with Vanderbilt: Consuelo, born in 1877; William Kissam Jr., born in 1878; and Harold Stirling, born in 1884. The two divorced in 1895.

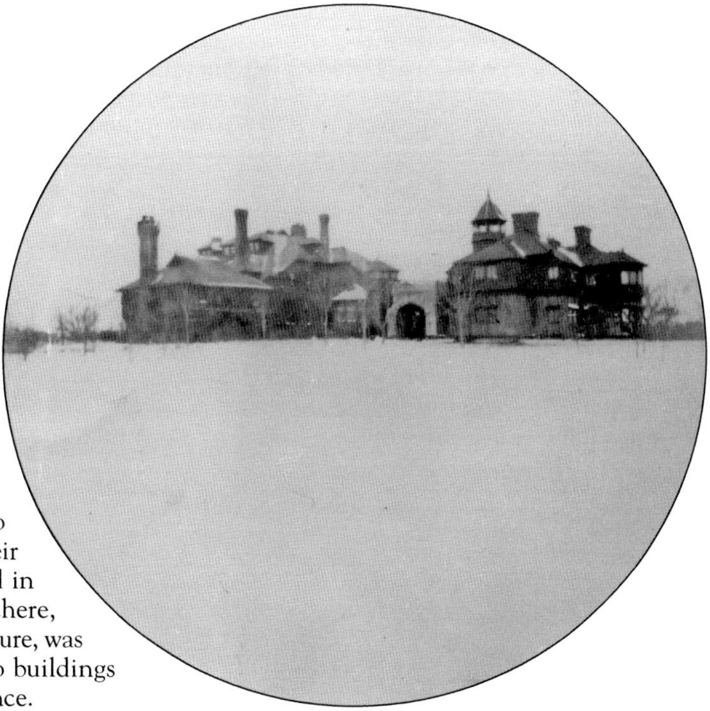

In 1892, in keeping with the social etiquette of the time, a large bachelor's wing, seen on the left side of the picture, was added to the original mansion. This wing served as an entertainment hub for unmarried men, or men who visited Idle Hour without their wives. Married couples stayed in the main house. A porte cochere, visible in the center of this picture, was constructed between the two buildings and served as the main entrance.

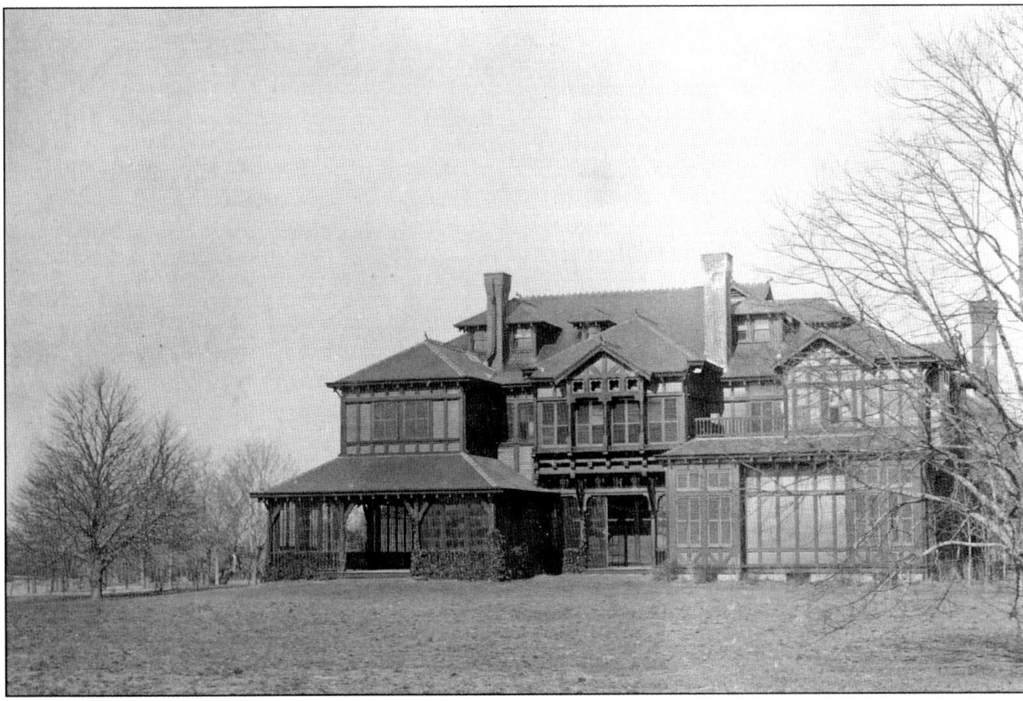

Alva Vanderbilt hired the architect Richard Morris Hunt to build a beautiful Queen Anne–style wooden house on the edge of the Connetquot River. This house was the first of many commissions that Hunt would take on for the Vanderbilt family and Alva. The house was completed in 1882 and was destroyed by fire on April 12, 1899.

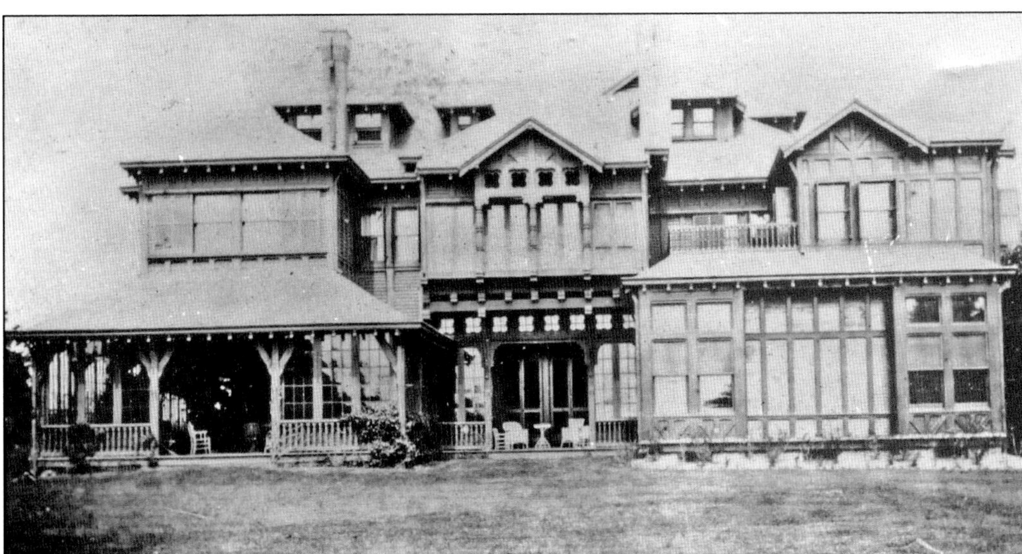

William K. Vanderbilt desired a country gentleman's existence. A member of the South Side Sportsmen's Club, he bought property in Oakdale in 1878. With Alva, he created a great working estate that served as a seasonal retreat for the family as well as a place for them to receive guests and entertain. This 1892 photograph shows the original Idle Hour mansion.

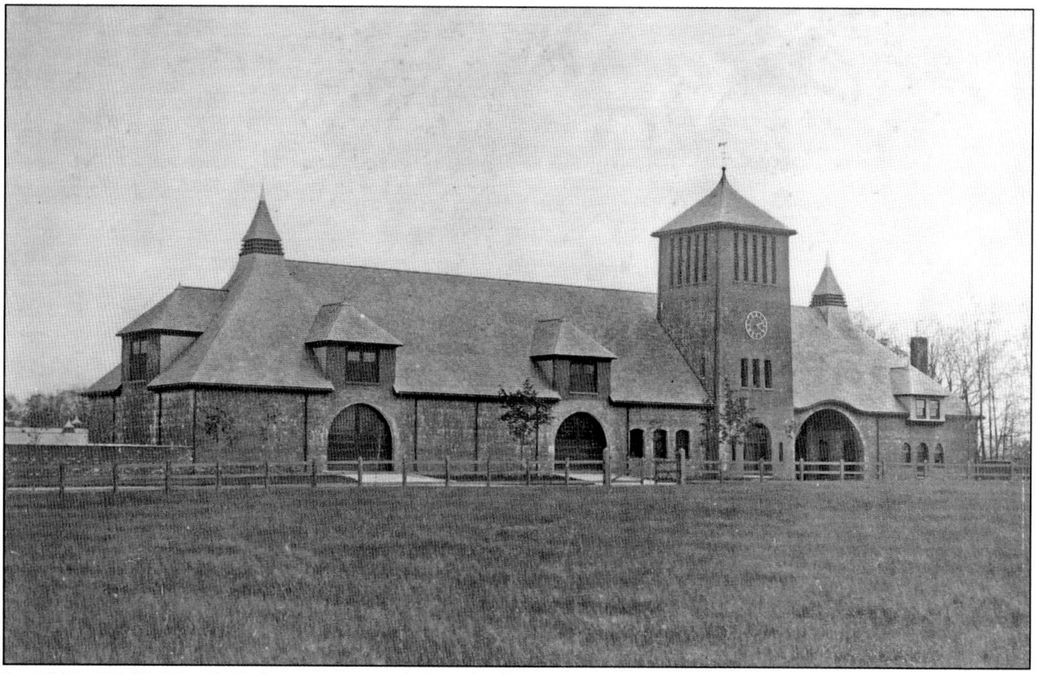

In 1899, W. K. Vanderbilt constructed the clock tower building in the farm complex. The clock itself cost $500 and had to be wound weekly by Mr. Terry, the Sayville jeweler. The building is believed to have been designed by architect Issac H. Green. The clock tower still stands today and is a private residence.

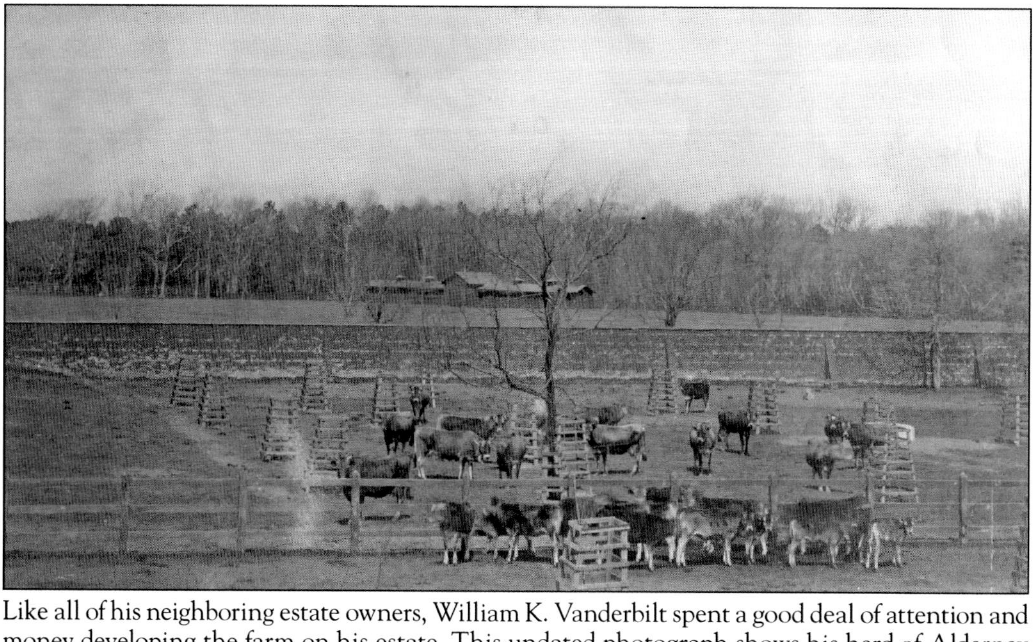

Like all of his neighboring estate owners, William K. Vanderbilt spent a good deal of attention and money developing the farm on his estate. This undated photograph shows his herd of Alderney dairy cattle. They are grazing on the southern portion of the estate grounds.

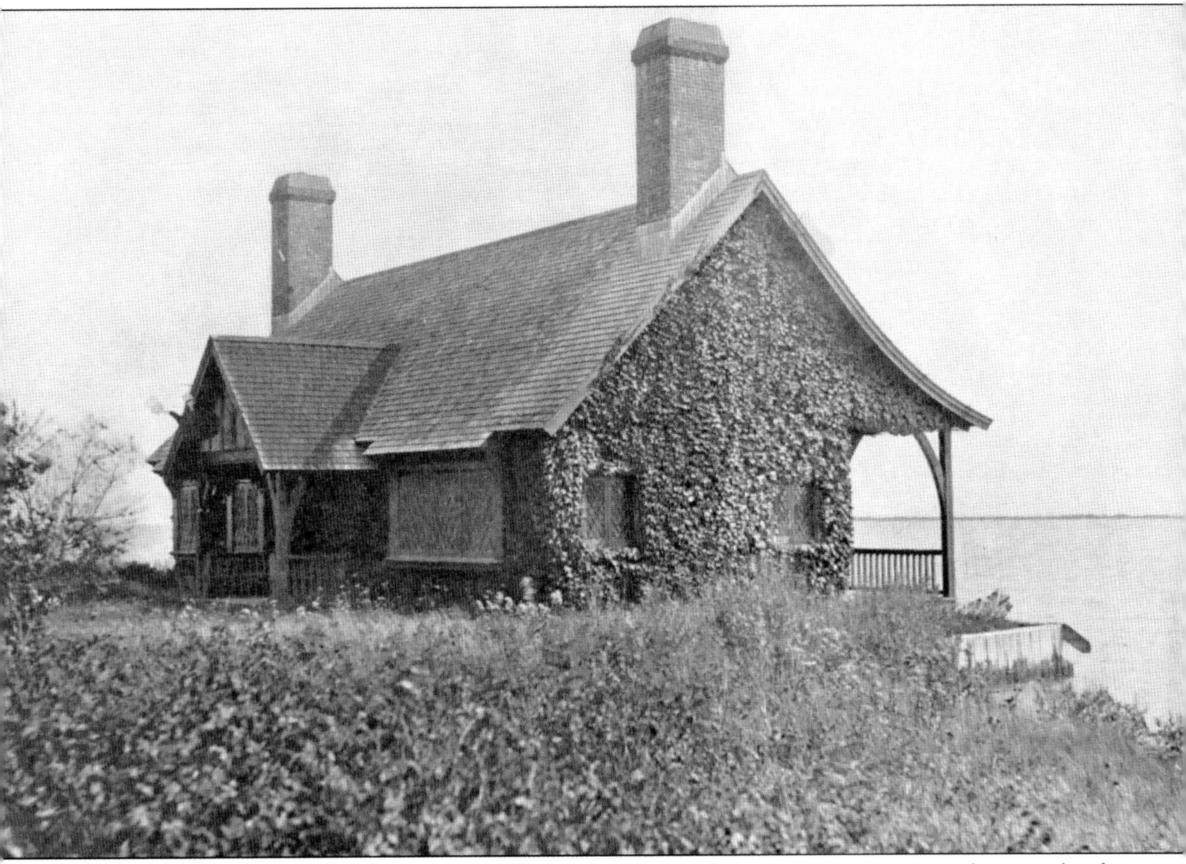

This undated photograph shows one of the outbuildings of the estate. Sitting on the mouth of the Connetquot River overlooking the Great South Bay, the tea house was designed by architect Isaac Green and built in 1888. Although the original structure is much altered, it survives to this day after many permutations as a restaurant. It has been the Singing Kettle, Hotel Pirnat, and the Saxon Arms and is now the Riverview.

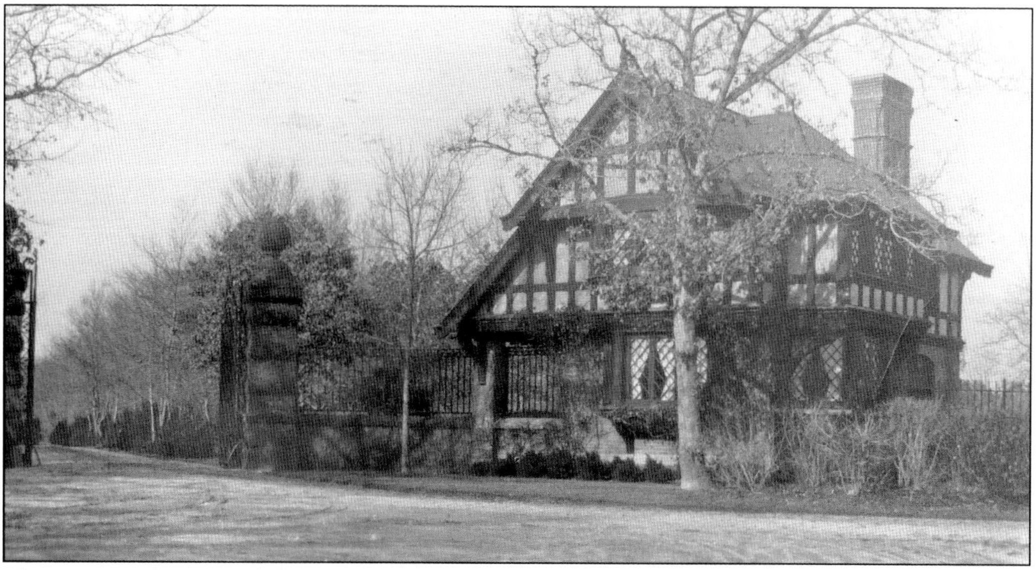

The west gatehouse and the entrance gate to Idle Hour was mostly likely designed by architect Richard Morris Hunt and built in 1882. Sometimes referred to as the "pouting house;" it is said Vanderbilt spent lots of time here once he discovered his wife, Alva's, affair with O. H. P. Belmont. Located very close to the Long Island Rail Road tracks, this gatehouse also served as Vanderbilt's personal train depot.

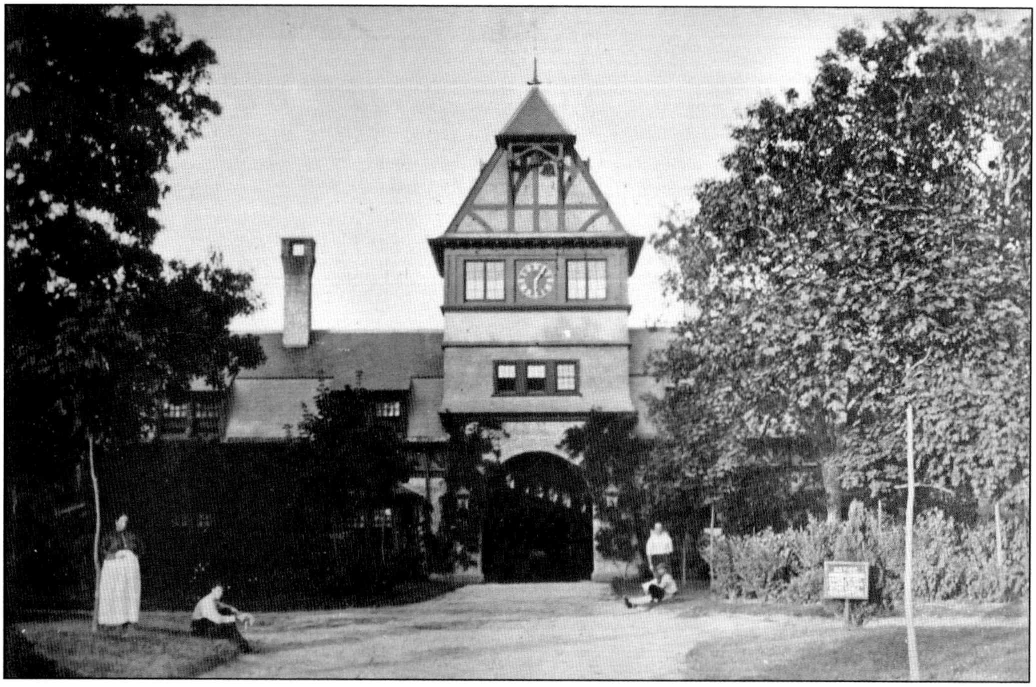

Built in 1882, the carriage house for the William K. Vanderbilt estate was located at the corner of Idle Hour Boulevard and Chateau Drive. Designed by architect Richard Morris Hunt, the initial cost of the building was put at $400,000. A fire in the 1950s destroyed the facade. (Courtesy of the Milstein Division of U.S. History, Local History, and Genealogy, the New York Public Library, Astor, Lenox, and Tilden Foundations.)

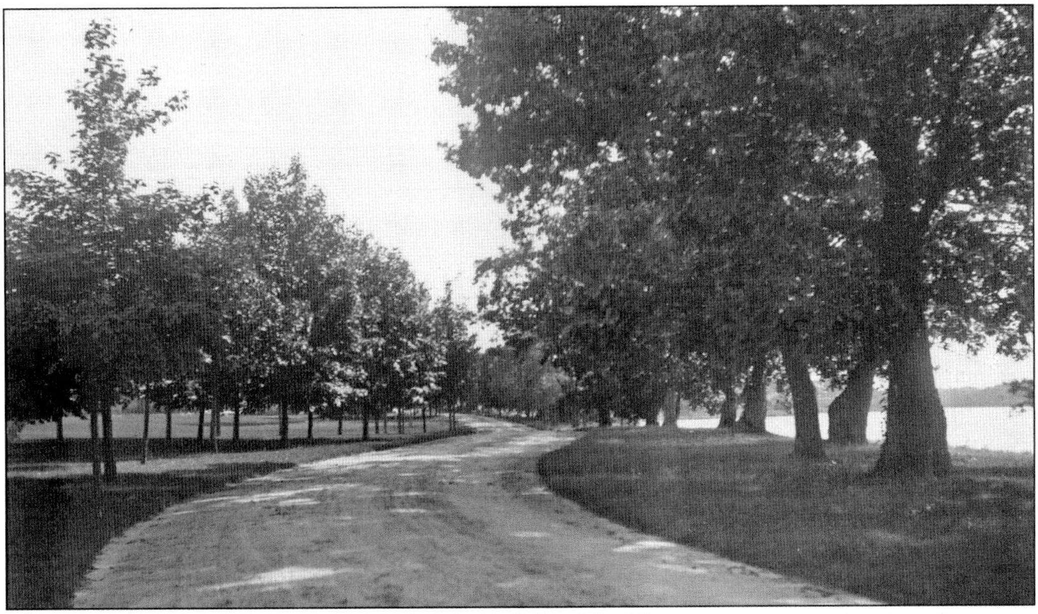

The land on which William K. Vanderbilt built his Idle Hour estate was undeveloped swamps and woodland. He eventually transformed it with walks and roadways stretching through the parklike landscape. The undated photograph above shows today's Shore Drive, which Vanderbilt had built along the east bank of the Connetquot River. (Courtesy of the Milstein Division of U.S. History, Local History, and Genealogy, the New York Public Library, Astor, Lenox, and Tilden Foundations.)

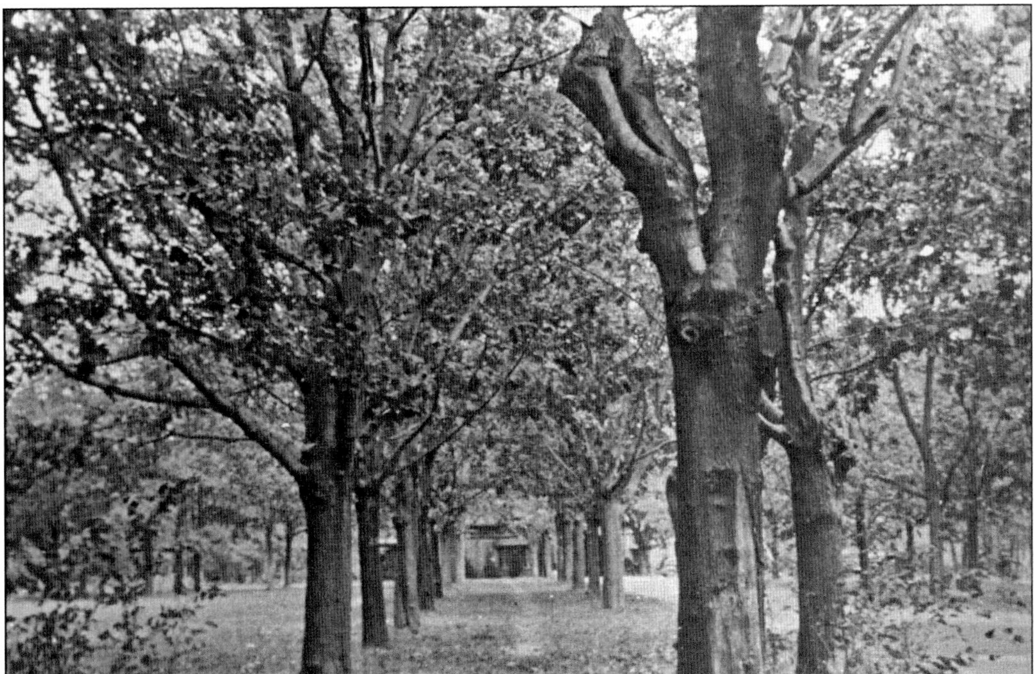

This photograph shows a path leading to the carriage house on the Idle Hour estate. Although dated to about 1940, little has changed in the bucolic nature of the surroundings.

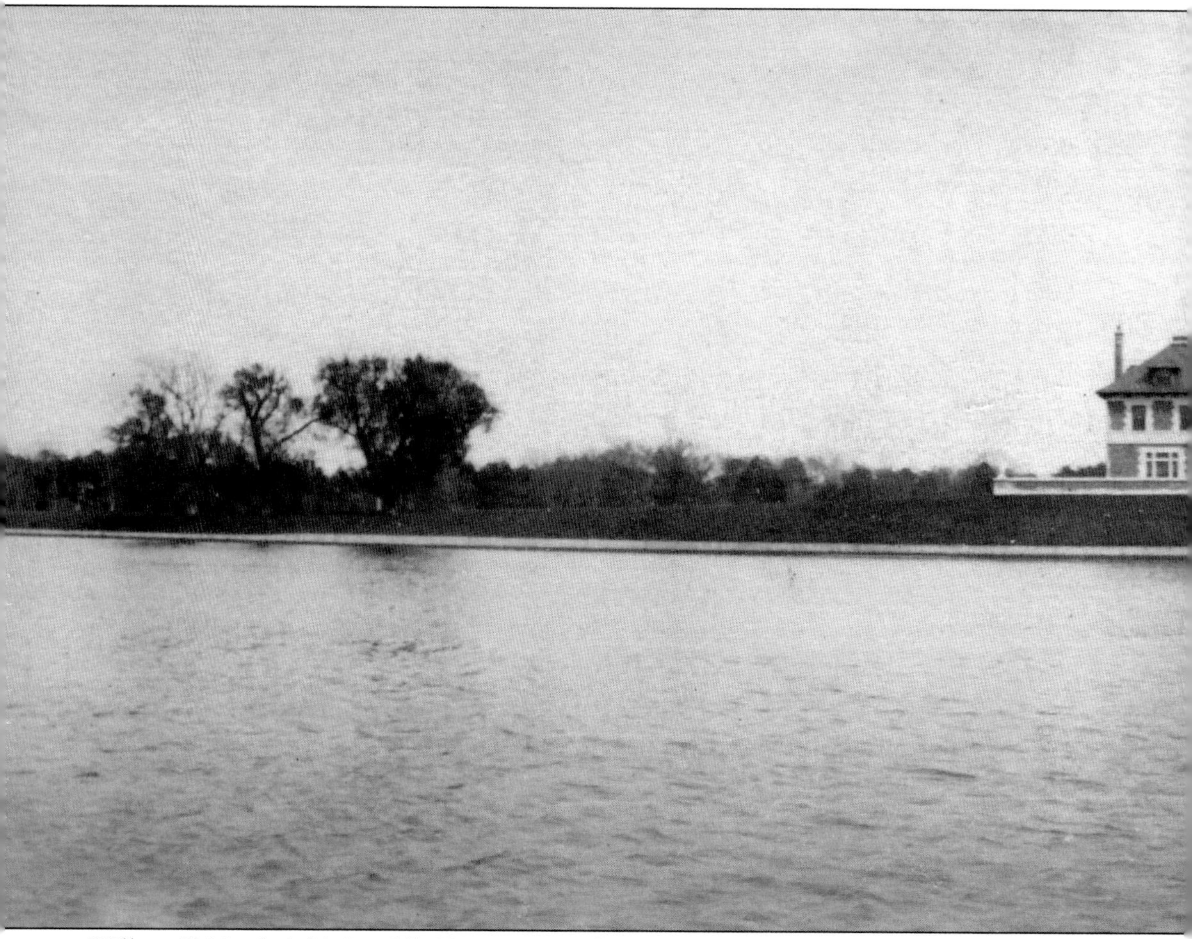

William K. Vanderbilt's first Idle Hour mansion burned down in 1899 while his son Willie K. was visiting during his honeymoon. Work was started immediately to rebuild a new and fireproof Idle Hour, seen here in this panoramic photograph. The palm court, bachelor wing, and tennis court

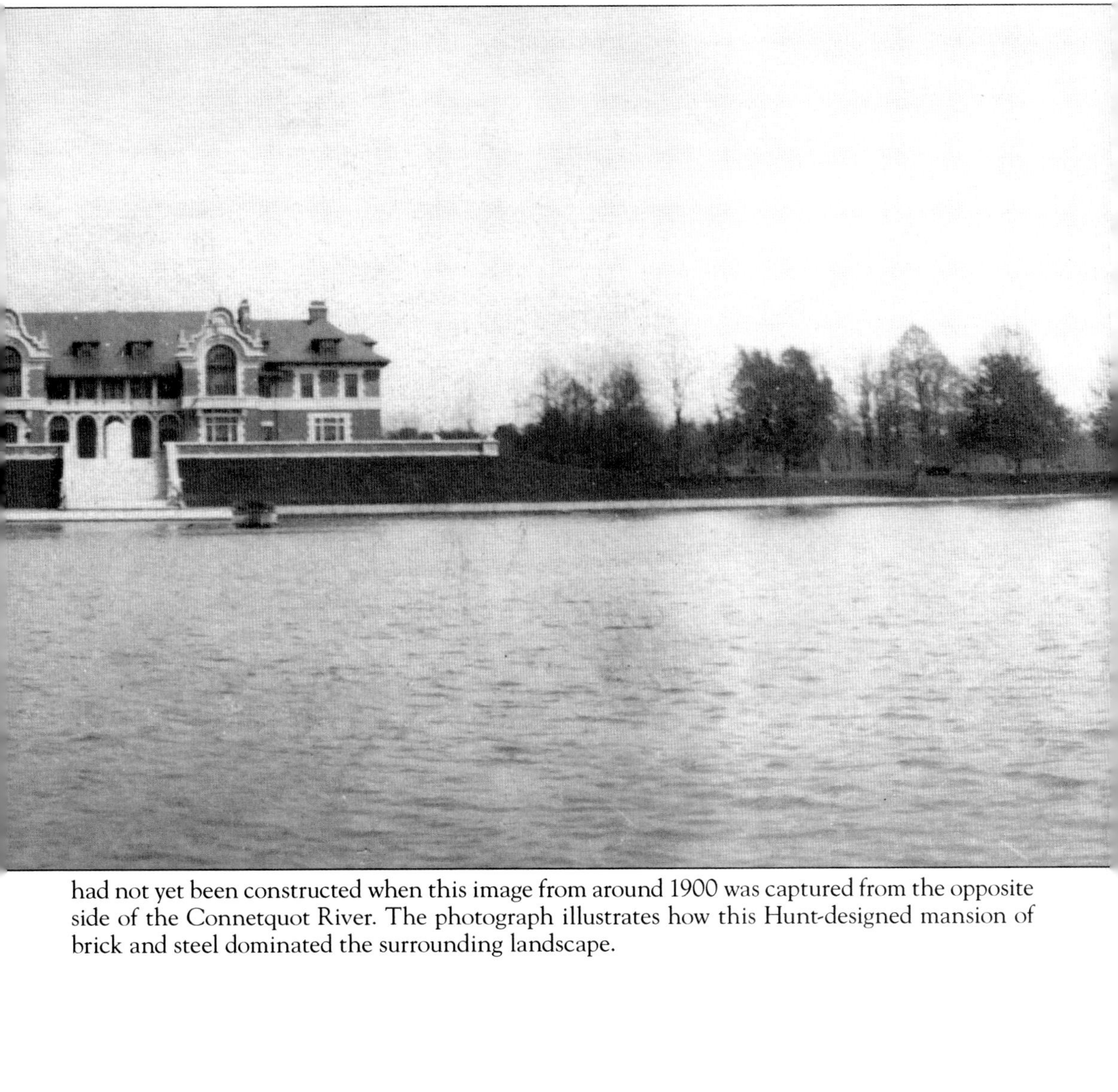

had not yet been constructed when this image from around 1900 was captured from the opposite side of the Connetquot River. The photograph illustrates how this Hunt-designed mansion of brick and steel dominated the surrounding landscape.

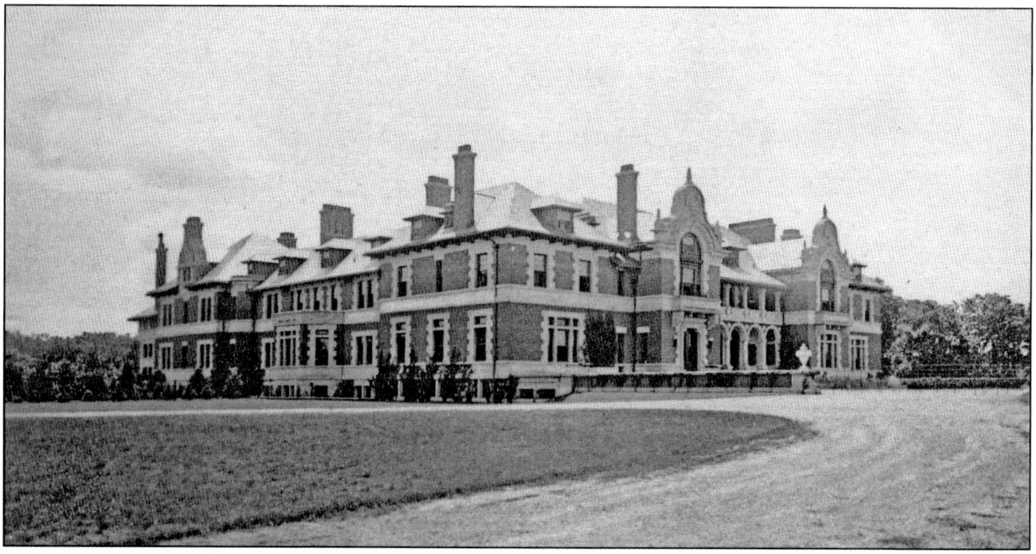

The two wings of Idle Hour are clearly seen in this photograph. On the left is the guest wing and behind it is the original bachelor's wing, where the smoking room and fives court were located on the first floor and bedrooms for single men were on the second floor. The wing on the right contains the public rooms of the house on the first floor and the family quarters on the second floor.

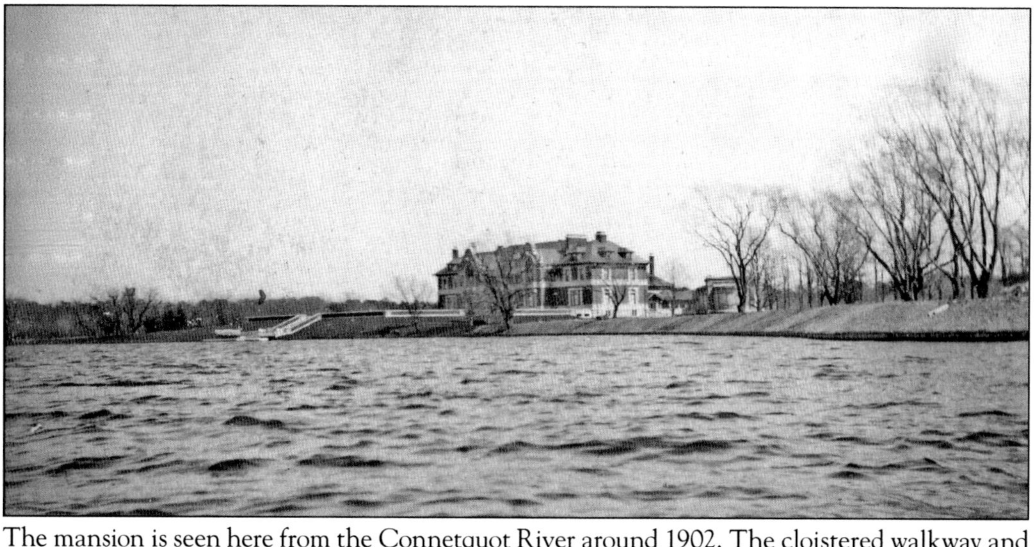

The mansion is seen here from the Connetquot River around 1902. The cloistered walkway and palm garden are visible on the right. Construction had not yet begun on the bachelor wing and tennis court when this image was taken, as they would appear further to the right of the palm garden. On the left side, the stairs leading to the mahogany dock are clearly visible.

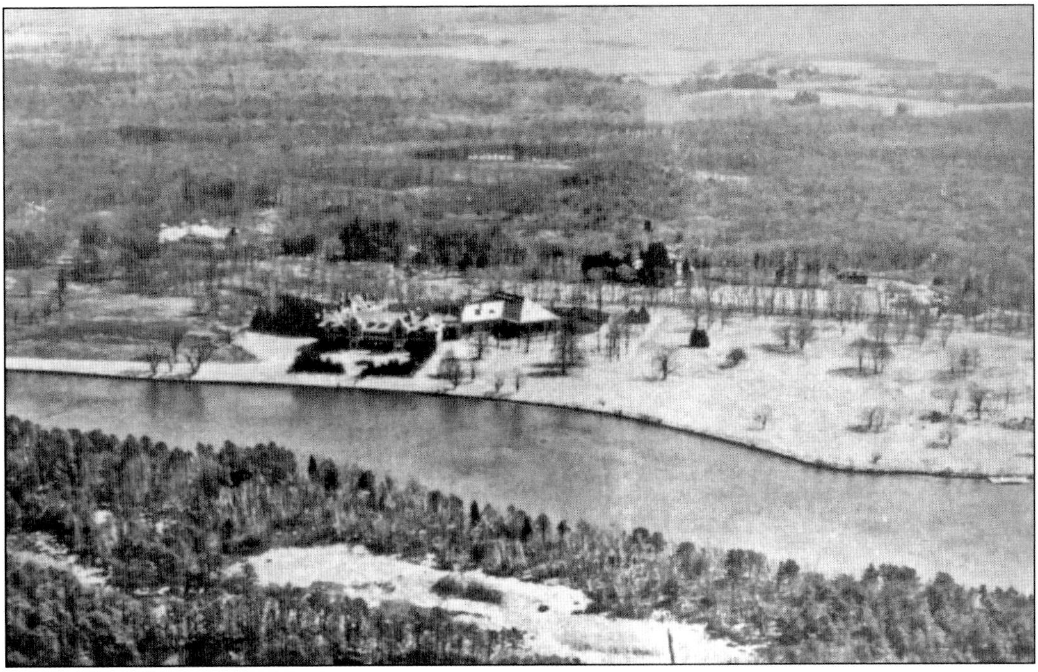

This early photograph shows Idle Hour from the air. In the foreground is part of William Bayard Cutting's property. Idle Hour, complete with bachelor wing and tennis court, are visible. The white roof to the left of Idle Hour is the stables and coach house. To the right in a small clearing is the palm house. In the upper right side of the photograph, in the far background, the outline of Christopher Robert's estate can just be distinguished.

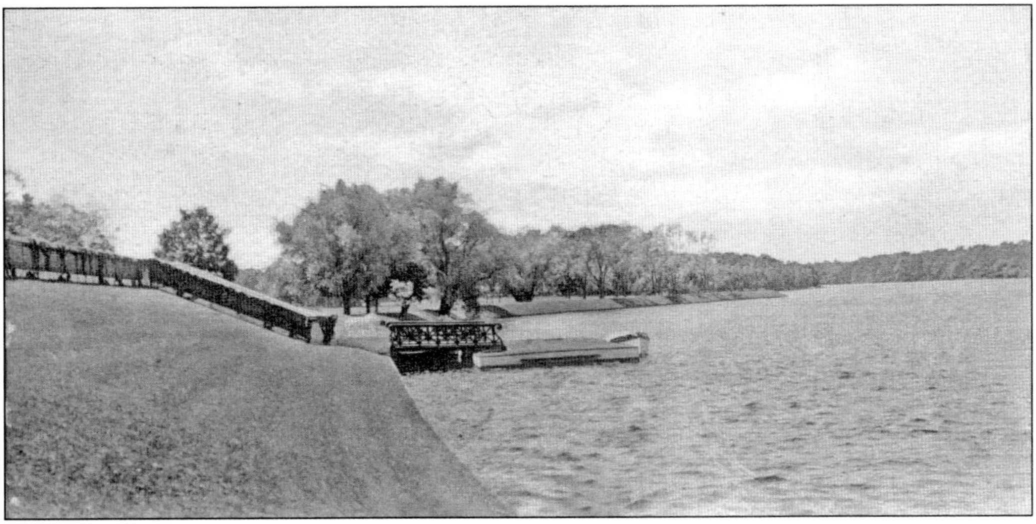

William K. Vanderbilt's Idle Hour mansion was designed by architect Richard Howland Hunt to face the Connetquot River, meaning that the front steps lead down to the water's edge. Vanderbilt dredged the river to allow for the passage of his boats to take him to his doorstep. This photograph shows the floating mahogany dock at which he would embark.

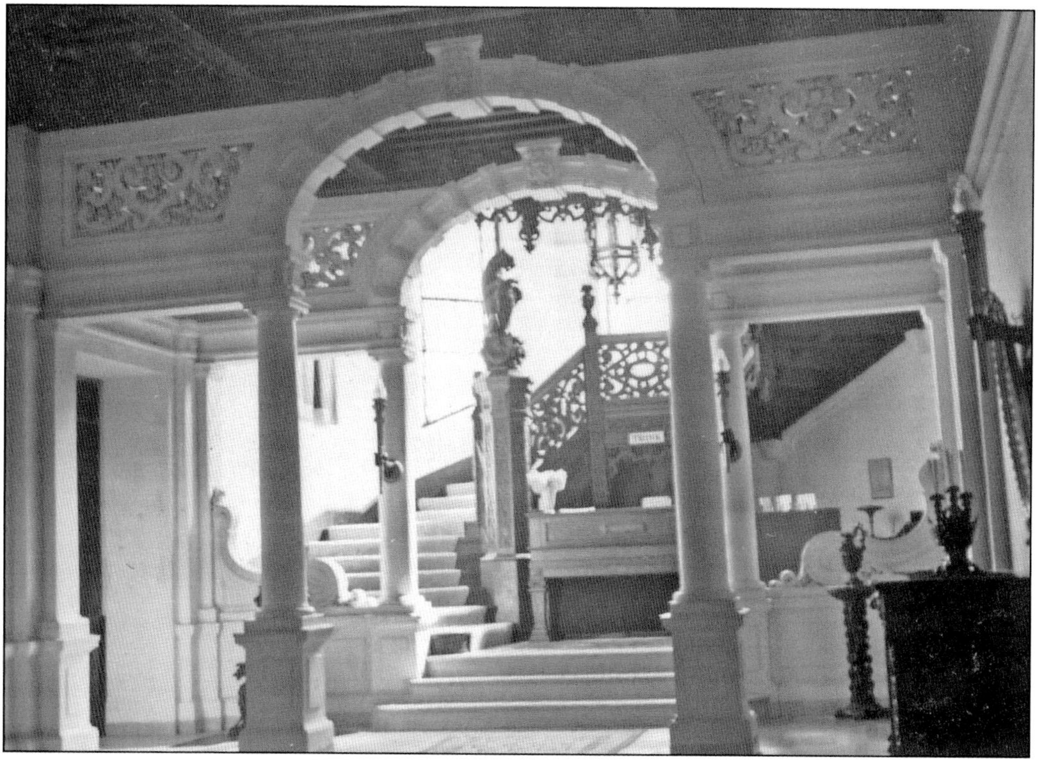

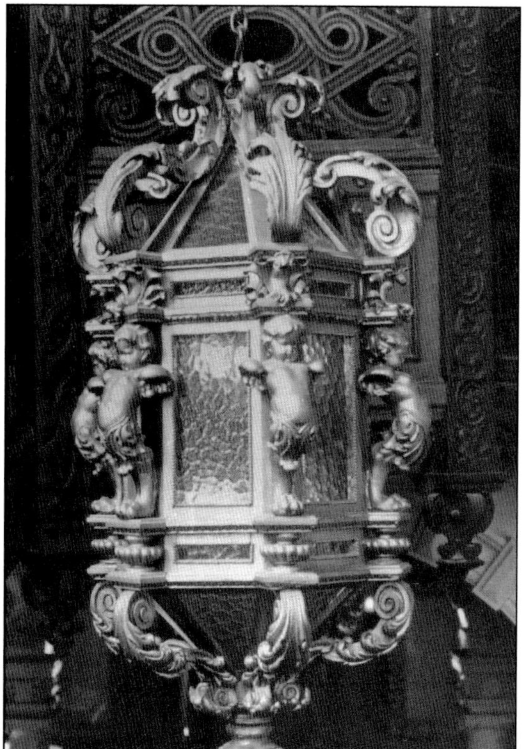

The main staircase of Idle Hour featured an intricately carved banister and newel post. Located just off the main entrance to the mansion, it also featured multicolored, diamond-shaped, stained-glass windows and a beautiful chandelier that featured intricate leaf motifs and many Putti, figures of infant boys often found in European Renaissance art. The chandelier and stairs were lost in a 1974 fire.

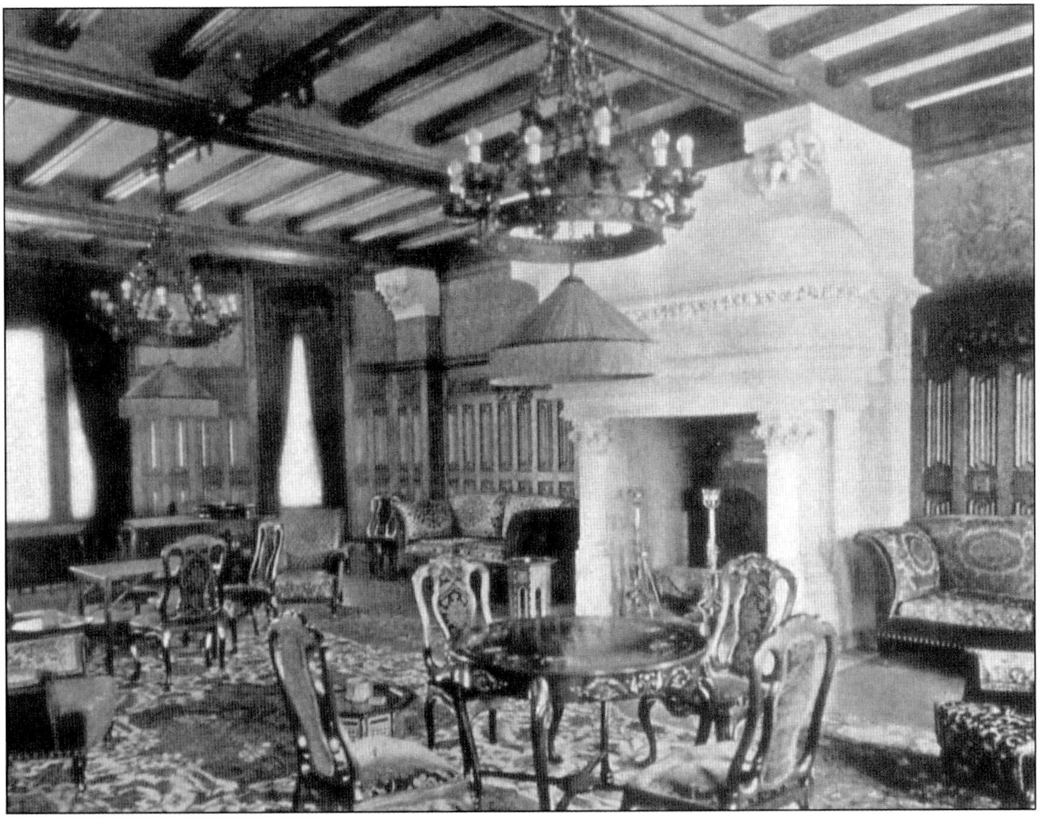

The smoking room was separated from the hall by a Gothic-style, carved oak screen. The room was dominated by a massive sandstone fireplace with carved stone, Grecian ornamentation, and antique furnishings. Not a room to be visited by women, it was located in what was then the old bachelor wing of the mansion. The room was lost in the 1974 fire.

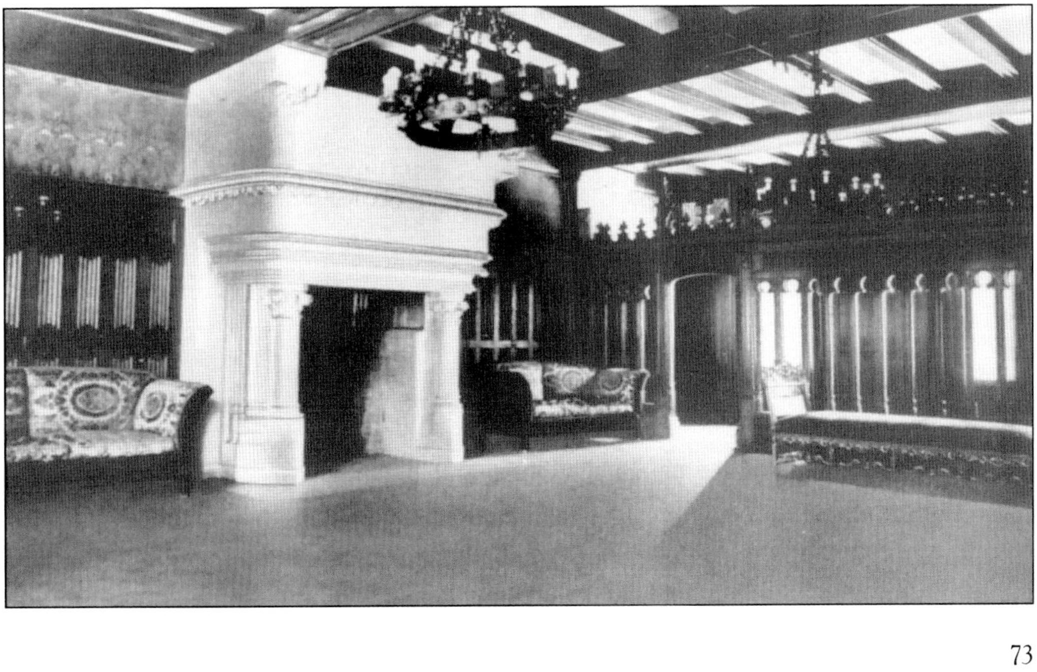

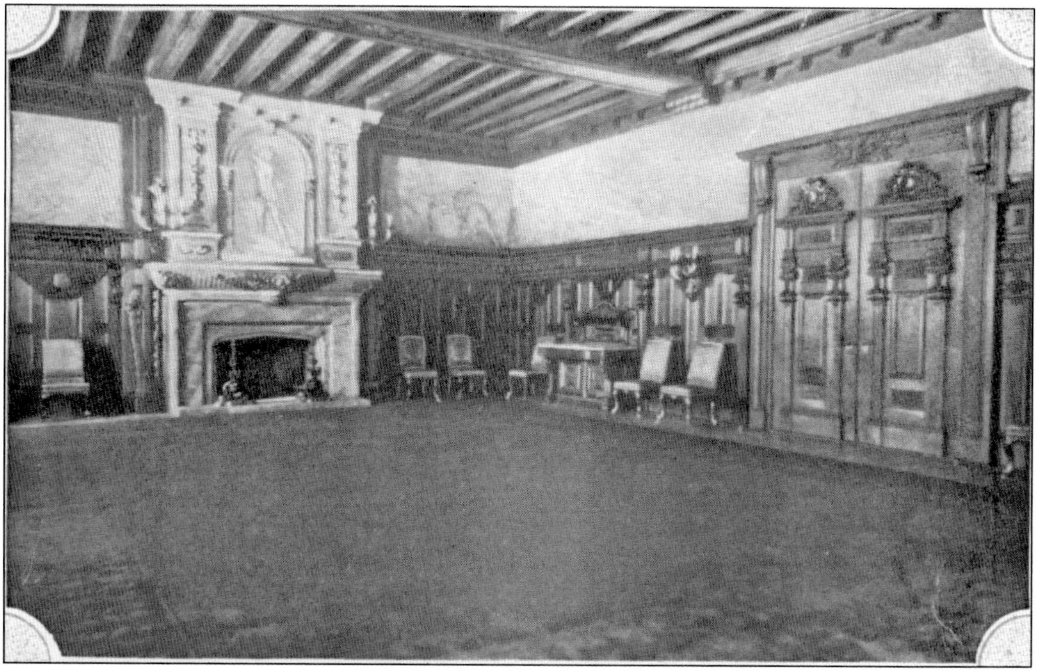

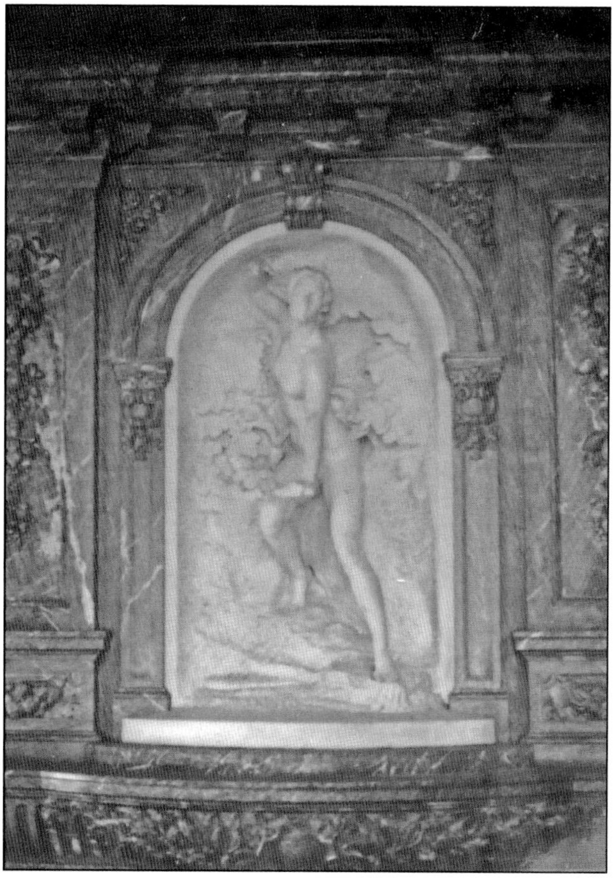

The dining room is dominated by the Karl Bitter sculpture of Diana above the fireplace. Karl Bitter also designed the ivory colored, cast-plaster harvest friezes surrounding the room. Below the friezes, the walls are paneled with hand-rubbed Circassian walnut. The photograph of Diana at left is from sometime in the 1960s. By this point, she had lost the bow she once held. The cast-plaster friezes were lost in the 1974 fire; Diana and the paneling remain.

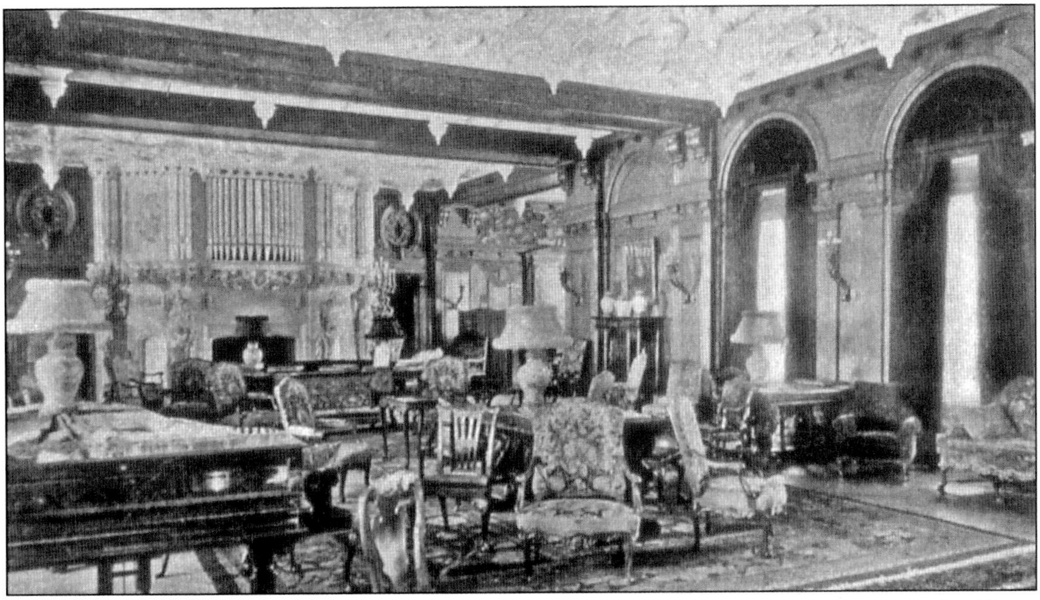

The white sandstone fireplace imported from Europe is the focal point of the living hall. Above the fireplace are the pipes of an Aeolian organ. The ceiling features intricately detailed pendentive plaster. The spacious living hall is furnished with antiques, which were relocated so that the room could be used as a ballroom. The walls were paneled with English oak. The ceiling and oak paneling were lost in the 1974 fire. The Aeolian organ is believed to have been relocated to Eagle's Nest, the Centerport, New York, estate of Vanderbilt's son.

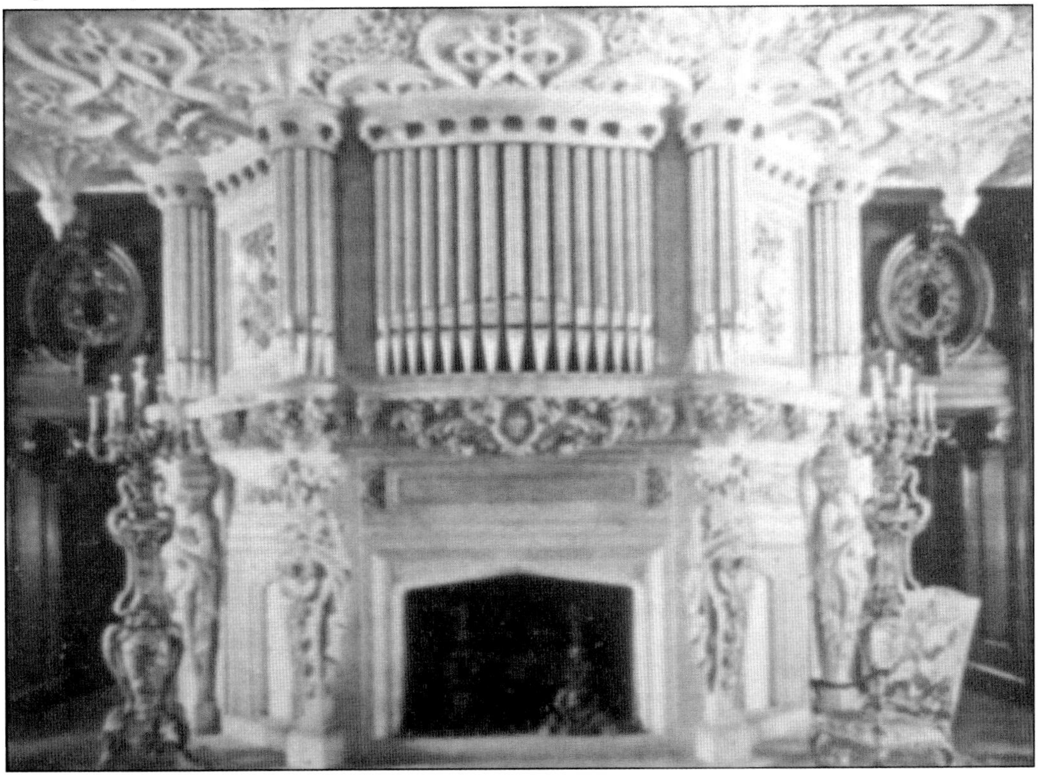

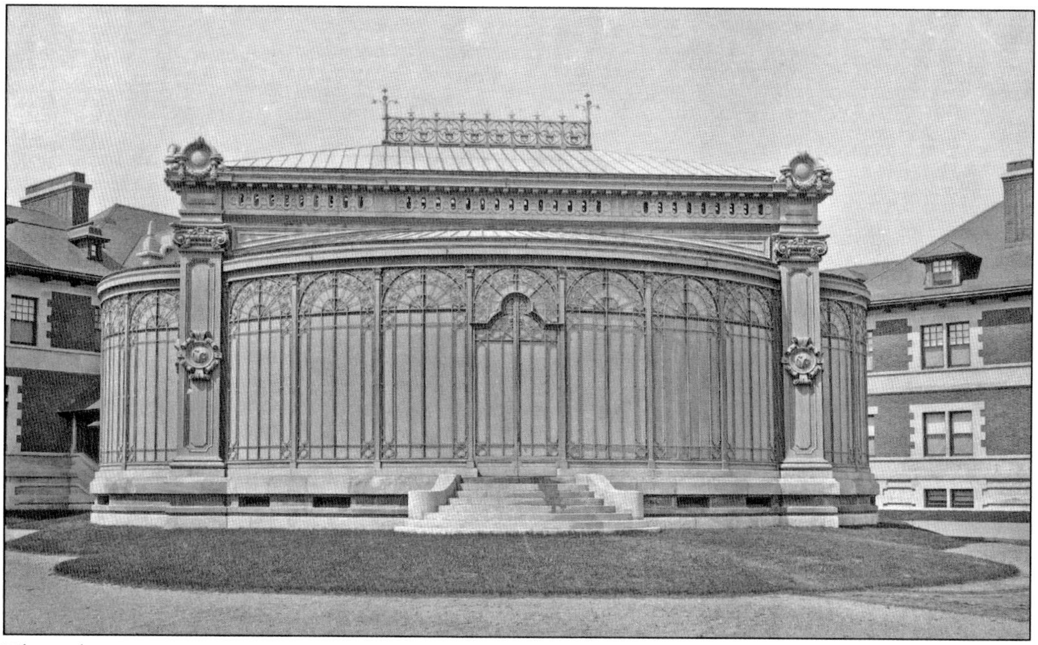

The palm court construction was completed in 1902. In this rare view, the outside entrance to the palm court is seen here with the wings of the Idle Hour main house framing it on either side. The photograph was taken before construction of the bachelor wing was begun, as the photographer of this image would now be standing inside the bachelor wing.

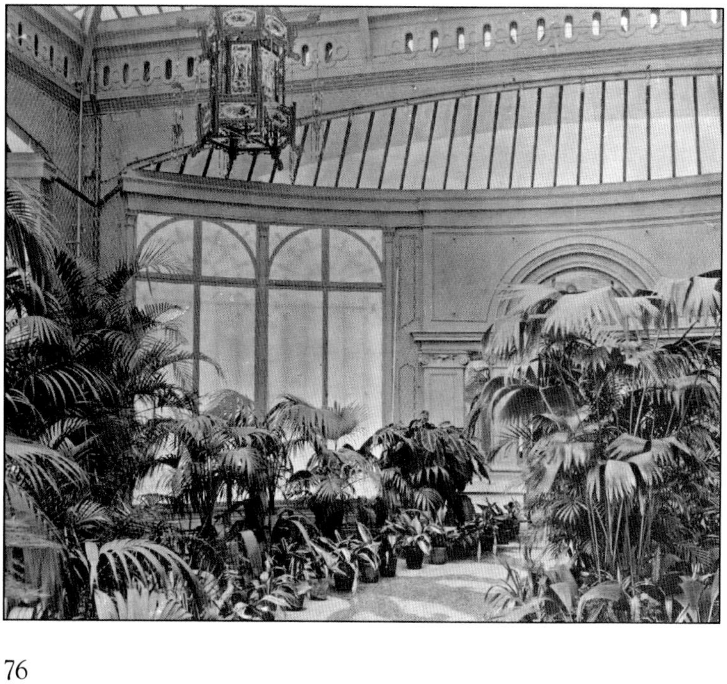

This photograph shows the interior of the palm court shortly after it was completed in 1902. The architect was Richard Howland Hunt. Decorative ironwork was used for the framework of the structure as seen near the roof. The walls were covered in lattice work and large decorative Chinese lanterns were used to light the space at night. In 1904, William K. Vanderbilt decided to build a larger palm house on the estate and converted the former palm court into a Turkish-inspired room.

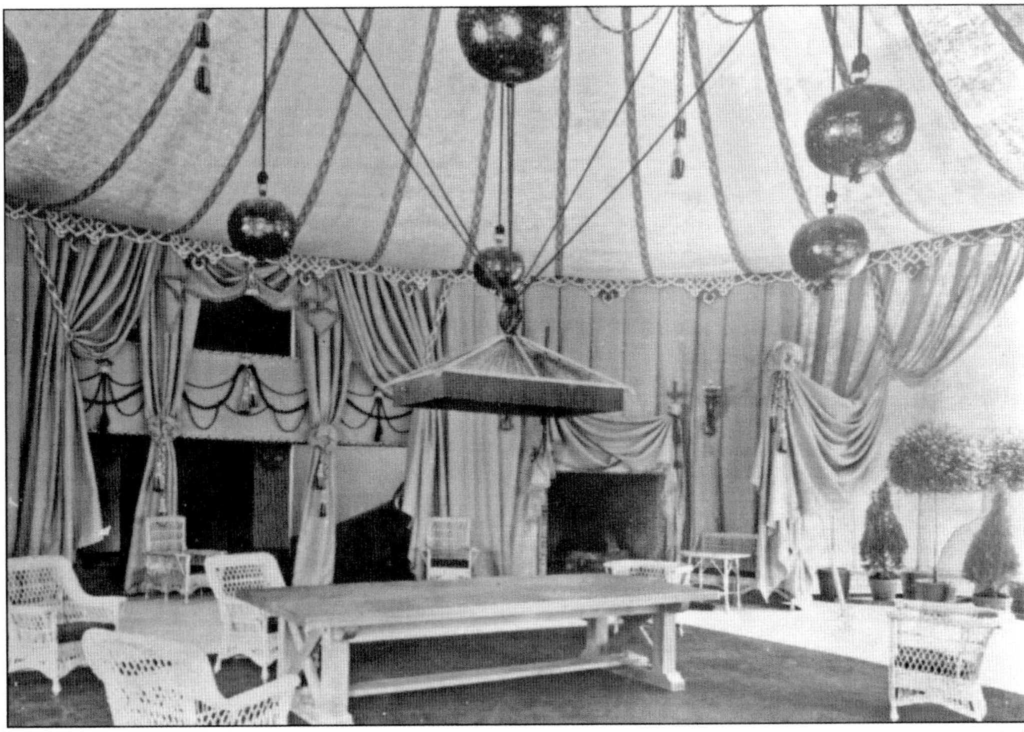

It was fashionable among country gentlemen to have a room in the house inspired by Middle Eastern decor. Architects Warren and Wetmore were employed to redesign the palm court. They tented the space with luxurious fabric, added large amounts of decorative trim and tassels, and replaced the Chinese lanterns with fabulous Turkish lamps.

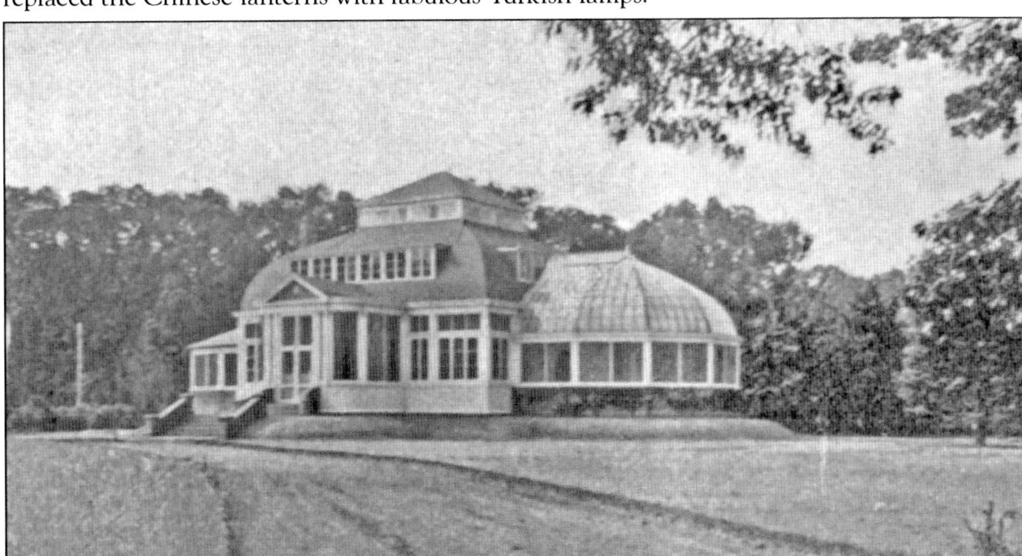

William K. Vanderbilt hired the firm of Lord and Burnham to construct this palm house conservatory near the mansion in 1904. This elegant structure replaced the smaller palm court that was constructed as part of the second Idle Hour mansion in 1902. Today it is a private residence.

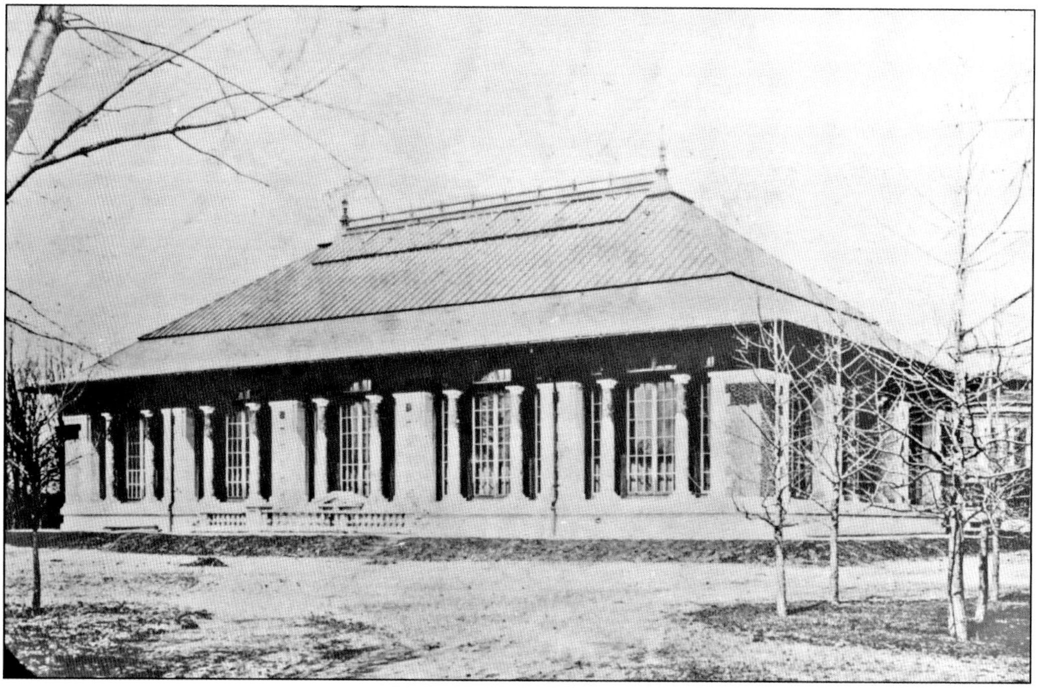

The tennis court and bachelor wing was the final addition to the Idle Hour estate, and it was completed in 1904. It brought the total number of rooms in the house to 110. Vanderbilt employed the architects Warren and Wetmore to create this vast play space for himself shortly before giving that firm the Grand Central Terminal commission. Design similarities can be seen between the design of this wing and the exterior design of the terminal.

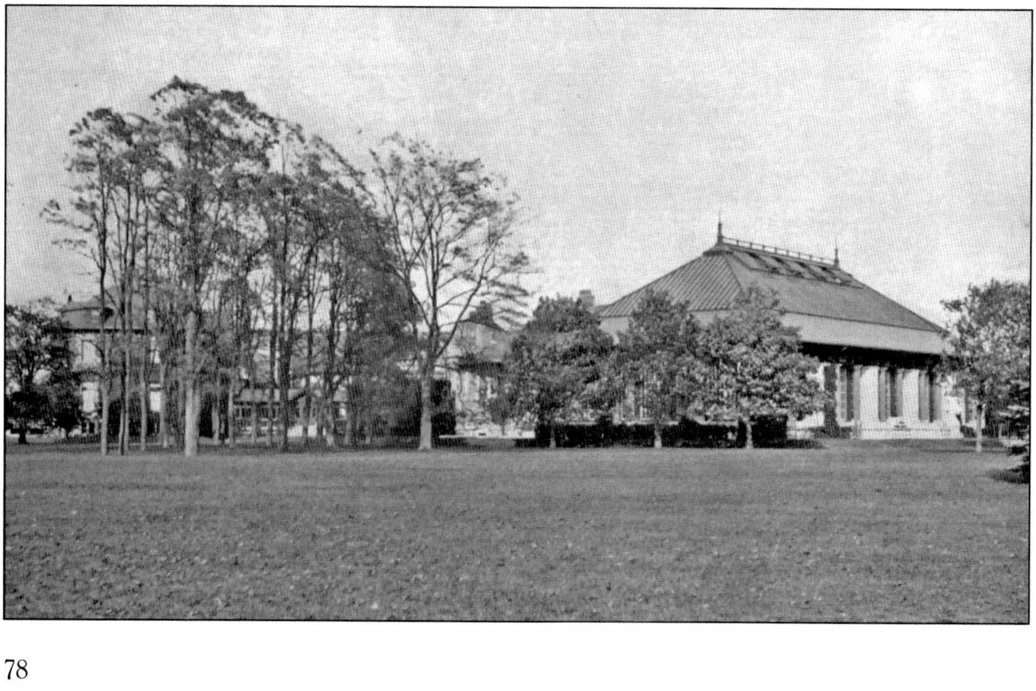

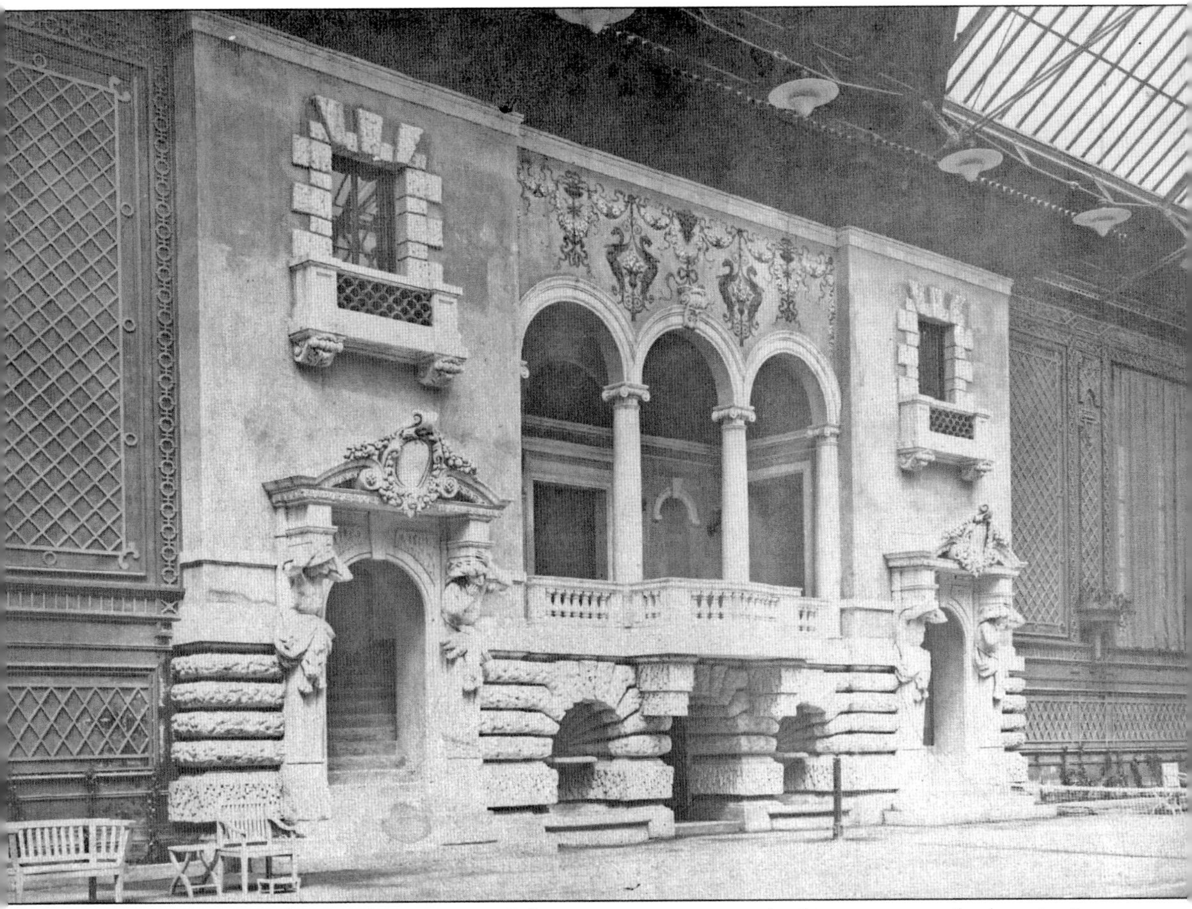

This picture was taken in the interior of the tennis court wing, looking up towards the viewing balcony and entrance to the bachelor wing. The tennis court wing ceiling was three stories tall, making the wing a voluminous space. The tennis court featured multiple seating areas, extensive use of lattice work, richly carved statuary, and utilized both electrical and natural lighting.

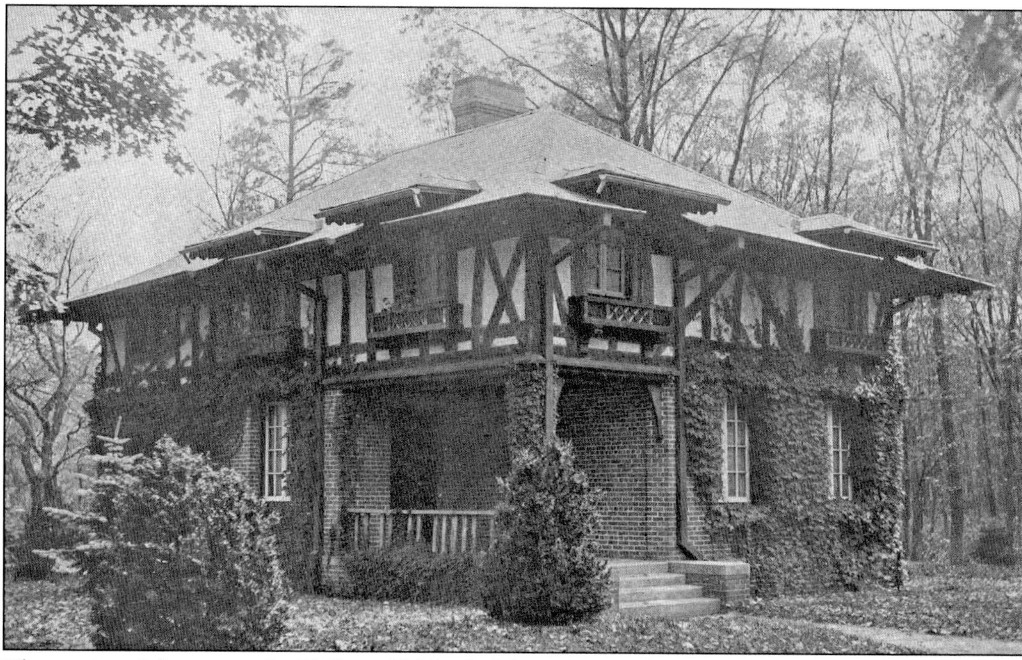

The engineer's house on the William K. Vanderbilt estate was built in 1904 shortly after completion of the second Idle Hour mansion. This pre-1920 photograph shows the building, which sits on Central Boulevard, and today serves as the Dowling College security office. Directly to the north is the powerhouse, which was built in 1900 and supplied heat and electricity to the Idle Hour mansion.

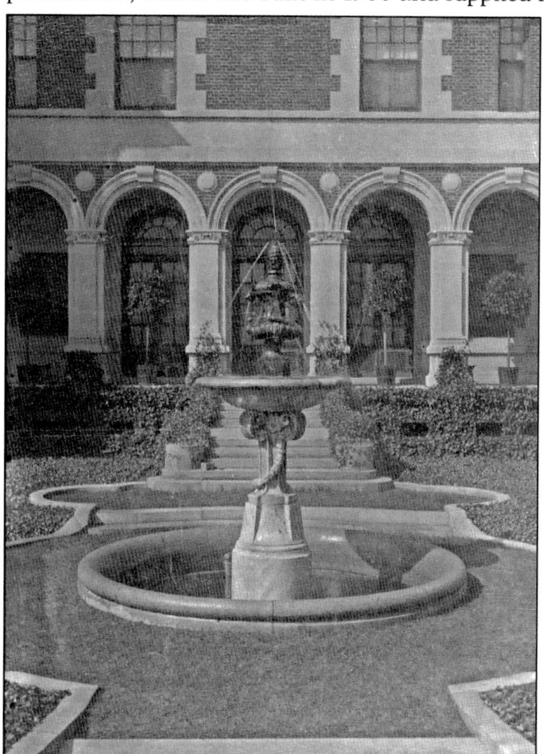

This carved carrerra marble fountain is original to the 1901 estate where it has presided over the cloistered Italian garden that is at the center of the Idle Hour mansion. The fountain was restored in 2003.

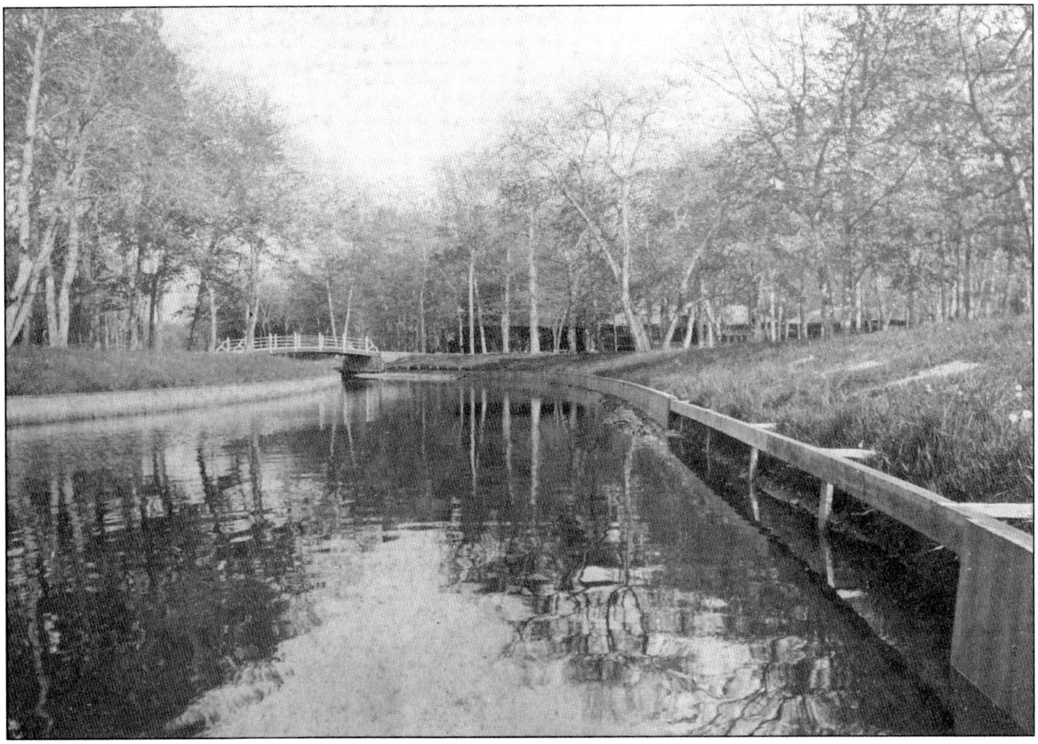

Oakdale is filled with swampy marshlands along the Great South Bay and the Connetquot River. All of the estates built here included some type of drainage system, but William K. Vanderbilt's solution was ingenious. In keeping with his desire to pay tribute to his Dutch roots, he had 5 miles of canals constructed to wind through the estate. These canals served his guests for recreation and were used by his workers to transport coal, ice, and provisions from the farm to the main house.

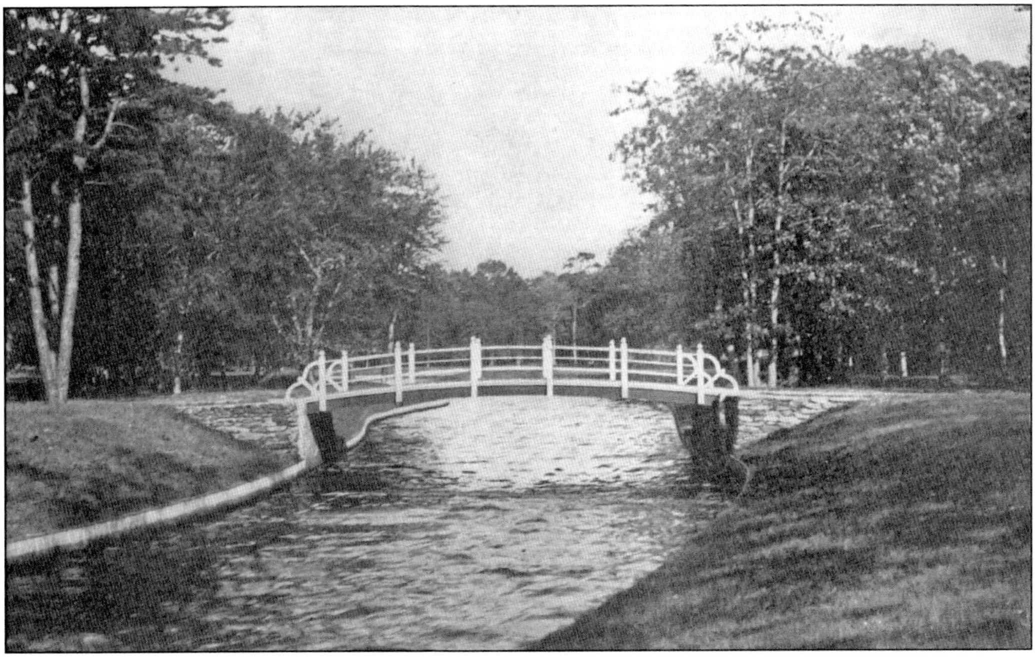

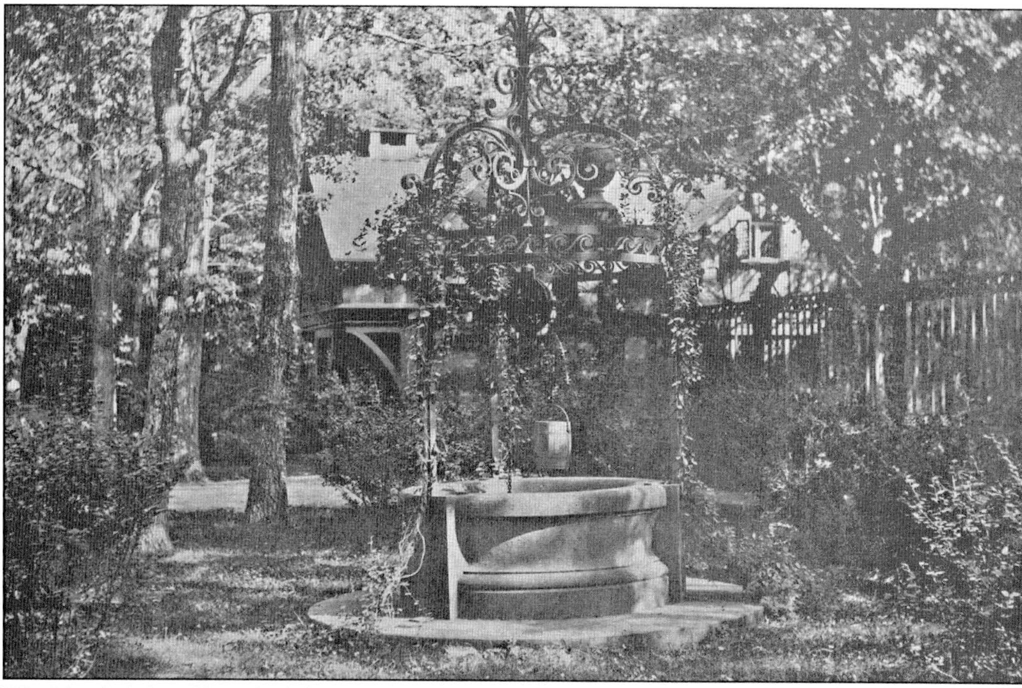

The Vanderbilt well marked the turning point in the Century Run, a 100-mile bicycle race between Brooklyn and Oakdale. In the background, the east gatehouse of Idle Hour is visible. The well was later moved to the entrance of Dowling College on Idle Hour Boulevard.

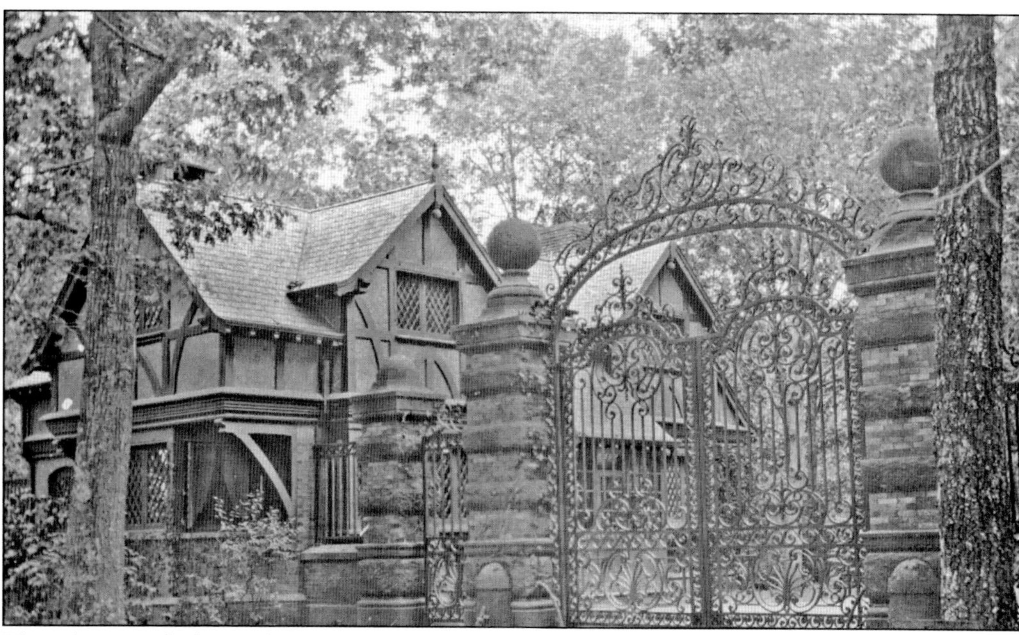

This photograph shows the east gatehouse and the entrance gate to Vanderbilt's Idle Hour estate as it appeared in 1907. This gatehouse is still in existence as a private residence at the corner of Vanderbilt Avenue and Montauk Highway. In 1920, the gate was moved to Eagle's Nest, the Centerport, New York, estate of Vanderbilt's son.

Six

Idle Hour and the Crazy Years

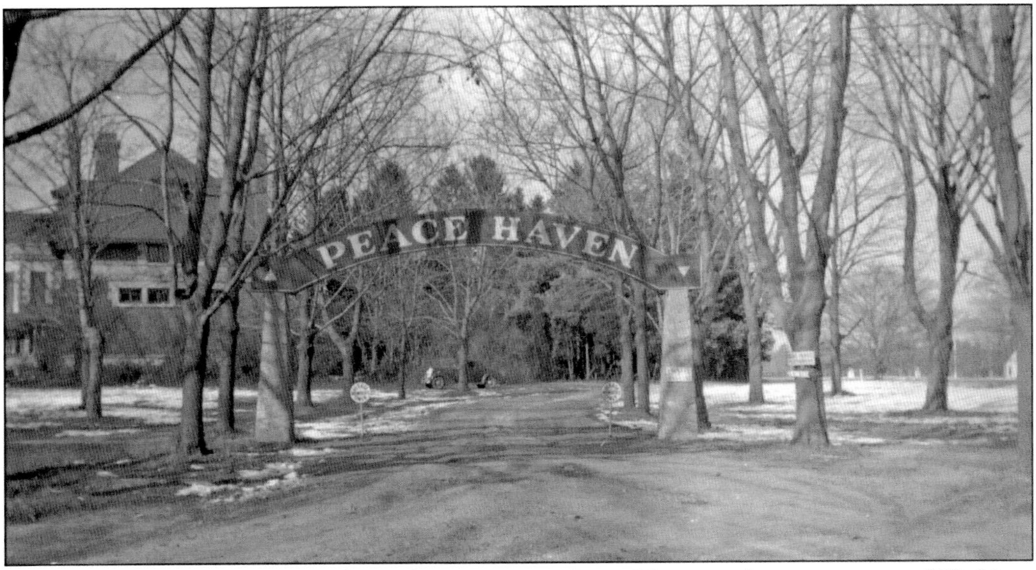

This photograph, around 1940, shows the entrance to Peace Haven at the intersection of Idle Hour Boulevard and Connetquot Drive looking west. In 1938, James B. Schafer bought the mansion for use as a retreat for his followers, naming it Peace Haven. In 1942, he was sentenced to five years in Sing Sing for grand larceny. He and his wife died in 1955 in an apparent double-suicide pact.

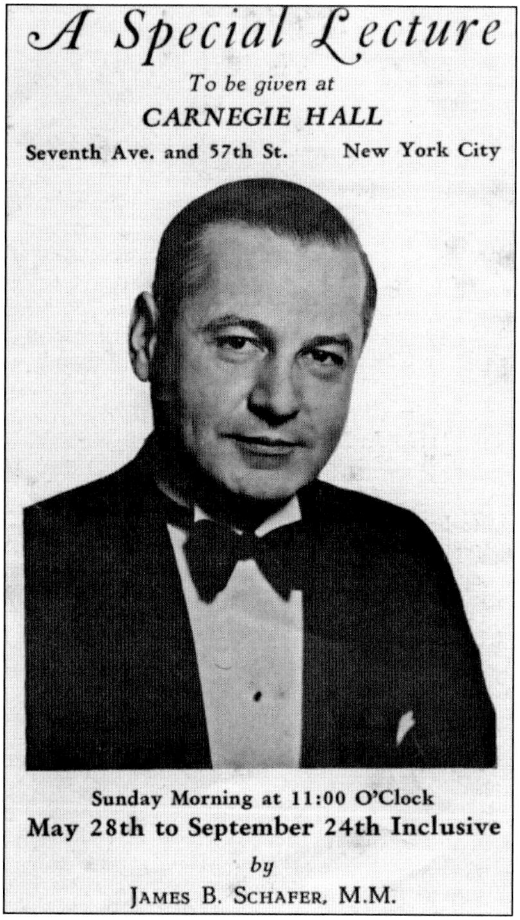

Born around 1890, James B. Schafer founded the Master Metaphysicians in the 1920s. Much of the money he used to purchase the Idle Hour estate came from member donations and the sale of $100 fellowship certificates. As his popularity grew, Schafer expanded from lecturing at Stenway Hall to speaking engagements at Carnegie Hall, as advertised in this undated pamphlet.

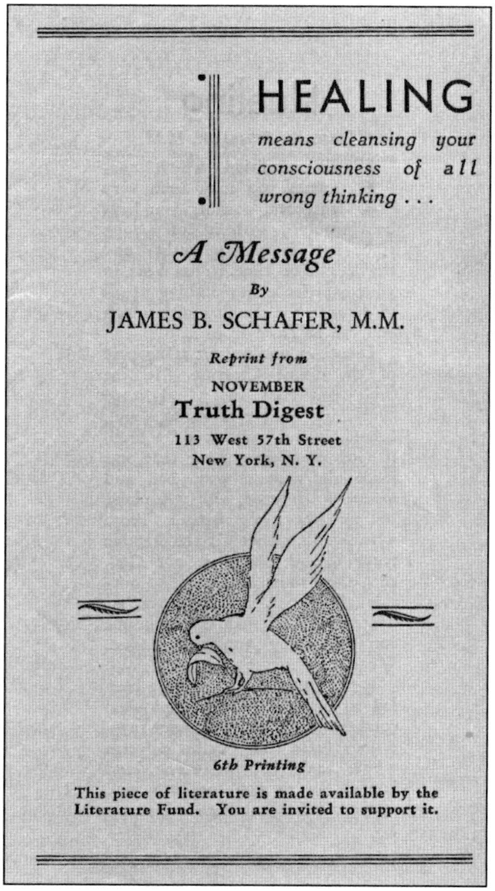

James B. Schafer produced a monthly *Truth Digest*, claiming a circulation of 10,000. This November 1940 edition, called *Healing*, outlines Schafer's ideas of using positive thinking to achieve one's goals. The greatest realization of this idea was Schafer's plan to raise a child to be immortal. To that end, the Master Metaphysicians adopted a baby girl named Jean in 1939. The baby was returned to her mother after a year.

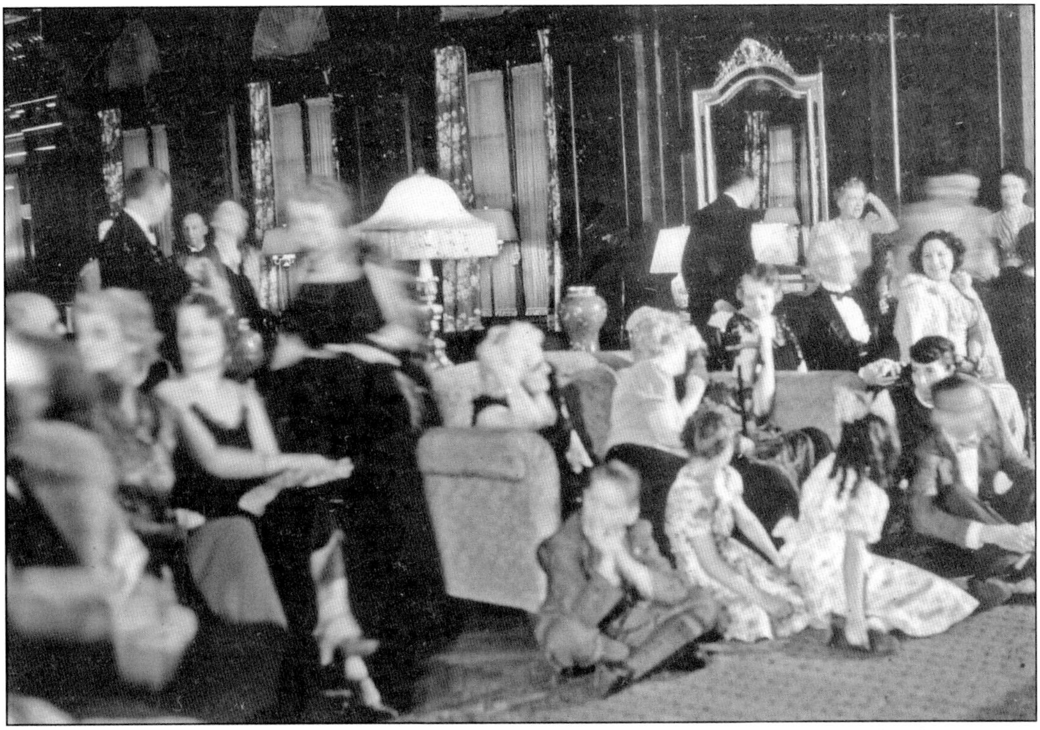

This photograph, taken around 1940, shows a group of Metaphysicians gathered to hear James B. Schafer speak. Schafer's Steinway Hall lectures were transmitted via phone line and played in the ballroom, now called Peace Hall. The sound system was hidden behind the main fireplace. The furniture and antiques were donated by Ann Tomlinson, a wealthy follower.

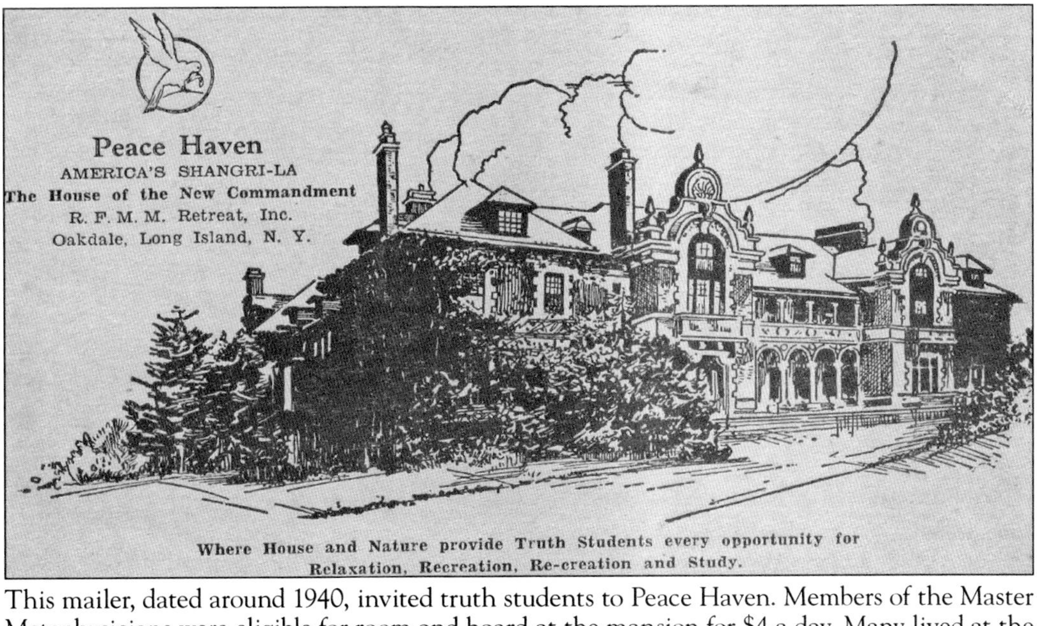

This mailer, dated around 1940, invited truth students to Peace Haven. Members of the Master Metaphysicians were eligible for room and board at the mansion for $4 a day. Many lived at the mansion permanently, commuting to their day jobs in New York City by the Long Island Rail Road. Most of the day-to-day operations of Peace Haven were handled by the Metaphysicians.

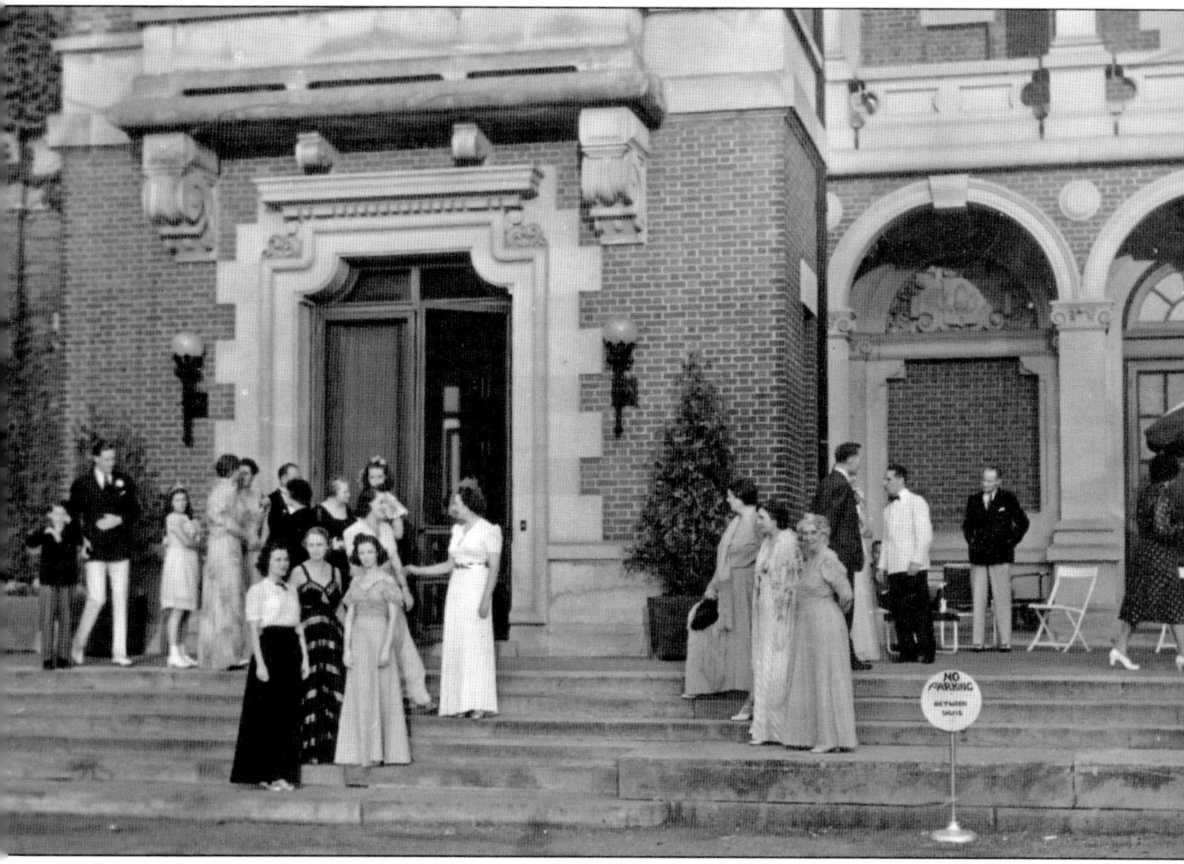

Som of the more anticipated events at Peace Haven were the Saturday night dances in the summer, held in the conservatory. This 1939 photograph shows a group of Peace Haven residents and guests in their evening dresses on the front steps of the mansion facing the Connetquot River. Throughout the Metaphysician's tenure as owners of the Idle Hour mansion, the atmosphere was more often than not one of a country club. The year after this picture was taken they established a junior lodge for the members' children. It was located in the former Vanderbilt carriage house across the street from Peace Haven.

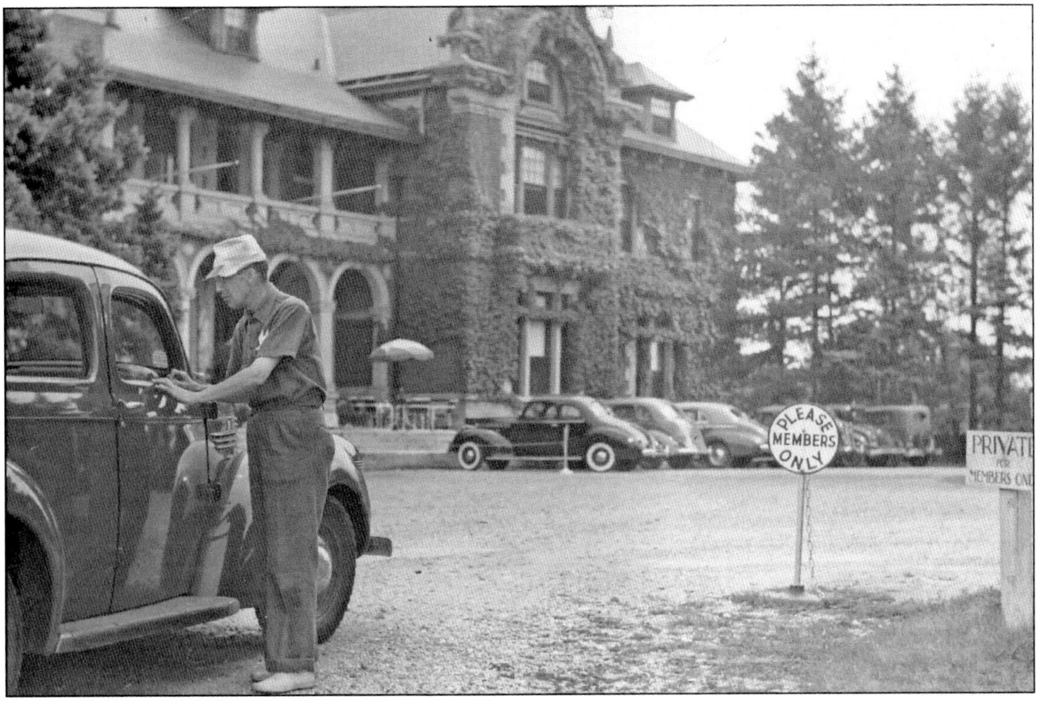

In this photograph from around 1939, local resident Ernie Brewer is seen attending to cars arriving for a Saturday night at Peace Haven. At this point, the main lawn of the estate included a circular driveway for extended parking. Other local residents who were employed on the grounds were Lavern Wittlock who, among other duties, lined the tennis courts, tended the outdoor swimming pool, and took care of unwanted pigeons.

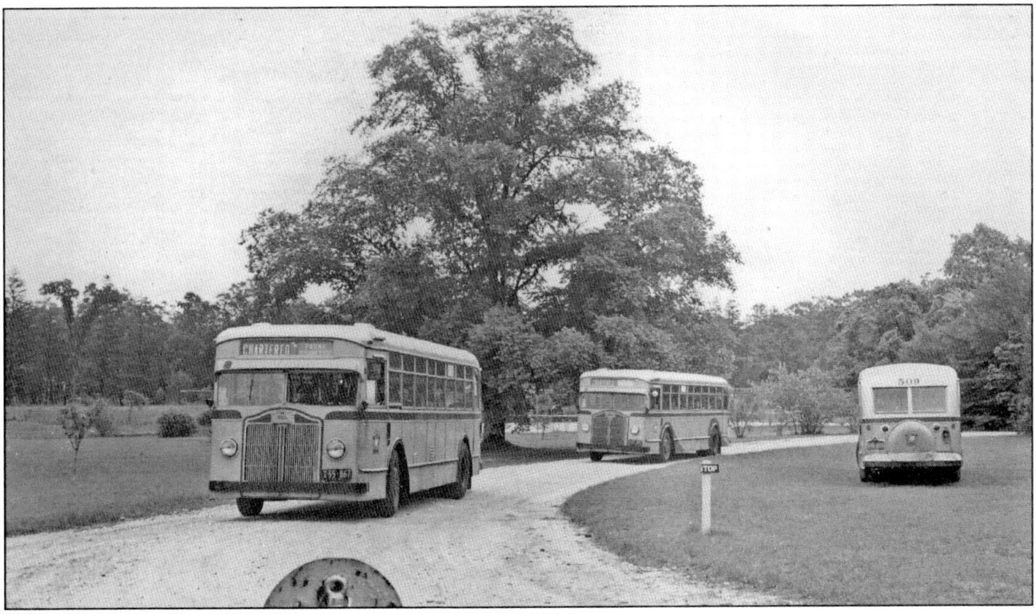

This photograph from around 1940 shows charted buses arriving at Peace Haven for an event. Contemporary accounts record a cross section of the guests who came to stay at Peace Haven, from an unemployed Broadway actor to a beautician and a retired chemist.

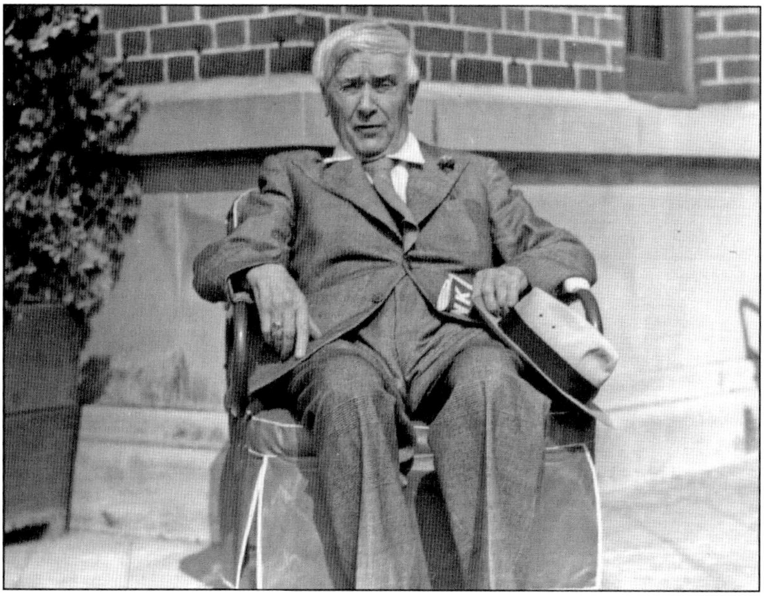

One of the distinguished guests who made an appearance at Peace Haven was Maurice Maeterlinck. This Belgian author and poet won the 1911 Nobel Prize for Literature. Among his most important works was *The Blue Bird: A Fairy Play in Six Acts*, an allegorical story of two children on a quest through a fantasy landscape. He is shown here, around 1940, sitting on the front loggia of Peace Haven.

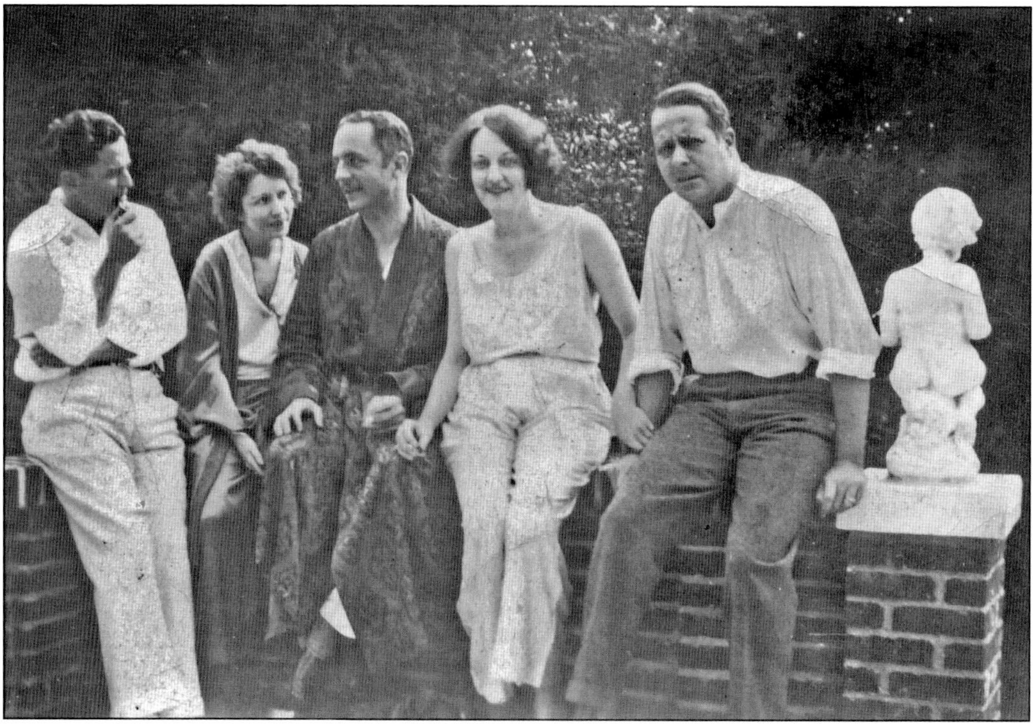

In 1930, Corinne Olivette Cartier (in white), the former wife of Louis P. Cartier, rented the Idle Hour mansion. In this undated photograph taken on the mansion grounds, she is visited by actor William Powell (in robe) and his costar in the *Thin Man* series, Myrna Loy (in bi-tone outfit), who had a home in St. James on the North Shore of Long Island.

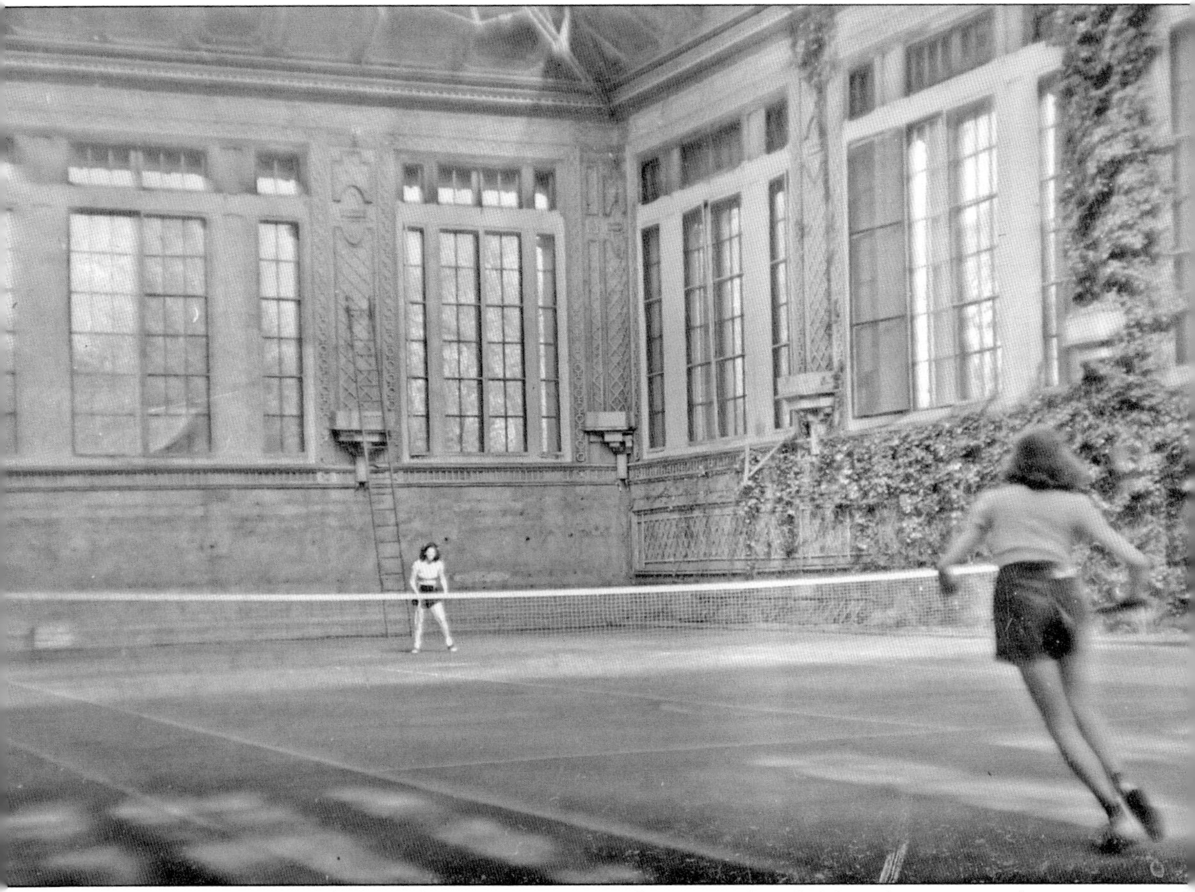

This undated photograph from the Peace Haven era shows two female Metaphysicians making use of William K. Vanderbilt's indoor tennis court, showing that little had changed since the early 1900s. There were many amenities available to attract guests and visitors, from horseback riding and shuffleboard to boating on the Connetquot River and outdoor tennis courts.

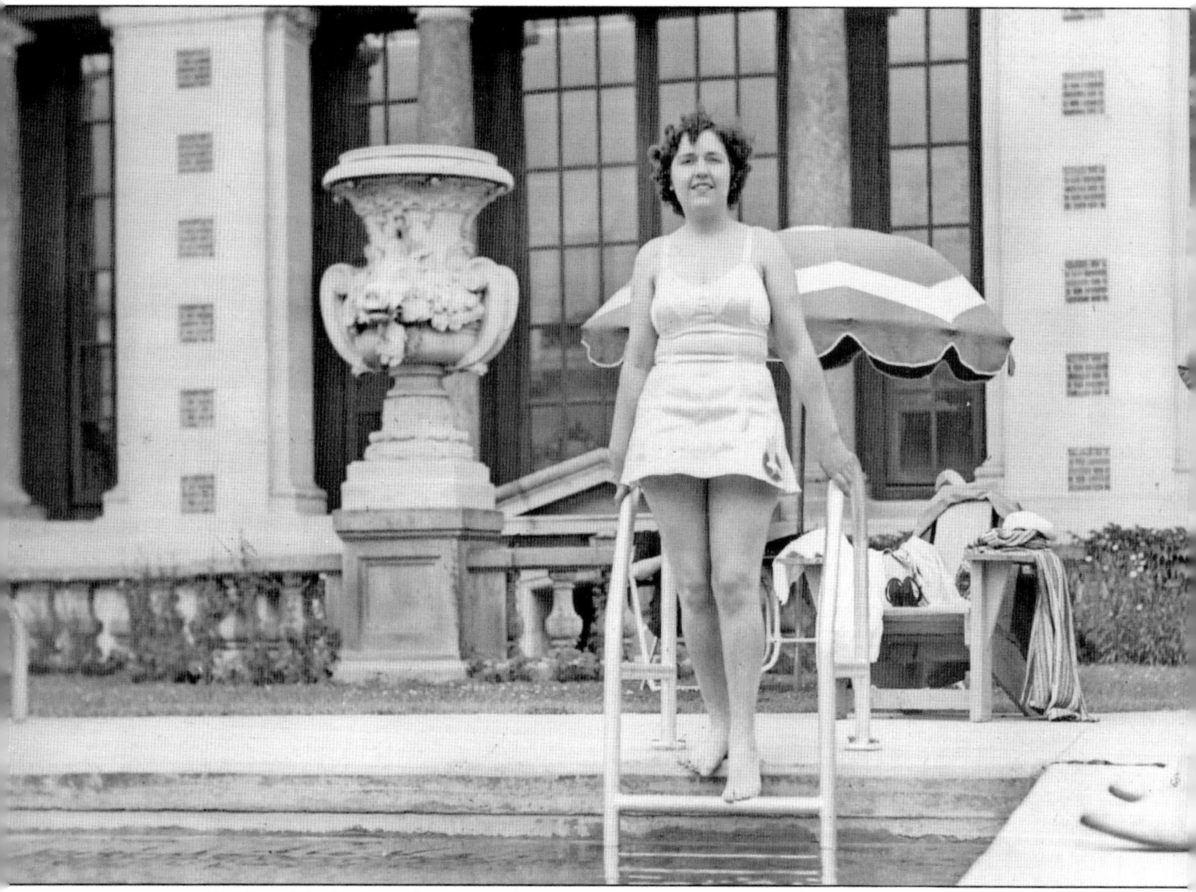

James B. Schafer added an outdoor pool to William K. Vanderbilt's Idle Hour estate between 1938 and 1940. It stood just to the south of the indoor tennis court. In the winter months, the pool would be drained and filled with hay. The pool was filled in sometime in the 1950s and today is a grassy area overlooking a parking lot. This photograph of the era shows a young Metaphysician about to take a dip.

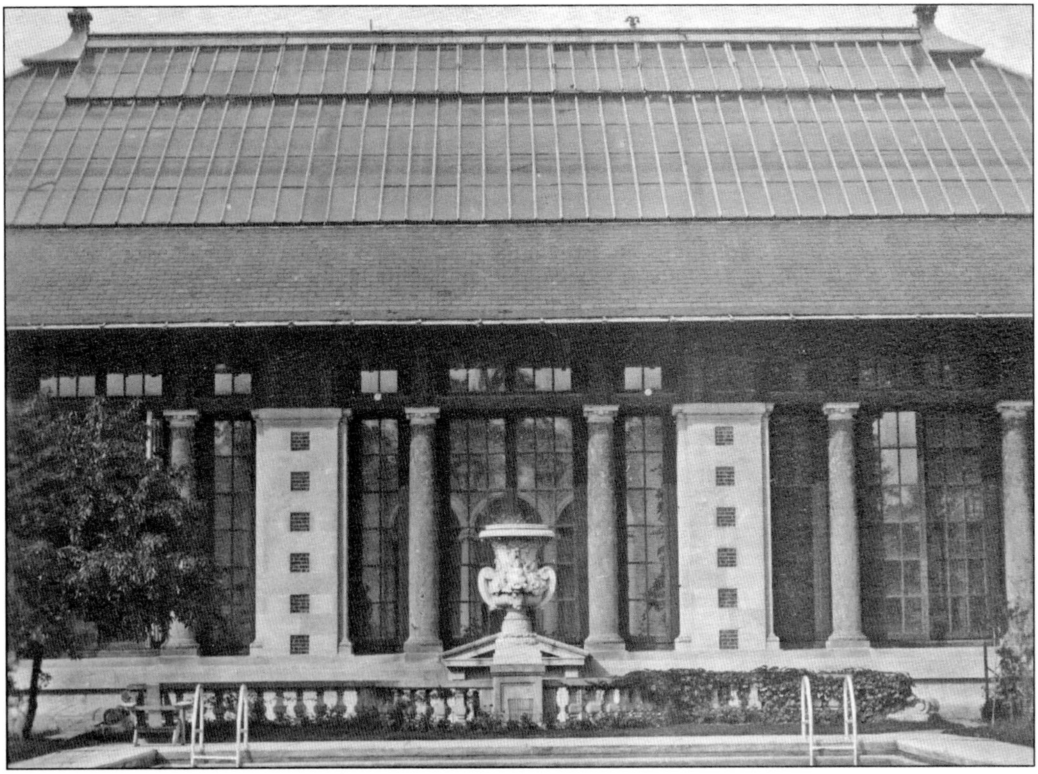

This photograph, dated around 1940, looks north over the pool to the south facade of the indoor tennis court. The large urn, which still stands there today, was designed by the French sculptor Sylvain Salieres. He often worked with the tennis court designers Warren and Wetmore. Salieres also spent five years working on decorations for Grand Central Station in New York City.

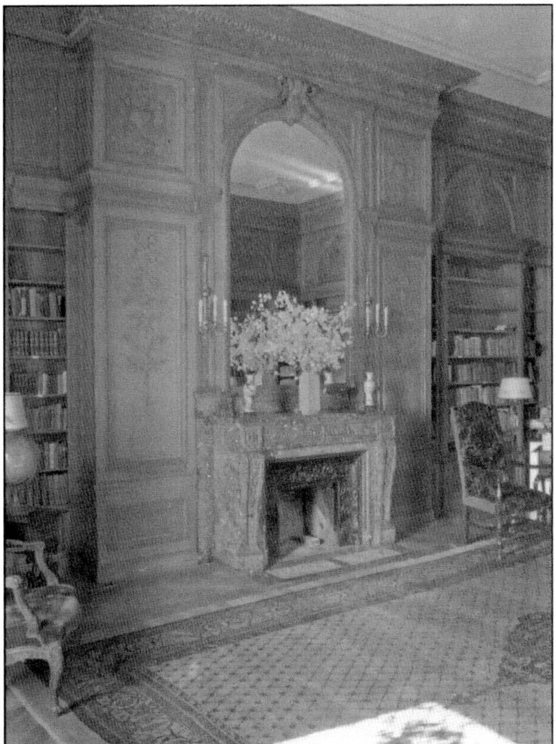

James B. Schafer had a penchant for renaming things in the abstract to reinforce his teachings. Not only did Idle Hour become Peace Haven but individual rooms received names. Throughout the mansion were doors marked integrity, sincerity, and joy. This photograph shows the library in William K. Vanderbilt's Idle Hour mansion during the Peace Haven period, when it was known as wisdom.

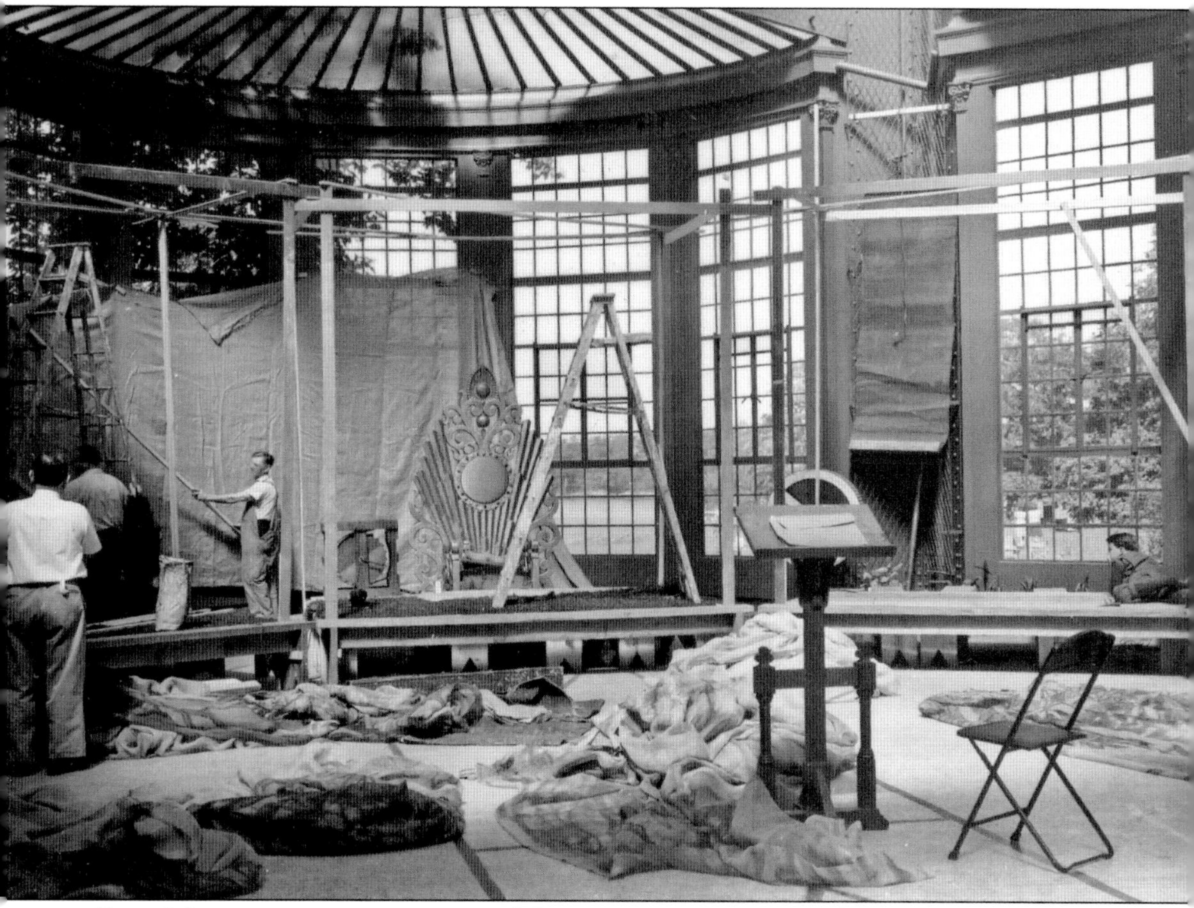

One of the more unique occurrences of the Peace Haven years was the staging of a Pageant of Truth, put on by a number of Metaphysicians with the help of local residents. The Pageant of Truth was performed only once and presented in the conservatory, the former site of William K. Vanderbilt's Turkish room. In this photograph, workers are preparing the elaborate stage and framework for the production.

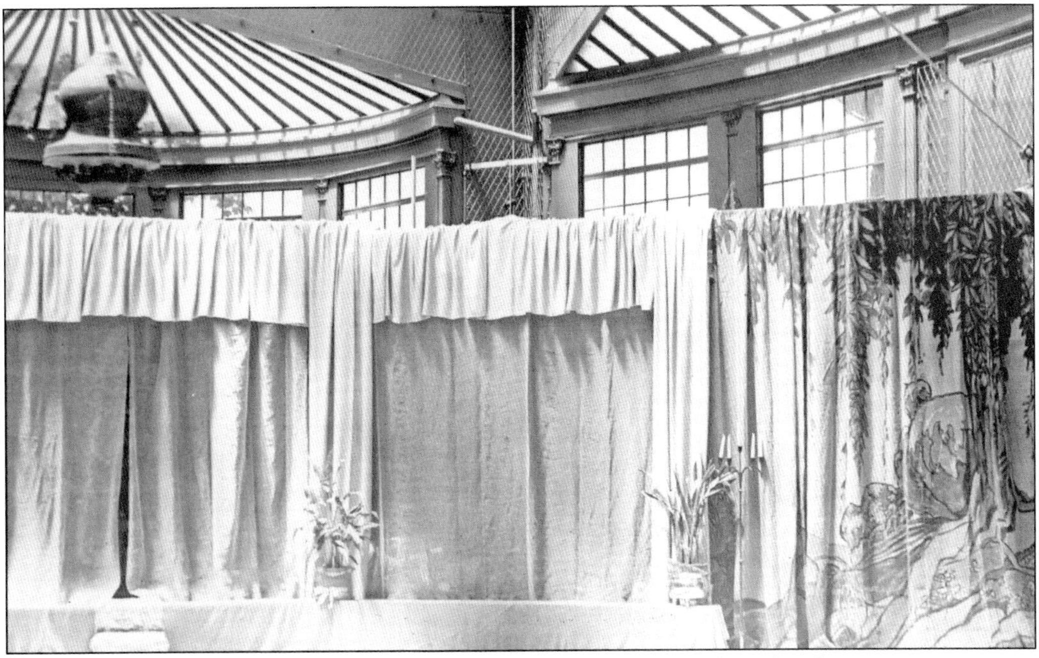

In this photograph, the curtains have been hung for the Pageant of Truth. The stage is occupying the northwest side of the conservatory.

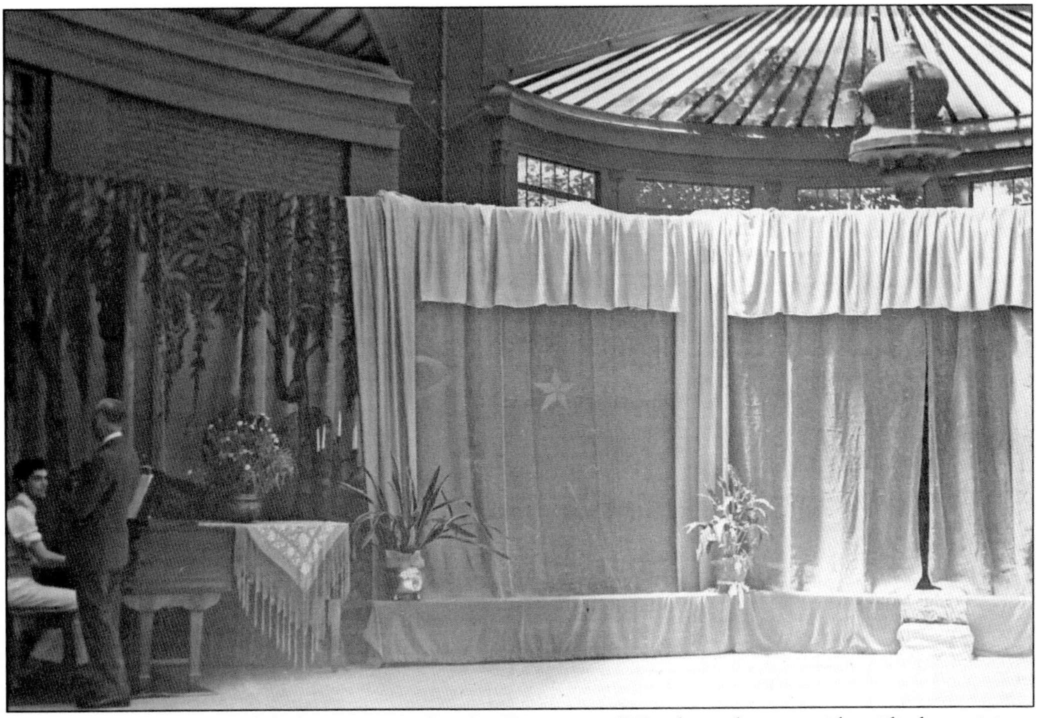

Eddie Astradour (right) helps prepare for the Pageant of Truth with an unidentified musician. This view is looking west from the middle of the conservatory. Behind the curtains at the far left is the entrance to the indoor tennis court.

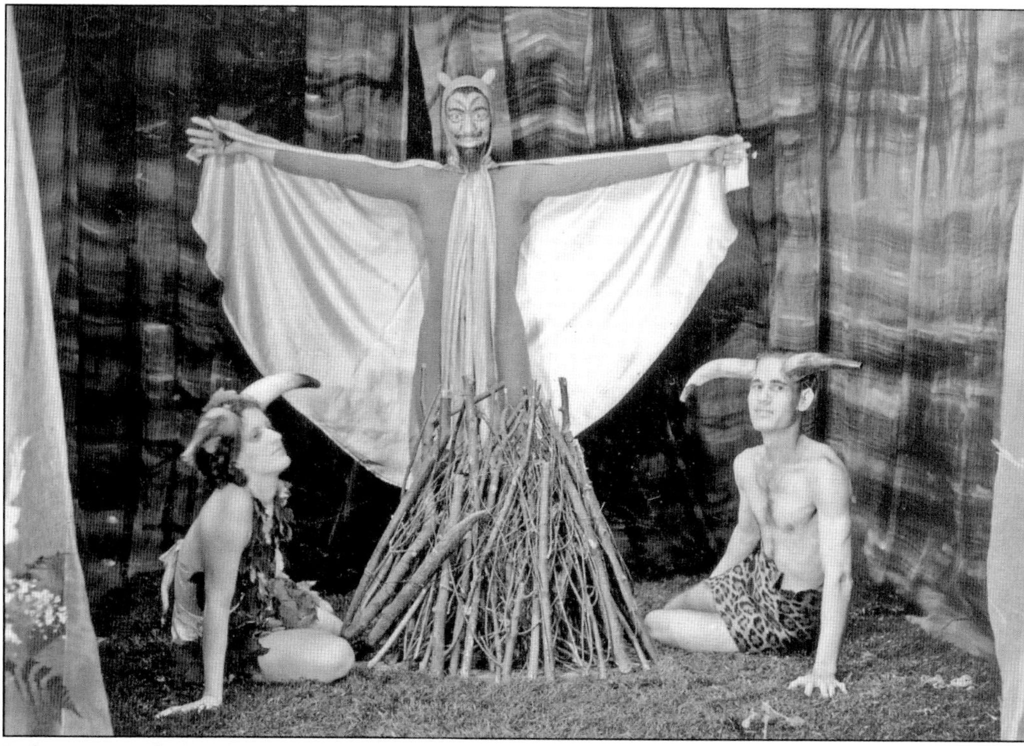

In keeping with the abstract tenants of some of James B. Schafer's teachings, the Pageant of Truth presented a series of silent tableaux depicting various human conditions. The photograph above depicts the scene "The Fall of Man/Evil" with (from left to right) Helen Anderberg, Carl Luckadoo, and Manuel Gonzalez. The photograph below features Conrad Kubat in "Clown/Folly."

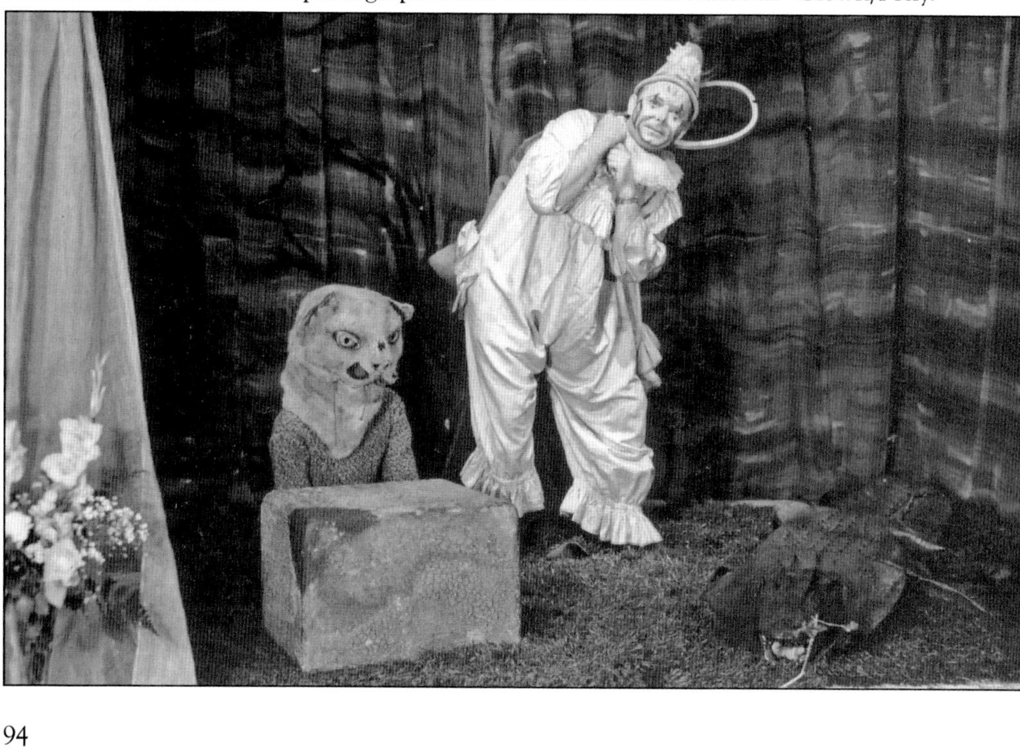

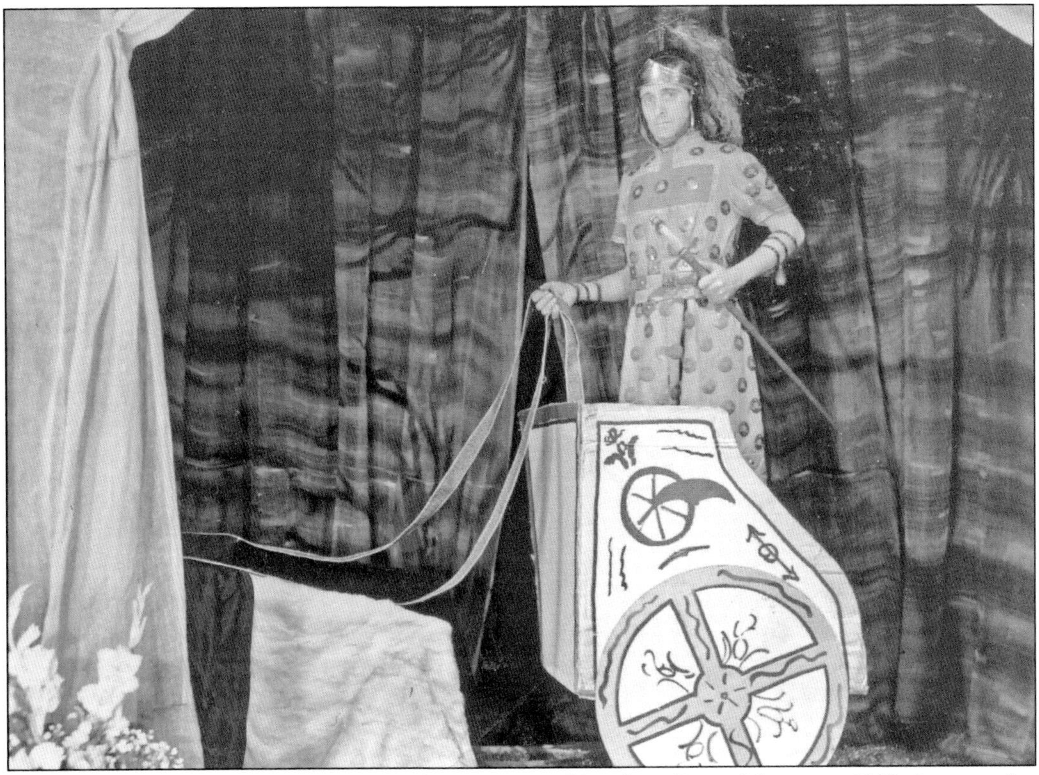

The photograph above, taken during the Pageant of Truth at Peace Haven in 1939, features the tableaux "Conqueror/False Quest" with Hale Burgess in the chariot. The photograph below shows the scene "Wisdom the Quest for Truth."

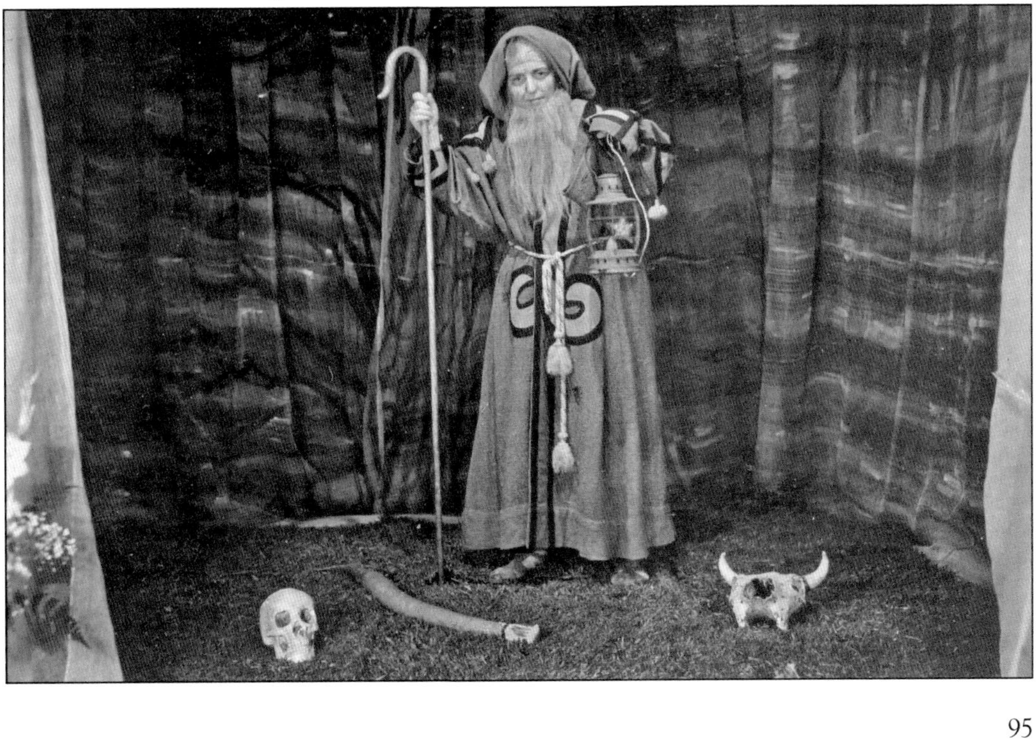

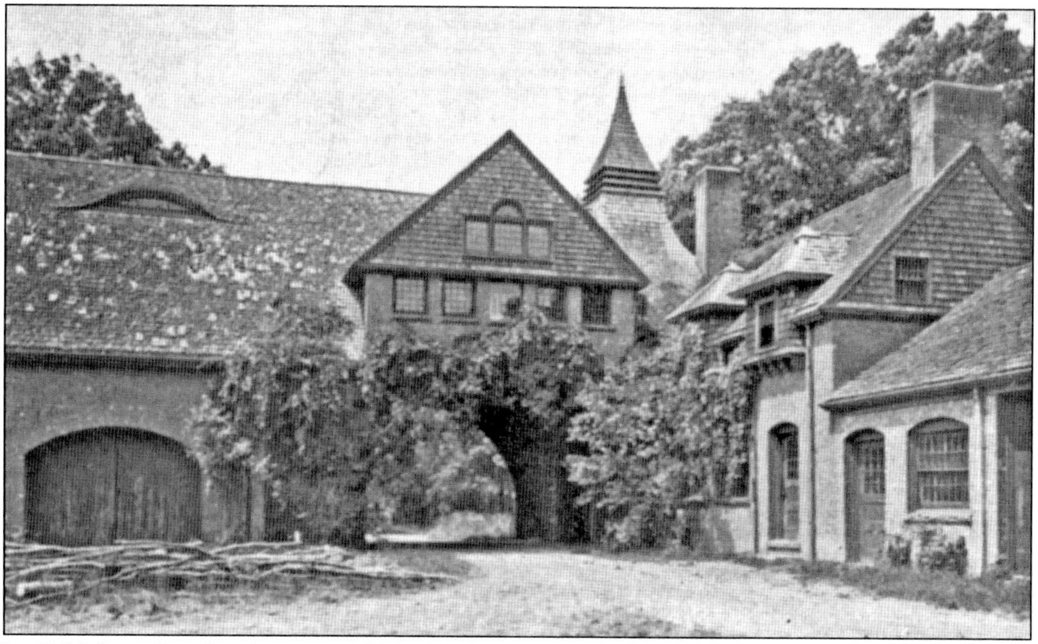

In 1926, Lucy Pritchard Sawyer Thompson, a wealthy widow active in the New York art world, purchased the 16-acre farm area of the William K. Vanderbilt estate. She proceeded to develop it into a community for artists and like-minded individuals to work and display their art. The photograph above shows the northeast corner of the complex with the clubhouse buildings.

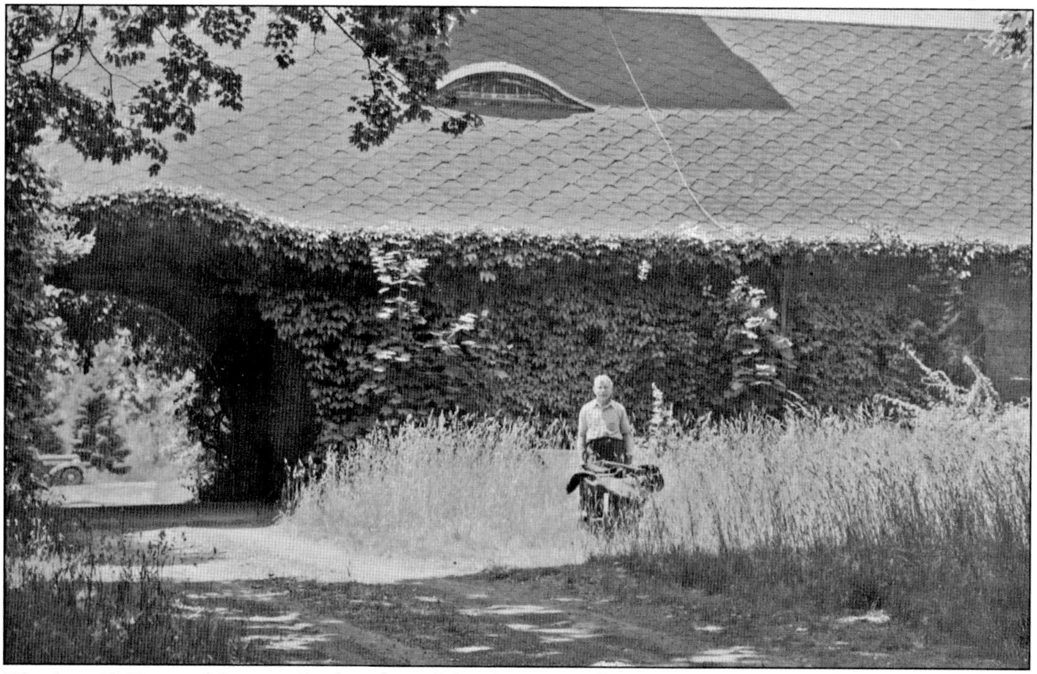

The late 1920s would prove the heyday of the Artists Colony. An art exhibition in the summer of 1927 drew some 1,000 visitors. This view of the Artists Colony from that time period is tentatively identified as looking south down Hollywood Drive at the eastern arch into the development. The man is unidentified.

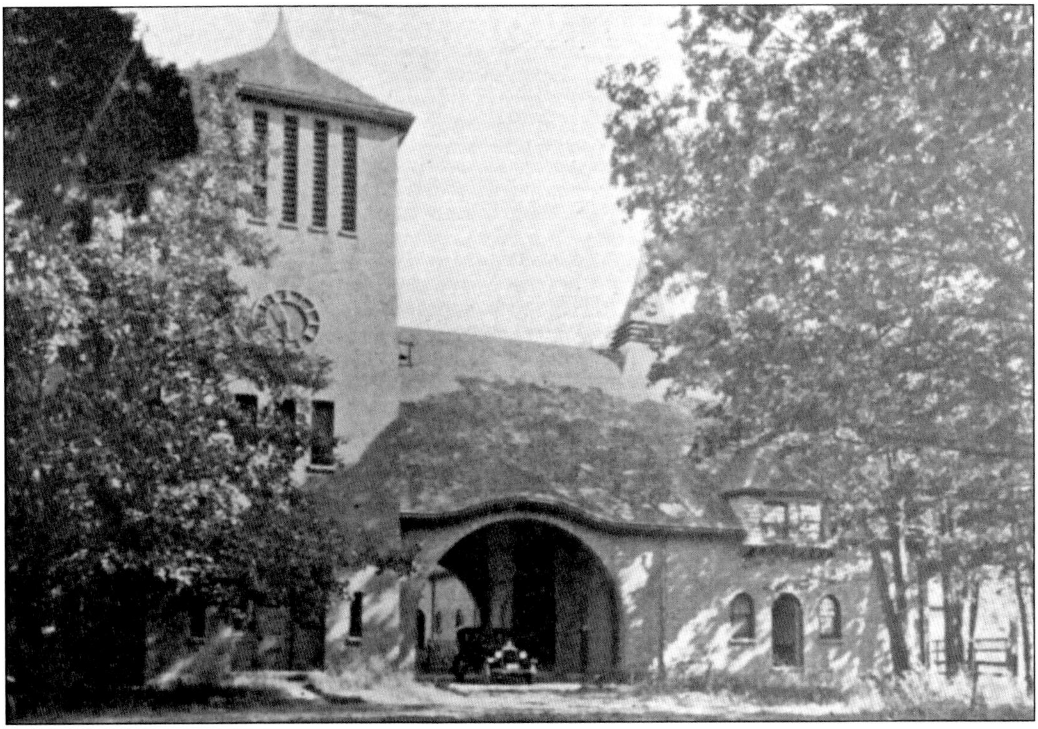

This photograph shows the clock tower entrance and western arch at the Artists Colony. The view is looking south. Idle Hour Boulevard runs through the arch becoming Tower Mews. Hollywood Drive proceeds along the face of the building to the left. The clock tower was actually built as a water tower for the farm buildings.

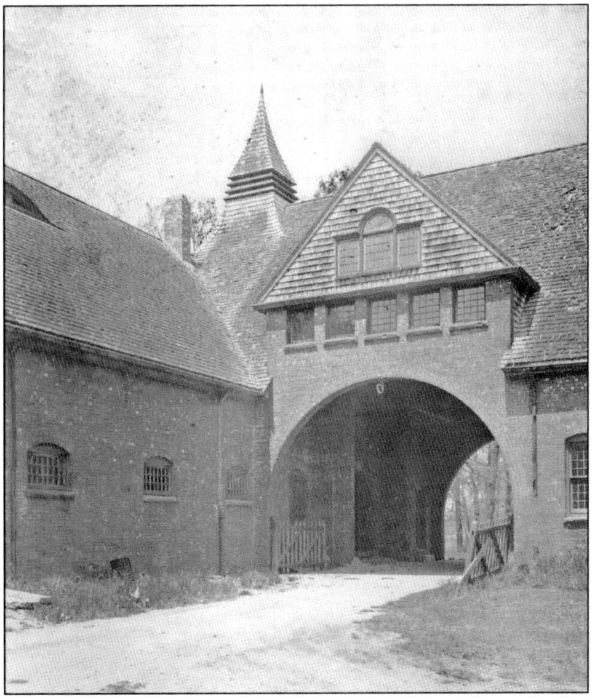

This is a view looking north from inside the Artists Colony towards the western arch. The street visible is Tower Mews, which becomes Idle Hour Boulevard on the other side. At one time the artist Harry Van Weston lived in this section, which featured the living space built into the arch itself.

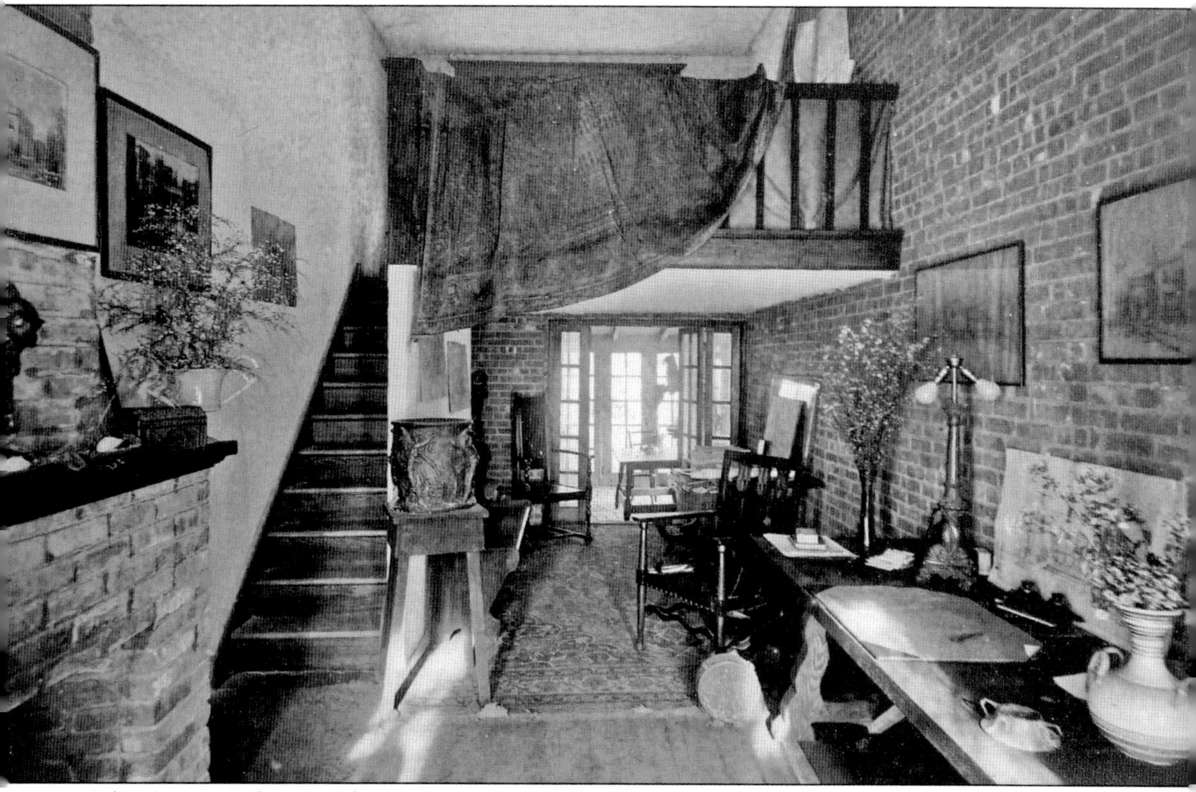

The Artists Colony was housed in a rectangular complex of buildings that had previously served the farming and agriculture needs of the Idle Hour estate. As the area developed under Lucy Thompson and her son, Bill, it became known alternately as Thompson's Village. They designed the interior of the development with a mix of literary sounding names such as Feather Bed Lane and Princess Gate while fashioning living spaces out of the former piggeries, poultry houses, and cattle barns. This handsome room along Jade Street was once part of an animal hospital and general service area. One of the artists who lived on Jade Street was Carl Nordell.

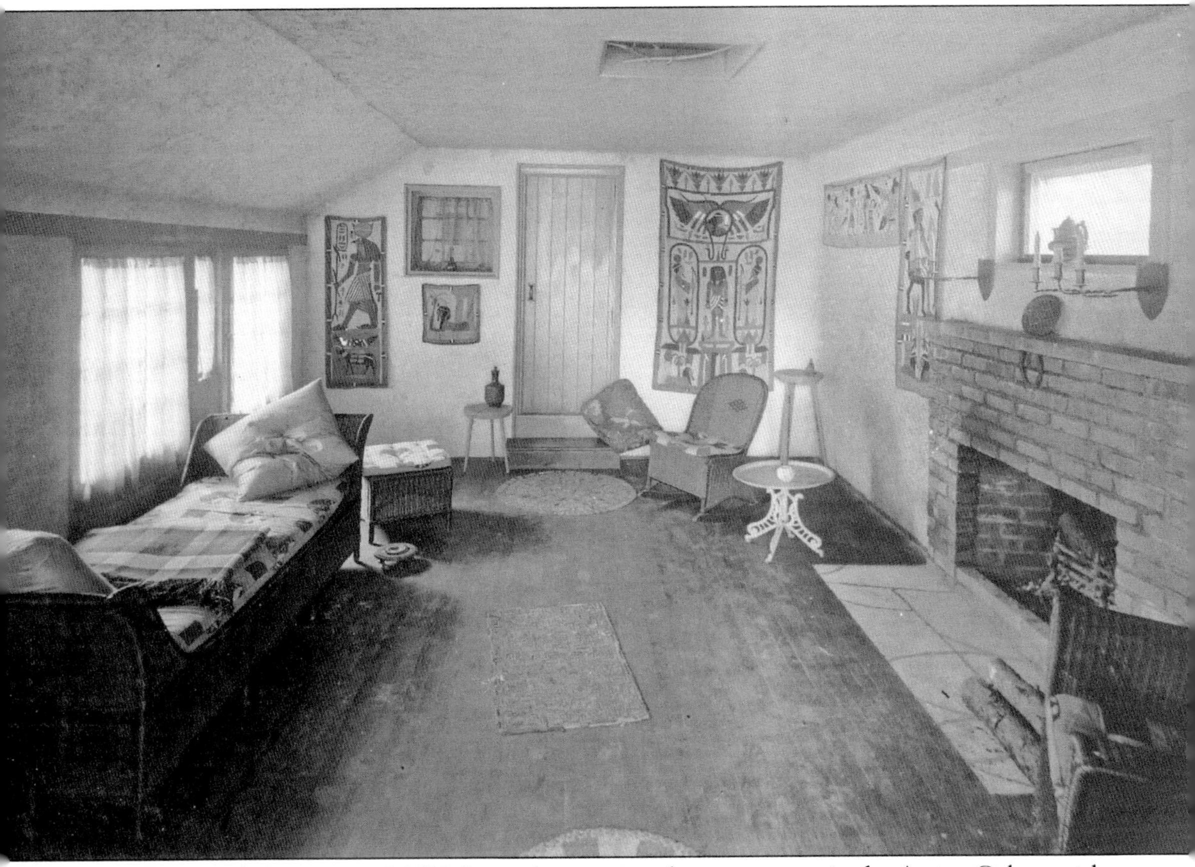

This photograph from around 1930 shows the interior of an apartment in the Artists Colony with its unique blend of rustic simplicity and artistic sensibility. Lucy Thompson who first bought the property that became the Artists Colony was a widow whose husband, William Andrew Thompson Jr., had been an executive for Texaco. She had a studio in Manhattan as well as Oakdale. An early prospectus for the Artists Colony set the price for dwellings starting at $800 and rising to $4,800 for duplexes. Thompson also took pains to point out that "the Idle Hour Artists Colony is not being exploited for profit by real estate promoters but is exclusively handled by artists and writers who comprise the board of administration."

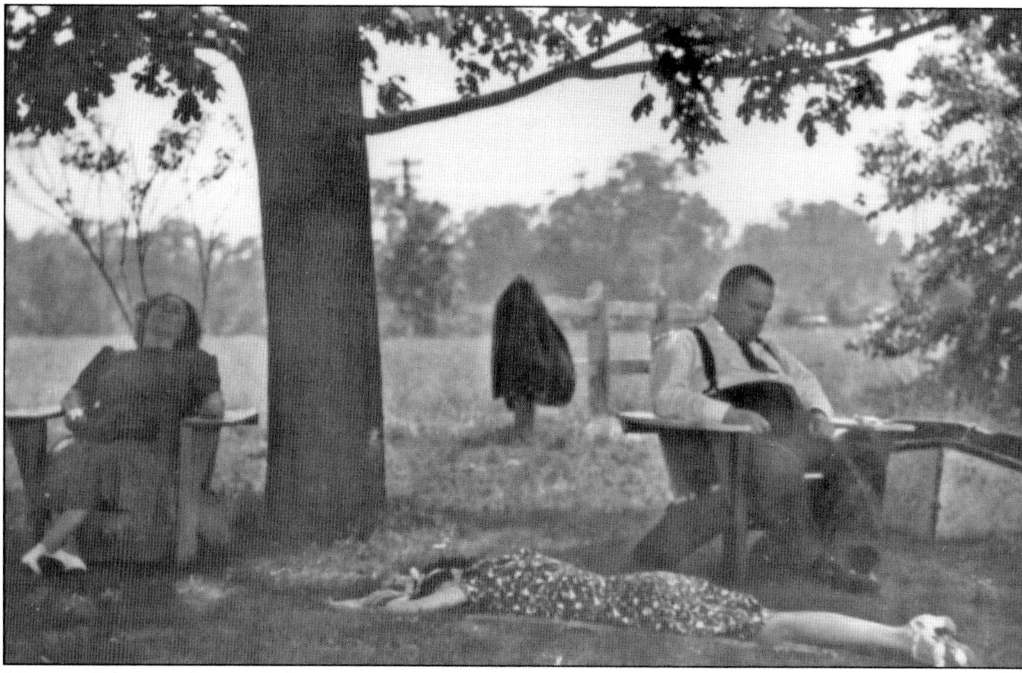

Many of the residents of the Artists Colony came out only for the summer months and while some worked on Long Island, many commuted to New York City some 80 minutes away by the Long Island Rail Road. Here a number of residents relax on a summer day around 1930. There were many communal areas open to residents, including a croquet court near the former pig wallow and tennis courts. One of the canals from the William K. Vanderbilt estate bordered the Artists Colony to the south.

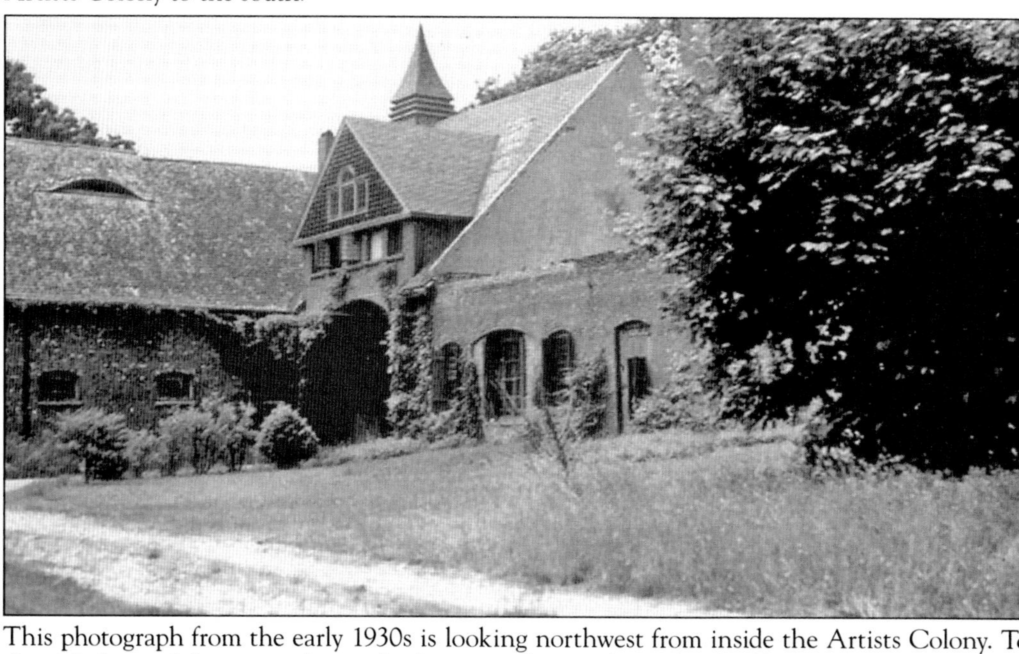

This photograph from the early 1930s is looking northwest from inside the Artists Colony. To the right beyond the tree is the result of a recent fire in a barn that had been serving as a theater and exhibition hall. The last production to be staged there was a puppet ballet entitled *Gawpy*.

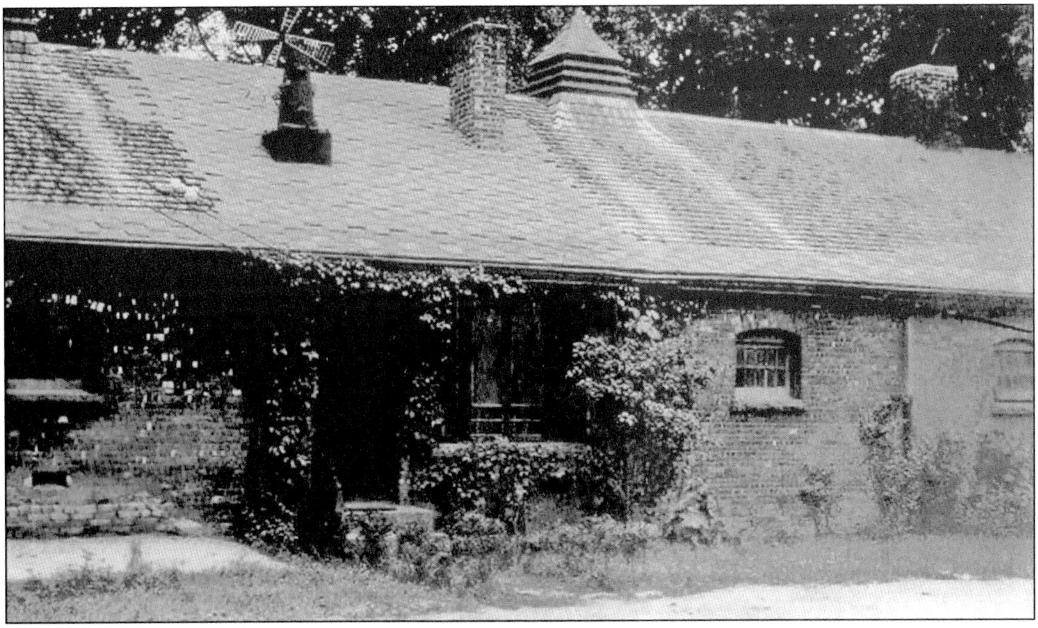

Taken around 1930, this is a photograph of the outside of the former piggery buildings along Princess Gate. It was not only painters who were attracted to living at the Artists Colony. In addition to people like Edwin Williard Deming and Roman Bonet (Bon) Sintas, residents included sculptress Catherine Lawson, costume designer Olga Meervold, and pianist Claude Govier.

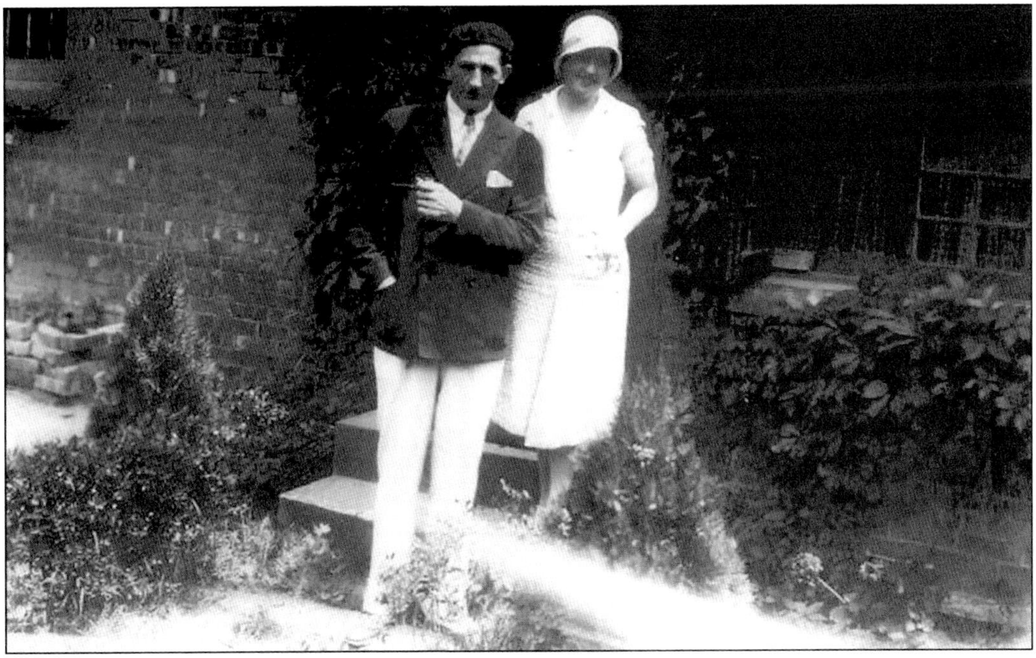

Francis Gow-Smith and his wife, Carol, stand outside their home along Princess Gate in this photograph, which dates to about 1930. They lived in the piggery. He was a noted explorer, having taken part in expeditions to Brazil and Borneo. He was also a member of the Explorer's Club in New York. After his death in 1939, Carol married artist Lynn Morgan and continued to live in the Artists Colony.

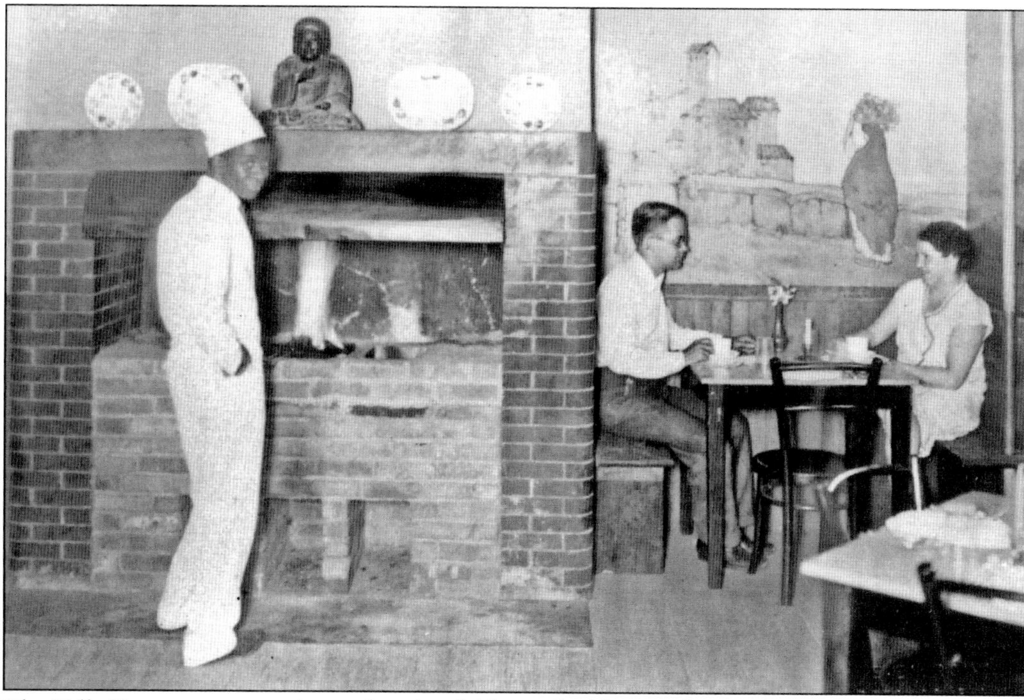

The Tally Ho restaurant was located in the clubhouse building in the northeast corner of the Artists Colony at the beginning of Jade Street. The restaurant was open to residents and nonresidents for an annual fee. This picture from around 1930 shows chef Emmet ? (left), Bill Thompson, and Betty Miller. Named for the tally ho carriages once owned by William K. Vanderbilt, the inn later was also known at one time or another as the Gypsy Tea Room and Chez Papa. The picture below, around the same period, shows the interior decorations.

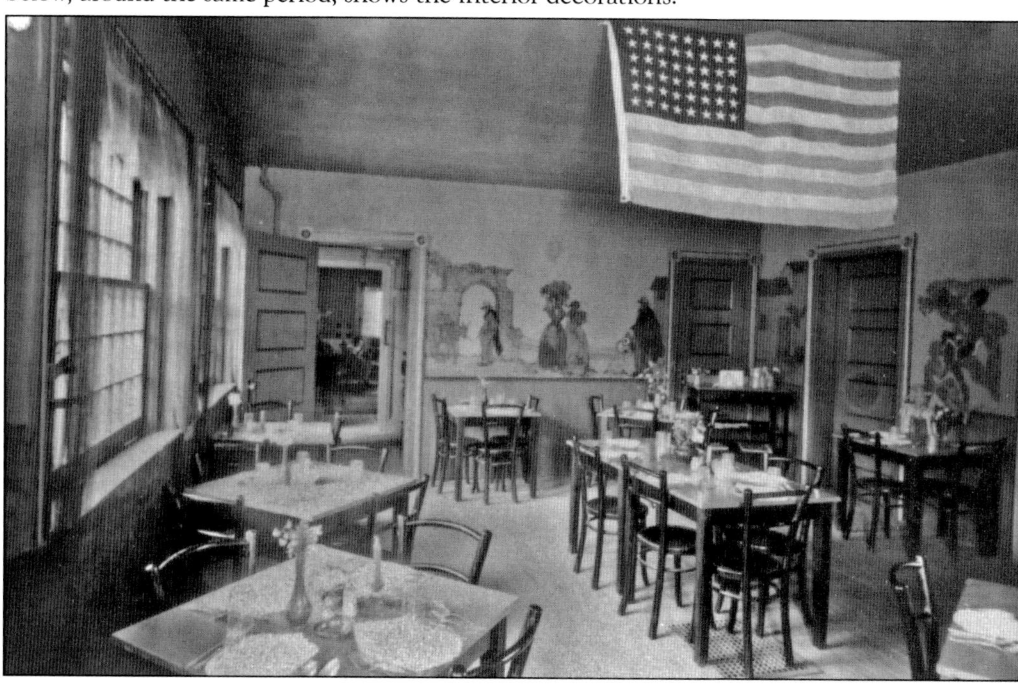

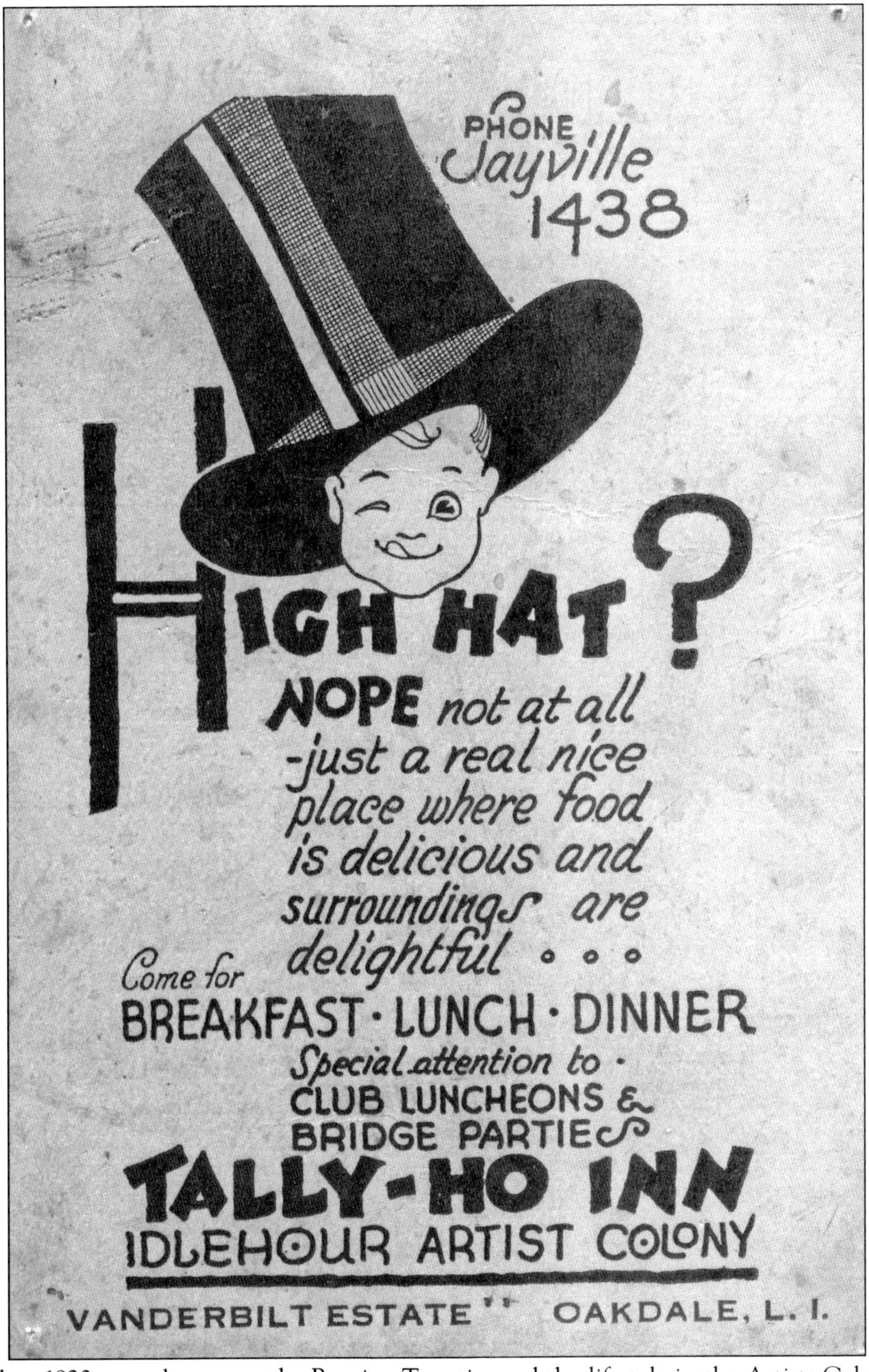

The late 1920s were known as the Roaring Twenties and the lifestyle in the Artists Colony fit the pace of the times as seen in this advertising card from the era. Writing in the 1980s, local resident LaVerne Wittlock recalled the Tally-Ho's specialty of the house: a cocktail known as the "Zaza" with gin, absinthe, or Pernad, Grenadine, and egg whites.

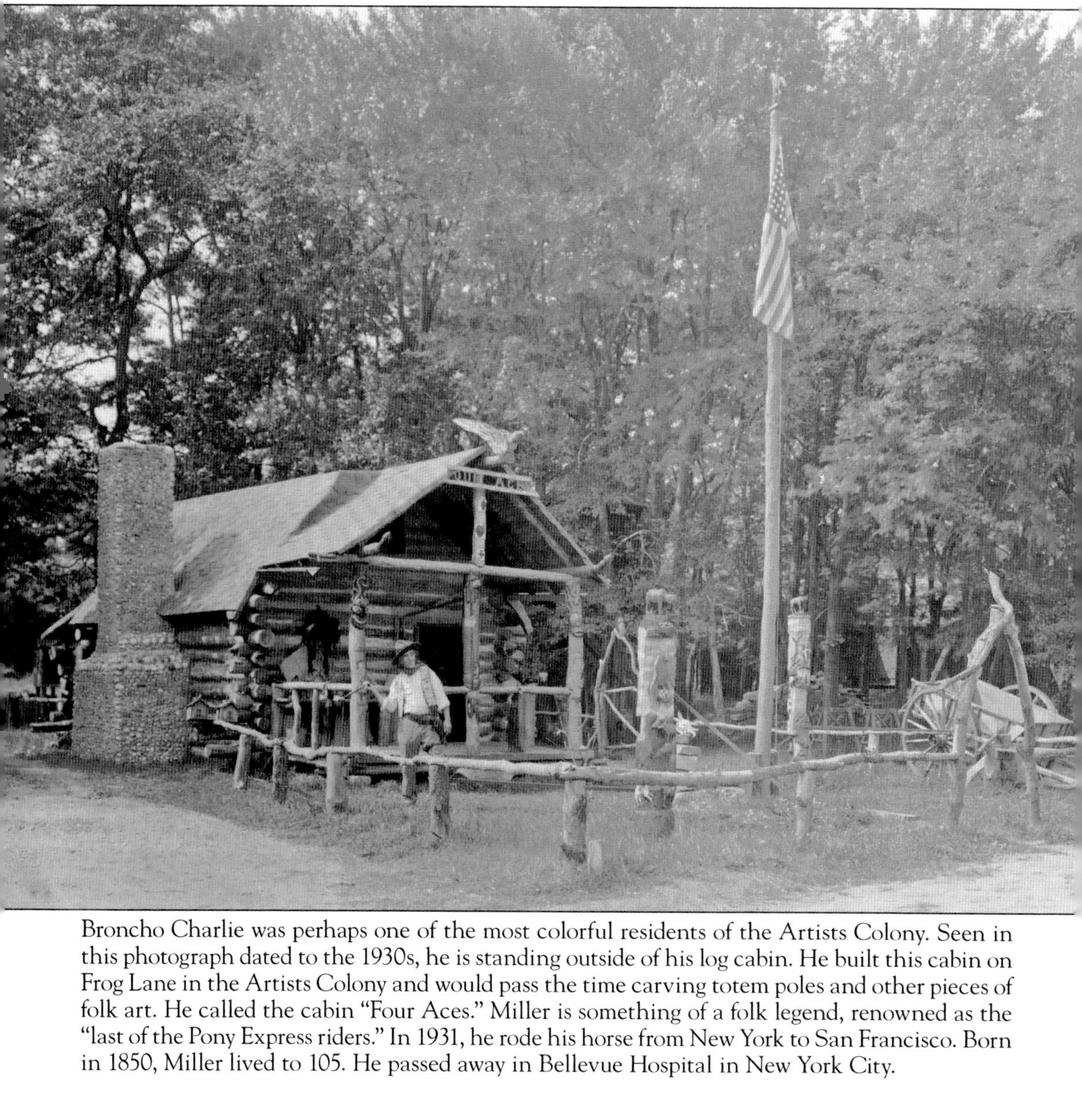

Broncho Charlie was perhaps one of the most colorful residents of the Artists Colony. Seen in this photograph dated to the 1930s, he is standing outside of his log cabin. He built this cabin on Frog Lane in the Artists Colony and would pass the time carving totem poles and other pieces of folk art. He called the cabin "Four Aces." Miller is something of a folk legend, renowned as the "last of the Pony Express riders." In 1931, he rode his horse from New York to San Francisco. Born in 1850, Miller lived to 105. He passed away in Bellevue Hospital in New York City.

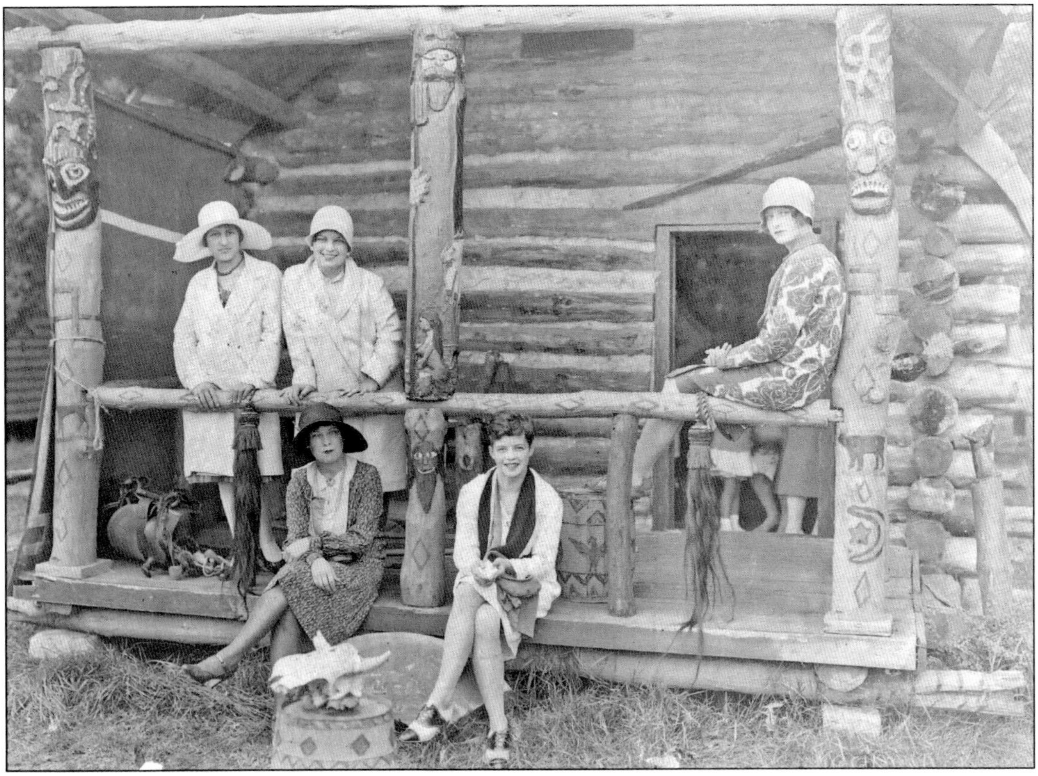

The five unidentified flappers in the photograph above, estimated to be taken sometime in the early 1930s, are seen posing on the front porch of Broncho Charlie's cabin on Frog Lane. In 1946, Broncho Charlie built a small log cabin simply called the "Log Cabin" on Montauk Highway to display his memorabilia and sell roadside refreshments. (Contrary to rumors, it was this cabin and not his residence that was converted into Bronco Charlie's Restaurant.) In 1948, Ferdinand and Tillie Marx purchased the Log Cabin from Bronco Charlie and turned it into a regular restaurant. The original Log Cabin Restaurant could seat only 24 people, but it was so popular that by 1951 an addition was added that increased seating to 500. The Marx family sold the restaurant in 1972.

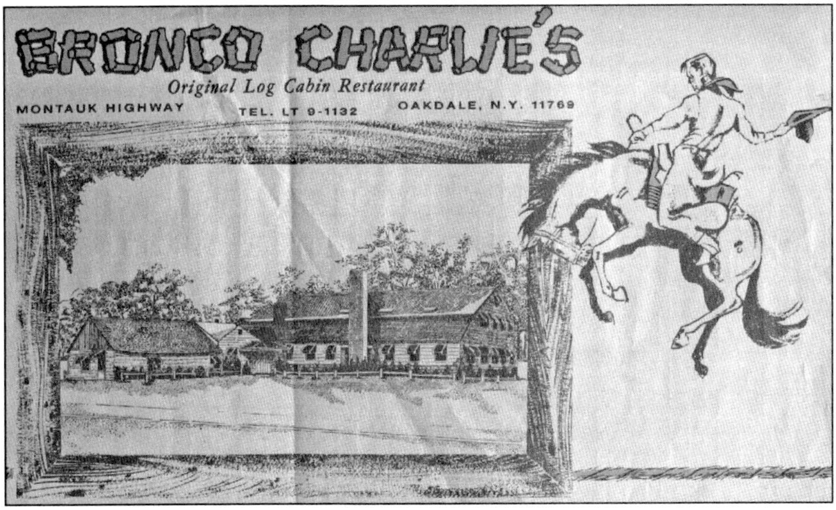

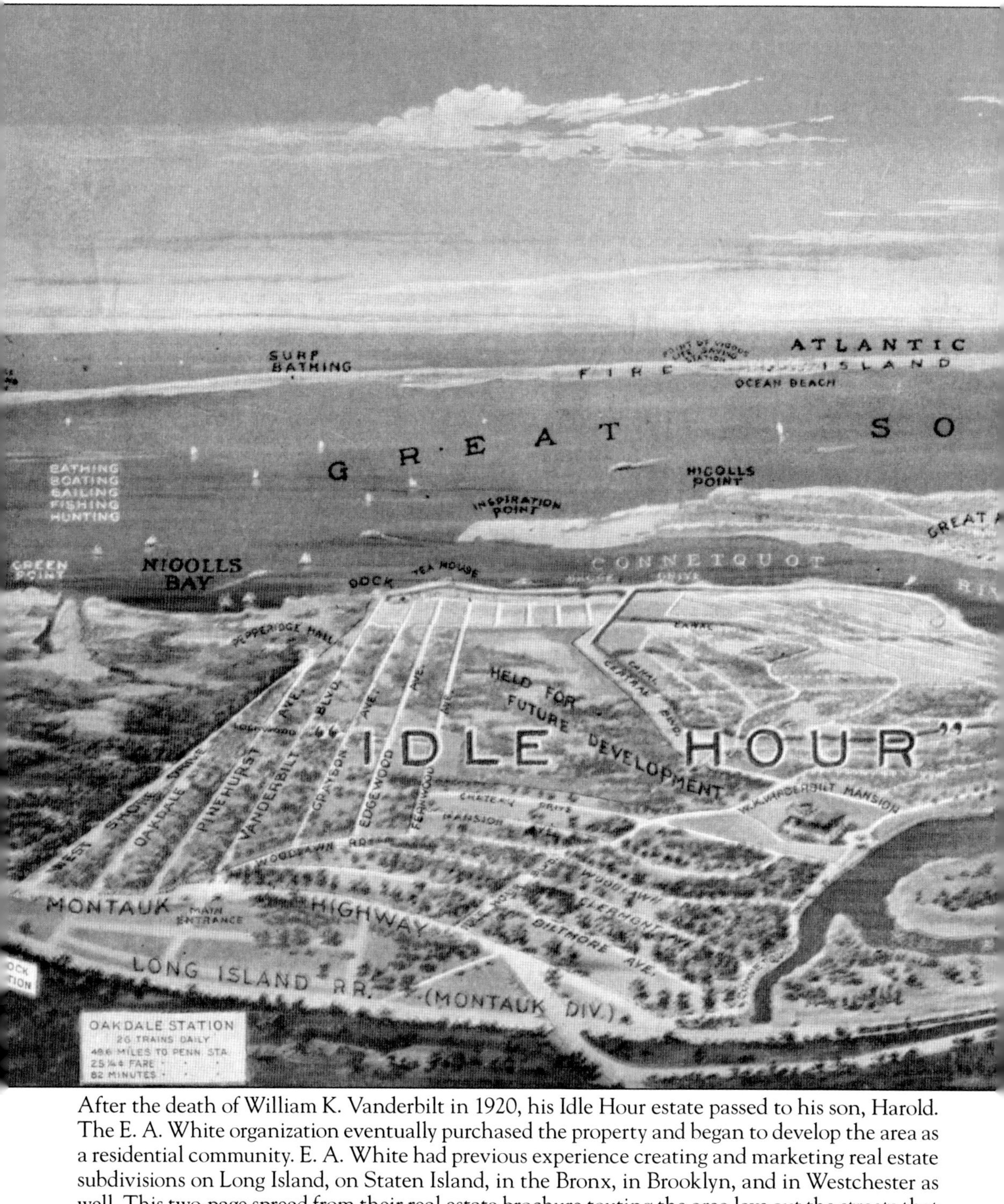

After the death of William K. Vanderbilt in 1920, his Idle Hour estate passed to his son, Harold. The E. A. White organization eventually purchased the property and began to develop the area as a residential community. E. A. White had previous experience creating and marketing real estate subdivisions on Long Island, on Staten Island, in the Bronx, in Brooklyn, and in Westchester as well. This two-page spread from their real estate brochure touting the area lays out the streets that

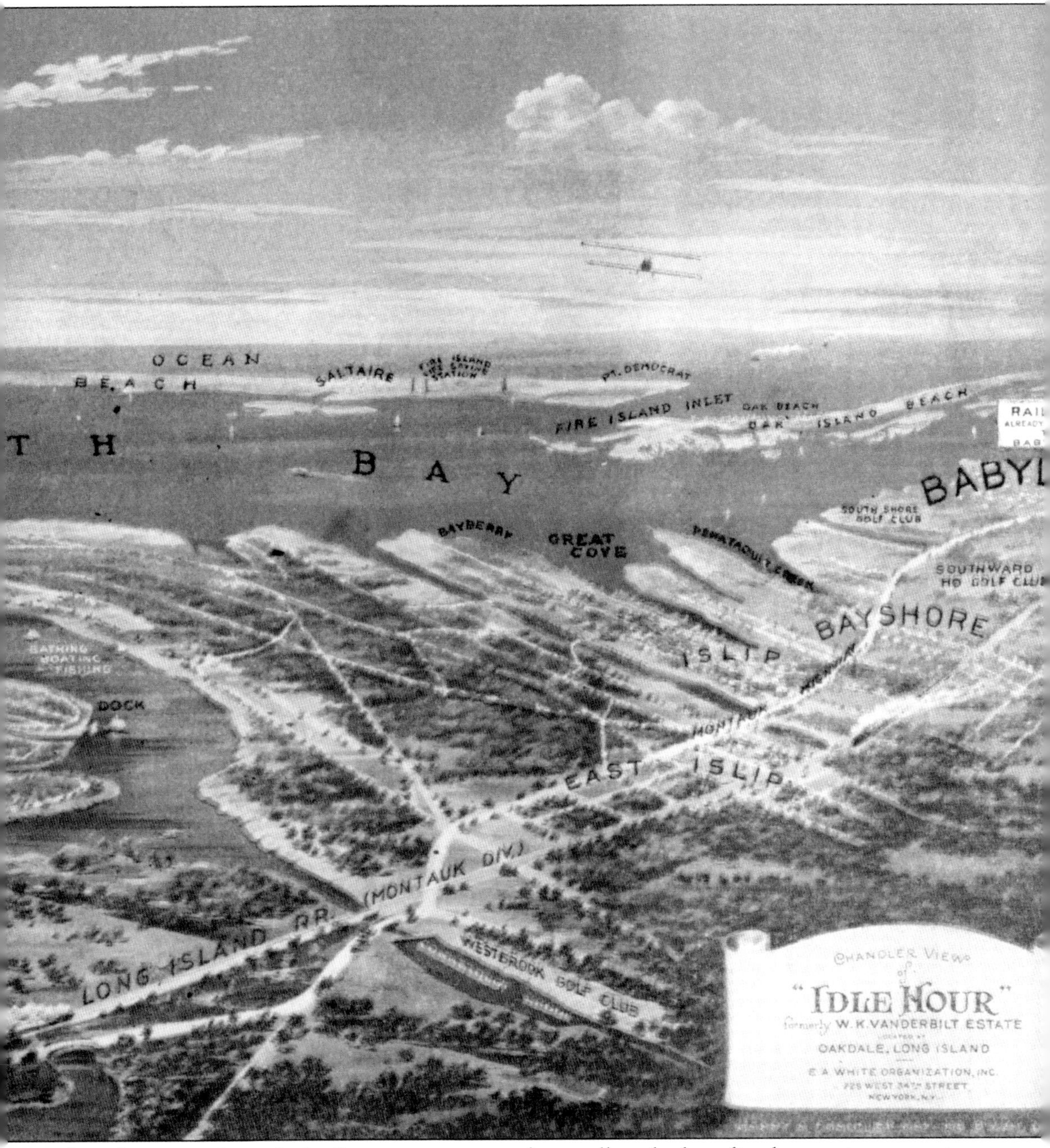

have been run through the former estate grounds as well as the benefits that await prospective buyers. Residents will receive exclusive fishing rights on the property as well as access to a private beach along the Great South Bay. The attempts at establishing an exclusive community did not stop the *New York Times*, in 1934, from speculating that the gangster Dutch Shultz had spent some time hidden somewhere in the neighborhood.

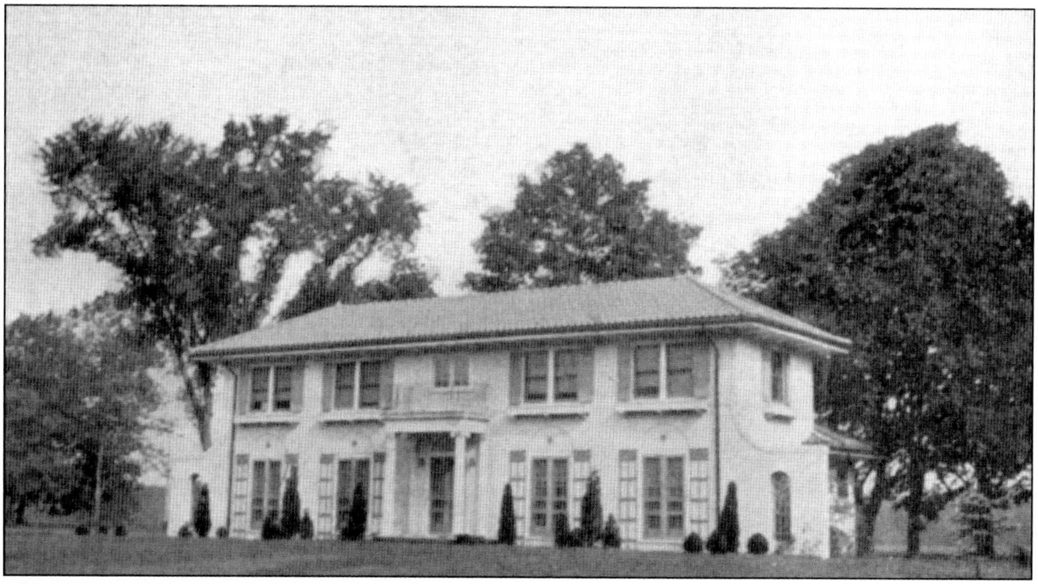

This Georgian Colonial Italianate–style home was designed by the first woman architect registered by the Brooklyn Chapter of the American Institute of Architects, Olive Tjaden. For decades, she was considered the most prominent woman architect in the Northeast. Construction of this home was completed in March 1927, after the Vanderbilt estate was subdivided. Neighborhood legend has it that perhaps the first owner of this home was a gangster.

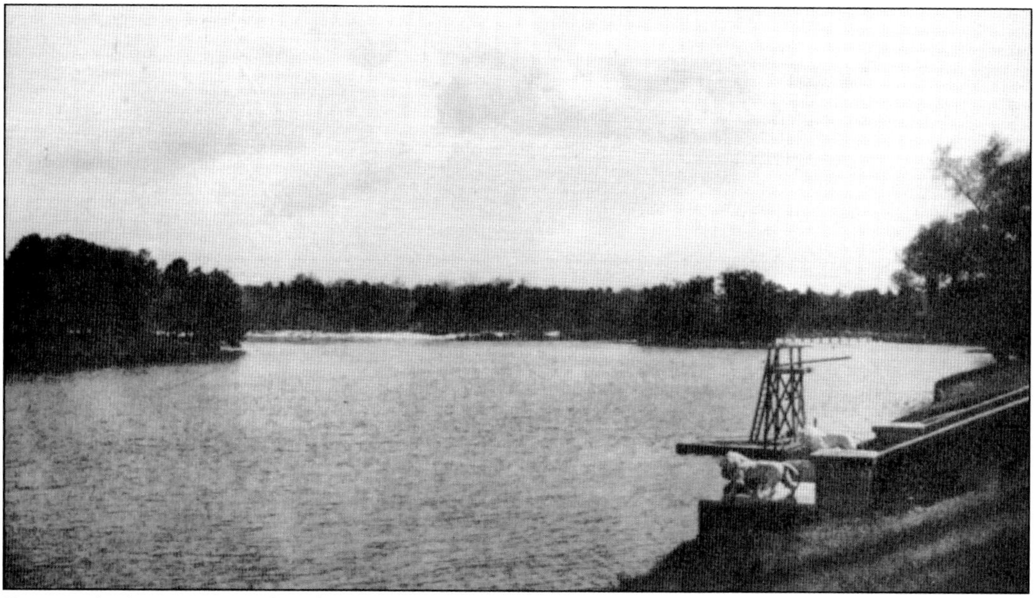

During the late 1920s and early 1930s, the Idle Hour mansion was marketed as a hotel. Note the lifeguard stand in the river. The stairs now lead hotel guests to swimming in place of Vanderbilt's mahogany dock. This 1933 postcard is one of the few artifacts of that period.

Seven

The Local Landscape

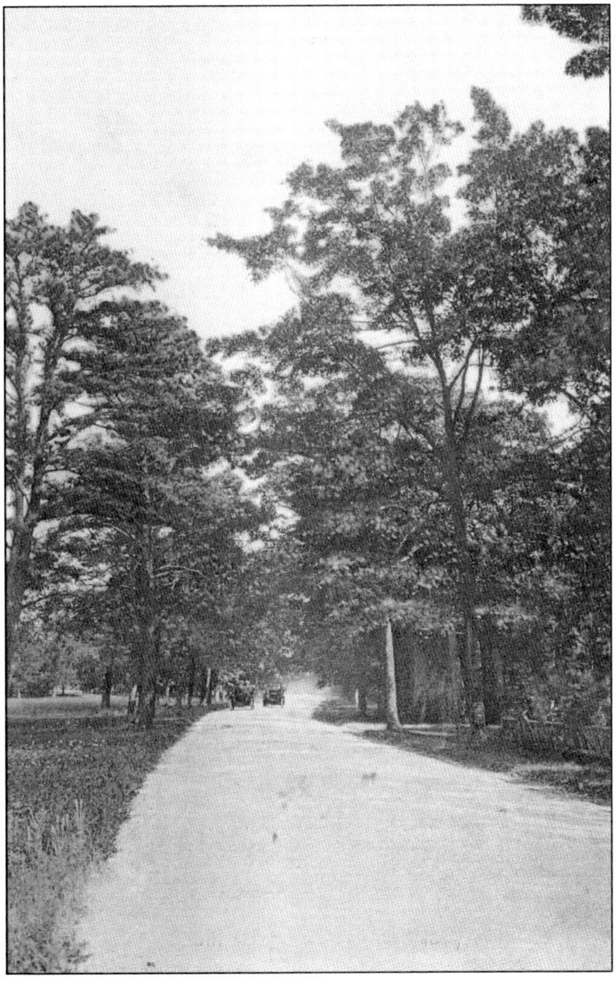

This postcard view from the early 1900s identifies Montauk Highway by its original name, the South Country Road. This was one of the three major thoroughfares laid out by the British to traverse the island, the other two being Middle Country Road (Jericho Turnpike) and the North Country Road (Northern Boulevard). This was the main artery, outside of the Great South Bay, that brought people to Oakdale. Liff Snedecor had operated an inn along this road back in Jamaica, Queens, before relocating to the Connetquot River in the 1820s. His clientele of outdoorsmen followed. It took the coaching club seven changes of horse to make it from New York City out to Oakdale to visit William K. Vanderbilt in 1888. Similar to the two early automobiles seen racing in the distance, the owners of Oakdale's estates used the road to test out their newest acquisitions.

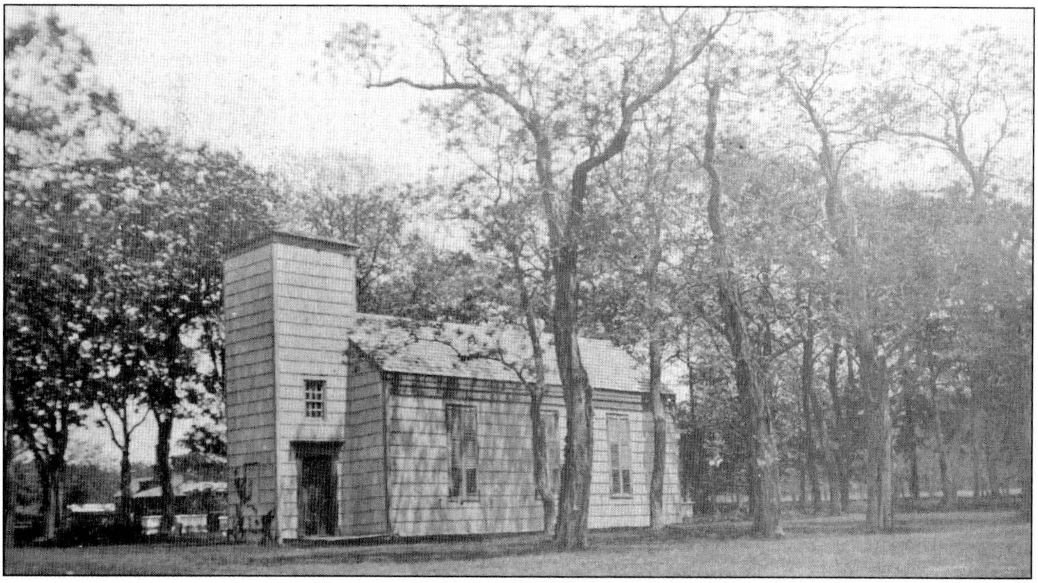

Located on the corner of Montauk Highway and Berard Boulevard, St. John's Church is the second oldest church building in Suffolk County. The current building was dedicated in 1843. The structure has been enlarged twice since it was known as the Charlotte Church, built in 1765 by William Nicoll, grandson of the patentee of the same name. The original church was consecrated by Rev. Samuel Seabury, the first Episcopal bishop of the United States. St. John's is the oldest church active in Suffolk County. Buried in the church yard is William H. Ludlow, once owner of much of the land in Oakdale. His home was located just north of the church.

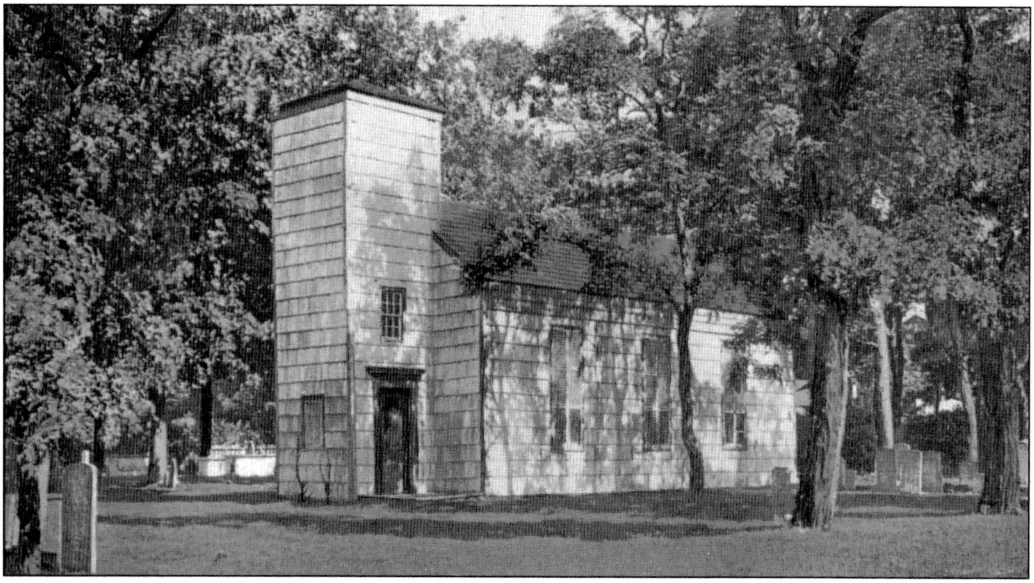

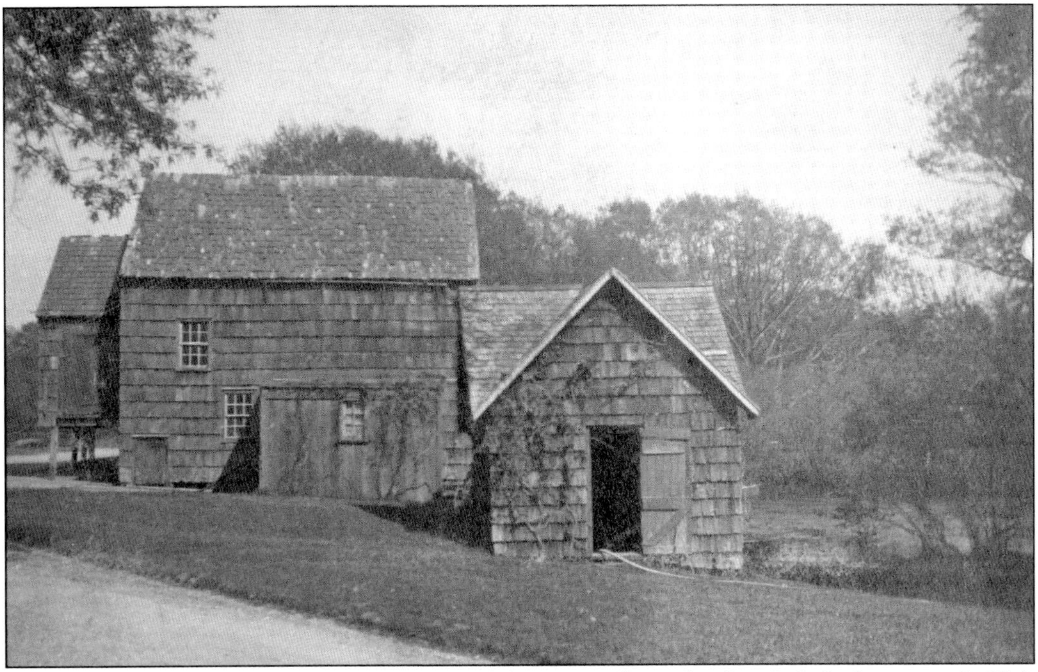

These two photographs provide two views of the gristmill on the South Side Sportsmen's Club property some time in the early 1900s. The mill itself is believed to date to the mid-18th century, built by William Nicoll and used to grind wheat and corn for the surrounding inhabitants. The mill is a tub wheel design in which the wheel is placed horizontally rather than vertically. Just southeast of the mill was the home of Stephen Murray, a Native American who worked at the South Side Sportsmen's Club as a guide for many years, as did his sons. The mill is currently undergoing restoration, and the hope is to one day have it returned to working order.

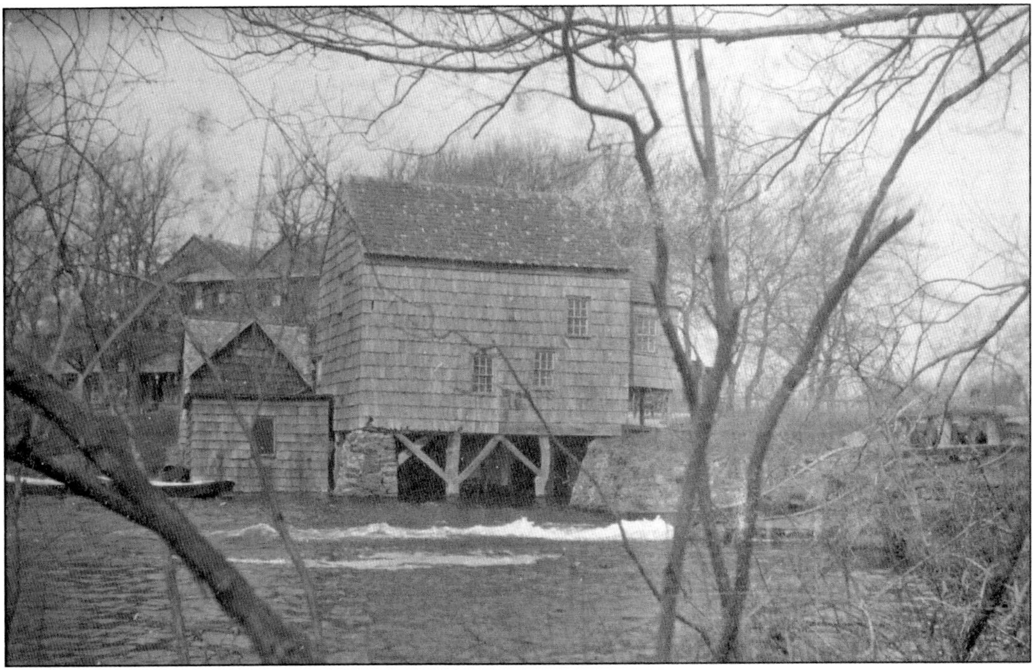

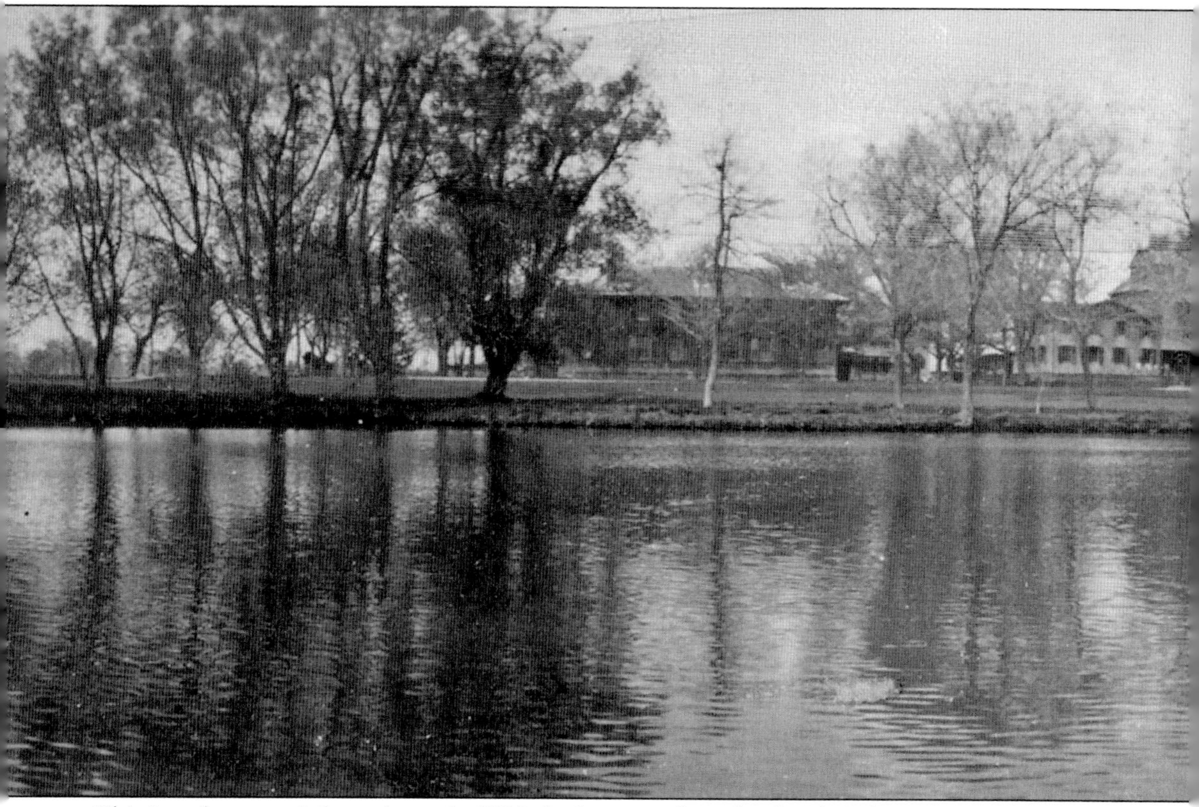

This is a photograph from the early 1900s looking north at the South Side Sportsmen's property across the lower pond. This pond was formed in 1881 with the re-routing of Montauk Highway. The Idle Hour mansion is just downstream to the south. Gherardi Davis, in his 1909 history of the club, sums up what attracted so many to this area of Oakdale: "I have rowed down the river at sunrise and seen the does come to the water's edge with their fawns and stare at the boat in silent wonderment; and one evening, coming back from bass-fishing, as we turned from the

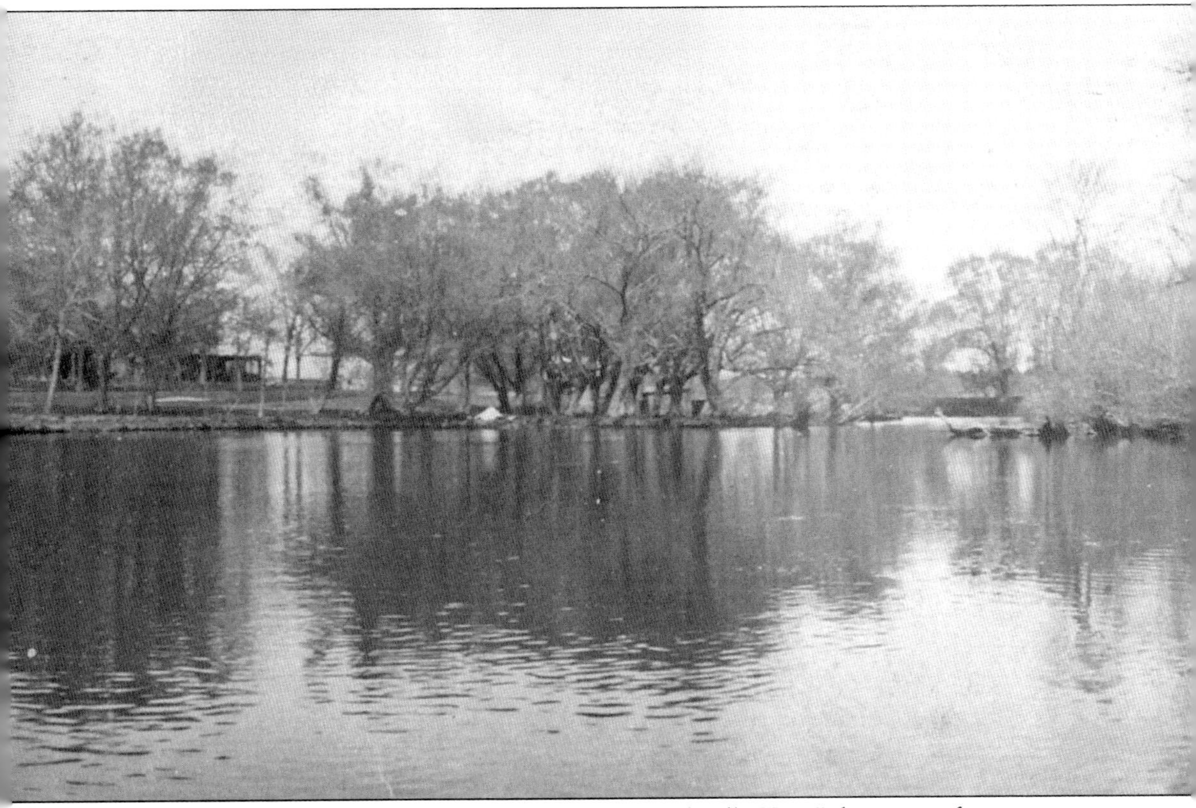

river (you will remember how, as you leave the river and "Idle Hour" disappears from view, you come into a stretch where there is no sign of man's having been there) I remember seeing a large deer standing on the East bank, with his head thrown back and his figure standing out sharply against the twilight sky . . . and I have met no one who does not agree that we are surrounded by a landscape in many respects beyond compare."

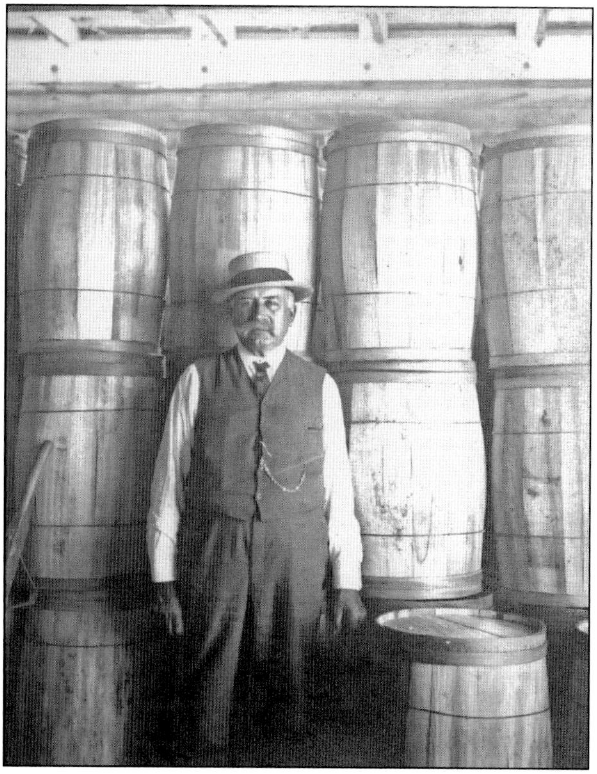

Jacob "Oyster King" Ockers was born in Holland in 1847. His father settled the family in Oakdale where Jacob learned the oyster trade. By 1900, he was exporting over 23,000 barrels of Blue Point oysters a year. One of the first to ship oysters over seas, he helped make Blue Point an international name. This undated photograph shows him posing with some of his wares. (Courtesy of the Long Island Maritime Museum.)

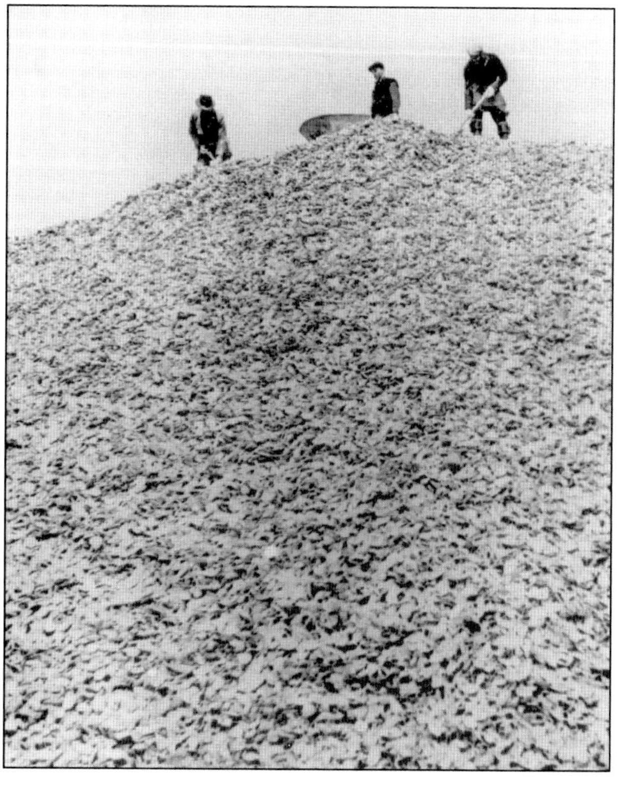

The stretch of the Great South Bay along Oakdale and West Sayville is synonymous with the golden age of oystering around the beginning of the 20th century. This photograph of workers outside an oyster house in the area from around that period illustrates how abundant the beds of the bay were. Along Montauk Highway, the streets were literally paved with oyster shells. (Courtesy of the Long Island Maritime Museum.)

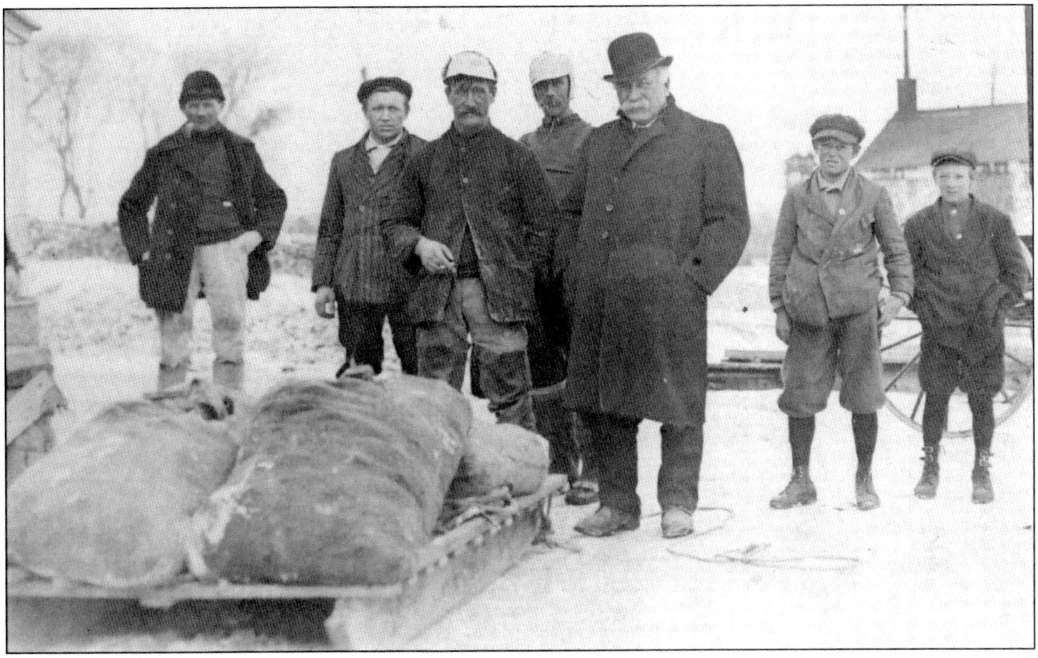

Jacob Ockers was a shrewd businessman. He began in the oyster trade working the bay, as did many others, off William H. Ludlow's farm in Oakdale. The cull houses and oyster shacks that go with the business did not match with Frederick Bourne's vision of Indian Neck Hall, which began to take shape in the late 1890s. Many of the oystermen were forced to relocate to West Sayville. When Ockers made the switch in 1908, he turned a $17,000 profit when selling his Oakdale shorefront to Bourne. These photographs date to the early 1900s, showing Ockers with his workers inside and outside the cull houses in West Sayville where he founded the Blue Pont Oyster Company in 1912. (Both, courtesy of the Long Island Maritime Museum.)

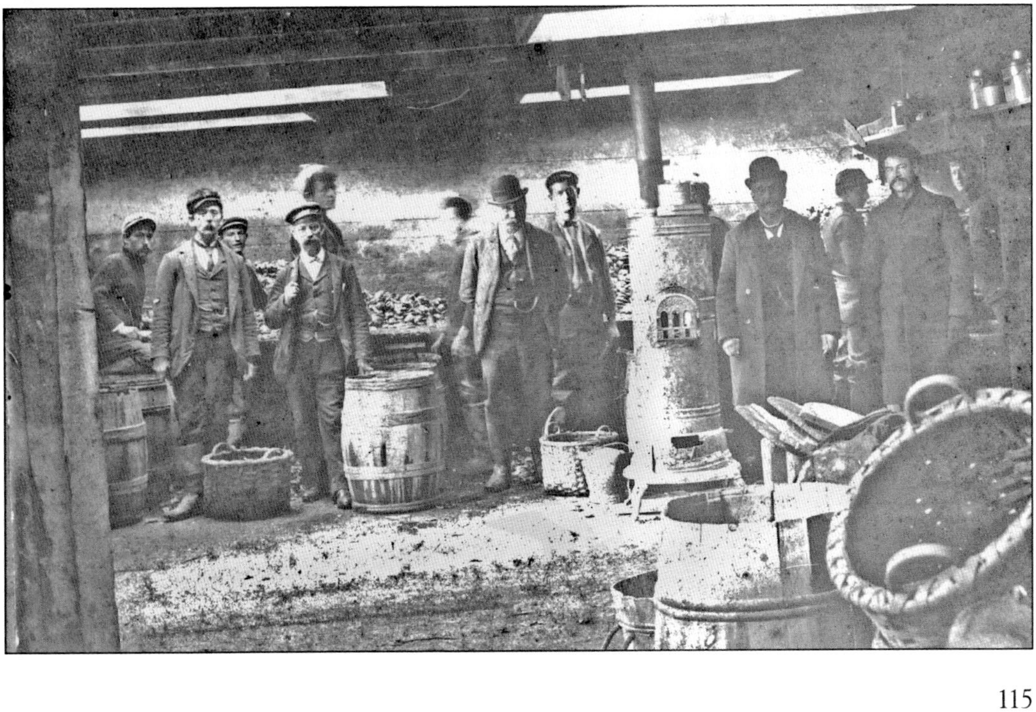

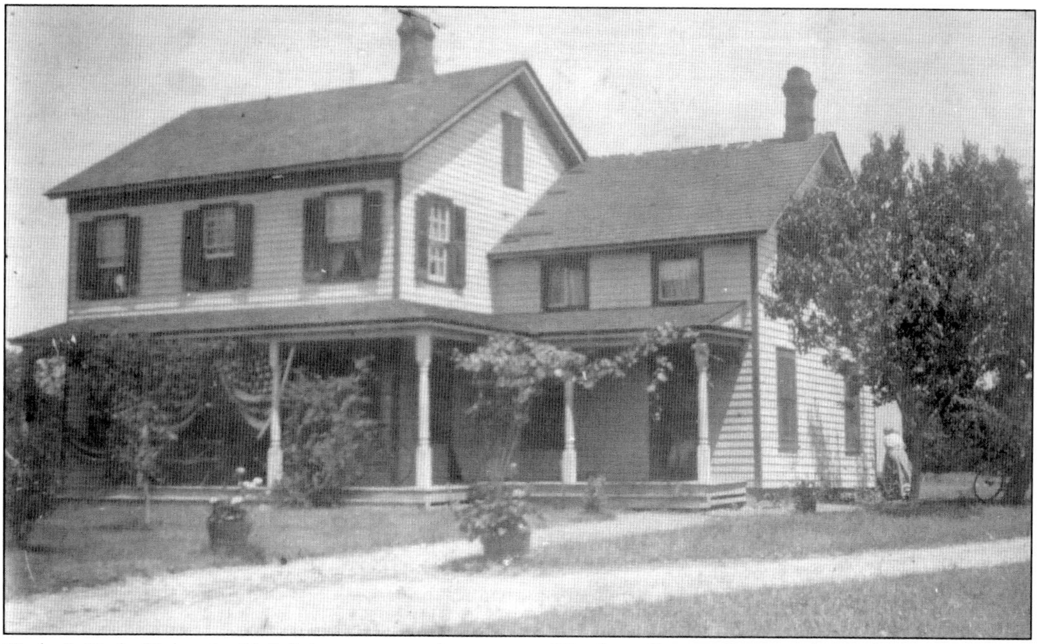

Today's Dale Drive in Oakdale was once known as Chicken Street. It served as a home for many immigrant families who were drawn to the area. The Dutch in particular settled in Oakdale to pursue the oyster trade. The first such settlers are recognized as the Hage family, who arrived from Bruinisse, also a center of shellfishing, in 1849. Other immigrants found work on the farms of William H. Ludlow and later Frederick Bourne. These pictures depict the homes of two similar families. The photograph above, dating to 1900, shows the Chicken Street home of John and Jesse Cochrane. The photograph below shows unidentified members of the Scherpenisse family standing on Chicken Street some time in the 1870s. (Both, courtesy of the Long Island Maritime Museum.)

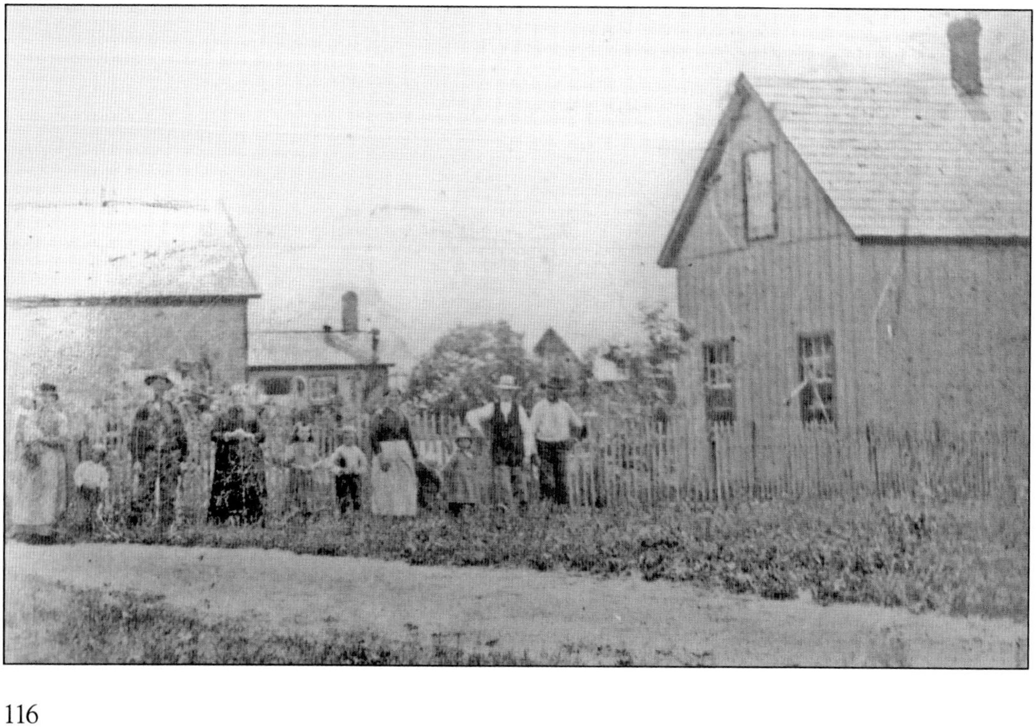

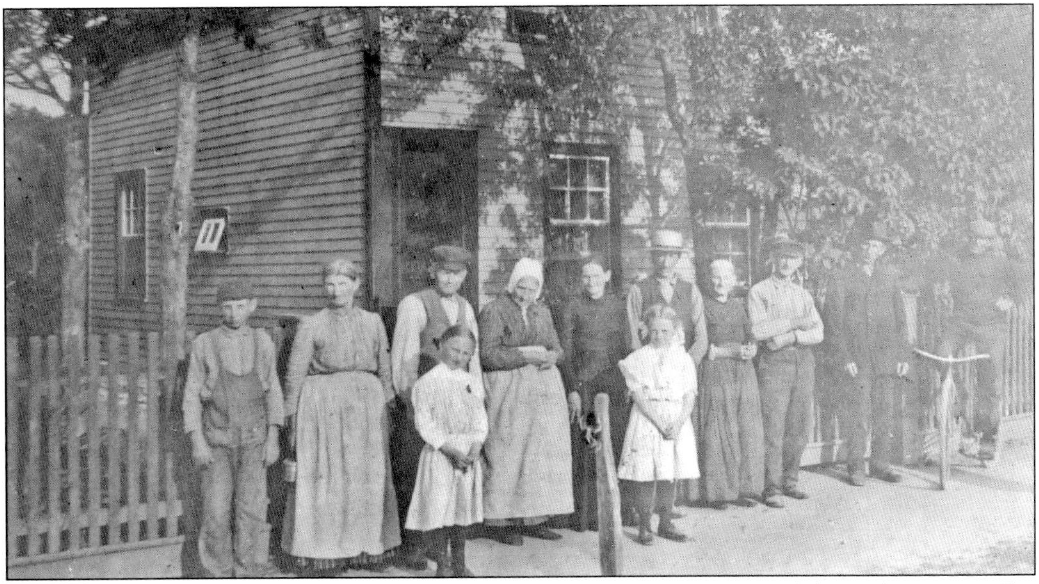

These two photographs show more Chicken Street residents at the dawn of the 20th century. The photograph above, dating to 1900, shows members of the Scherpenisse family and other Dutch residents of Chicken Street. Pictured are, from left to right, (first row) Anna Scherpenisse and Cornelia Scherpenisse; (second row) Leendart Scherpenisse Jr., Cathalina Hoek, Adrian Tiyse, Cornelia Tiyse, Nellie Scherpenisse, Leendart Scherpenisse, Anna Scherpenisse (grandma), William Scherpenisse, Adrian Scherpenisse, and Johannes Hoek. Below is a photograph of neighborhood children and an unidentified family from the same period. (Both, courtesy of the Long Island Maritime Museum.)

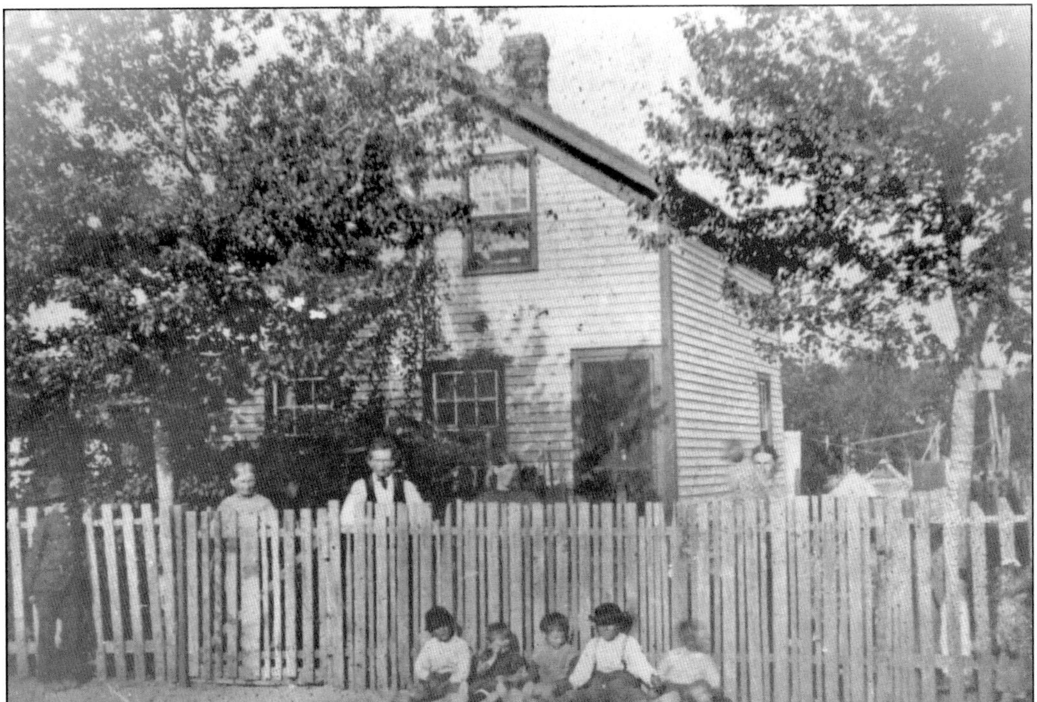

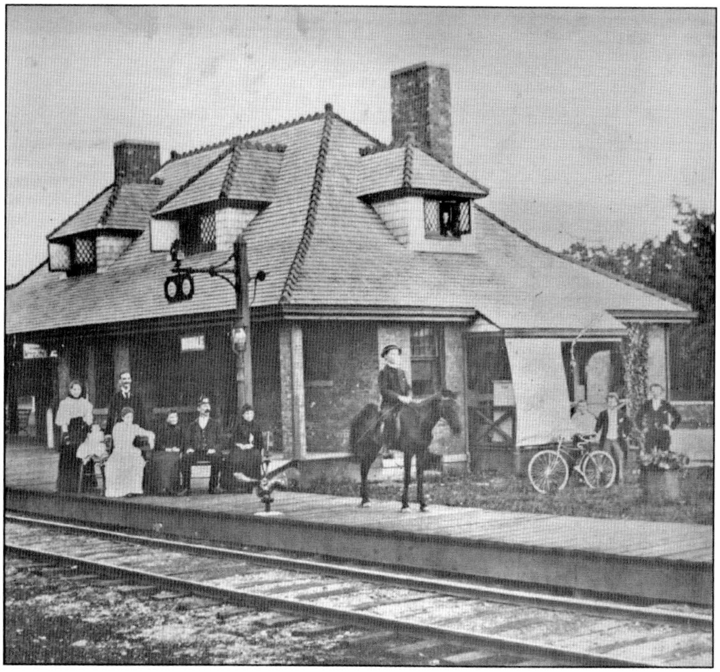

The Oakdale Station of the Long Island Rail Road is located on the northwest corner of Montauk Highway and Oakdale-Bohemia Road. This photograph, taken around the beginning of the 20th century and depicting several unidentified local residents, was taken from the north side of the tracks looking southeast. Contrary to local legend, the station was not built for Consuelo Vanderbilt's wedding.

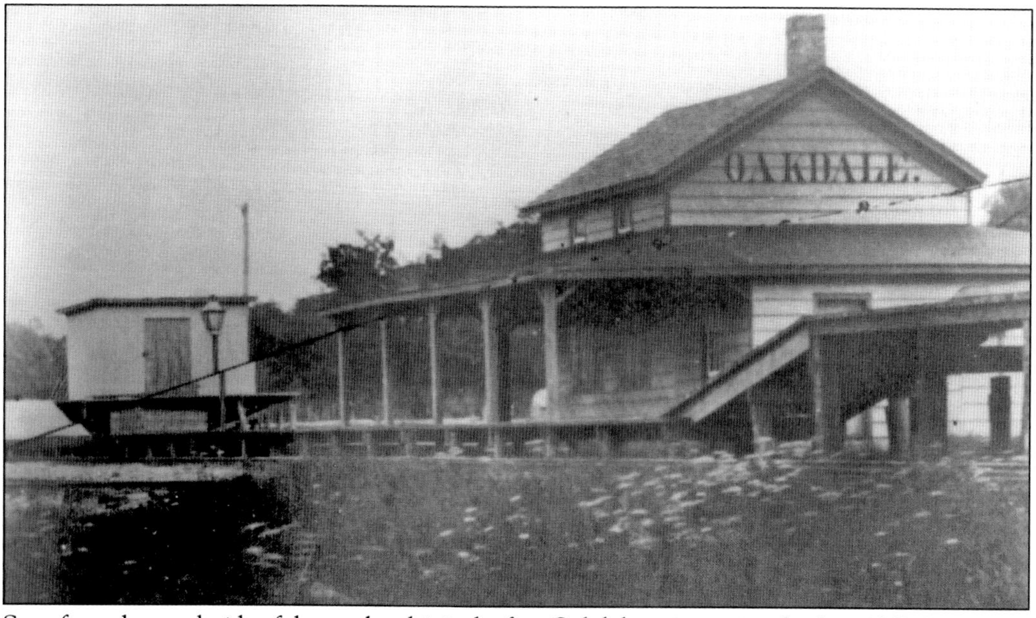

Seen from the north side of the tracks, this is the first Oakdale train station, built in 1869. It was part of the South Side Railroad line, operated independently of the Long Island Rail Road whose main line, built in 1844, traversed the middle of the island. Although undated, this photograph was taken before the demolition of the station in 1889. (Courtesy of the Long Island Maritime Museum.)

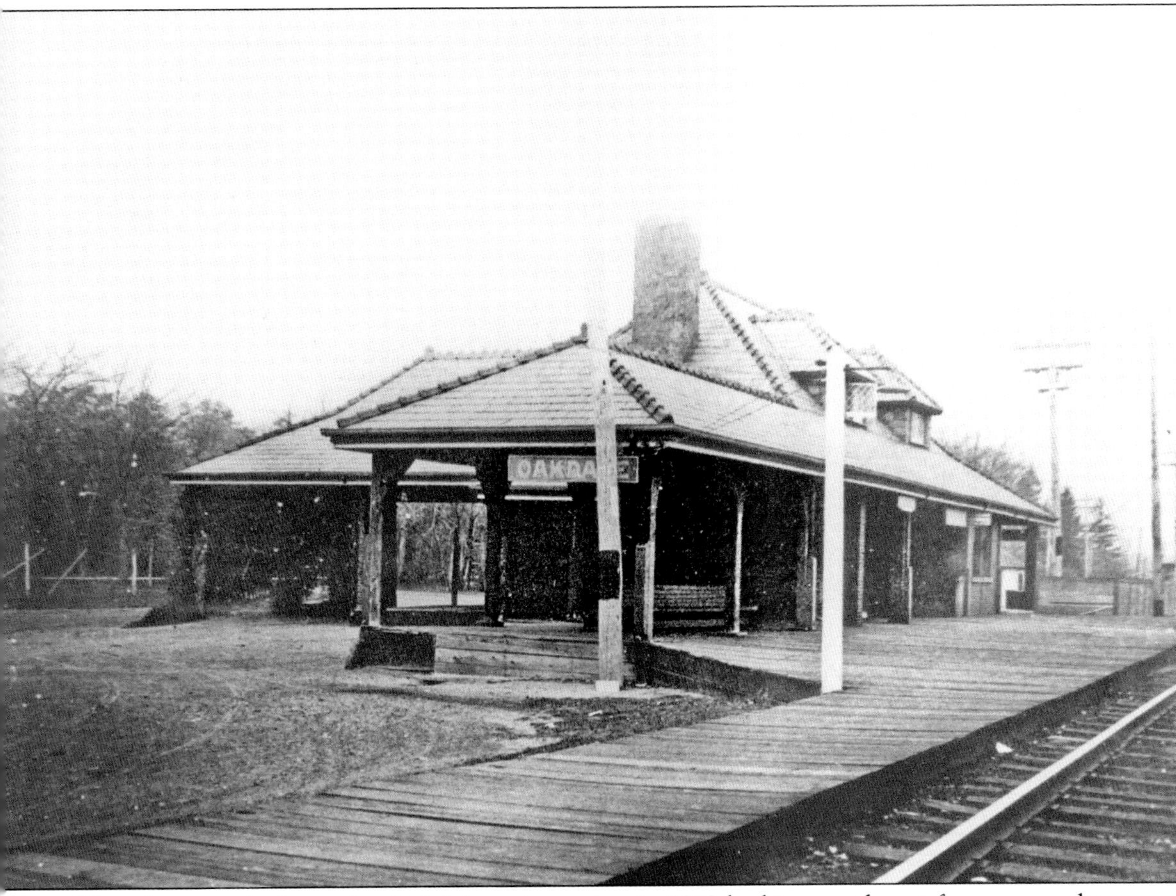

This photograph shows the Oakdale train station in 1918 looking southwest from across the tracks. Built in 1899, this structure replaced the earlier wooden station constructed in 1869. This second Oakdale train station was designed by Isaac Greene of Sayville at a cost of $30,000. It is said that Commodore Bourne paid to enlarge the second floor so the stationmaster could live comfortably there.

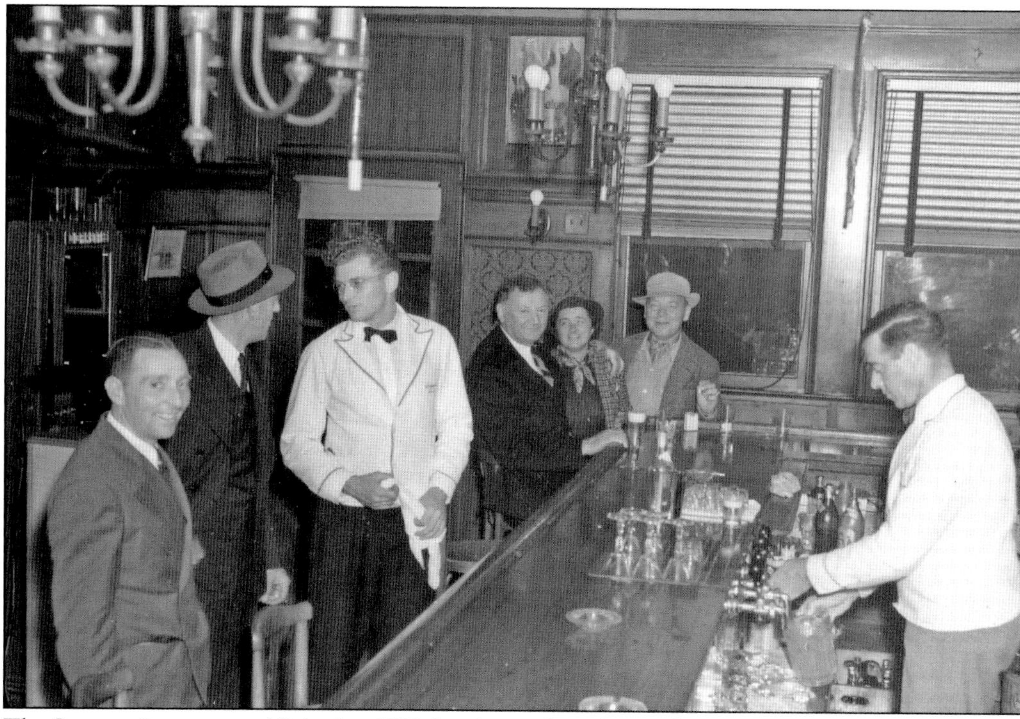

The Snapper Inn was established in 1929. It is located on the southern tip of William K. Vanderbilt's Idle Hour estate, along Shore Road overlooking the bay. It has been run by members of the Remmer family for over 80 years. Taken in 1939, the photograph above shows a crowd at the bar including, from left to right, "Spike" Lambin, "Doodle" Otto, George Remmer, Henry Remmer Sr., Addie Peterson, Billy Peterson, and Shelby Jones. The photograph below, taken in 1940, shows Frank Stokes (left) and George Remmer.

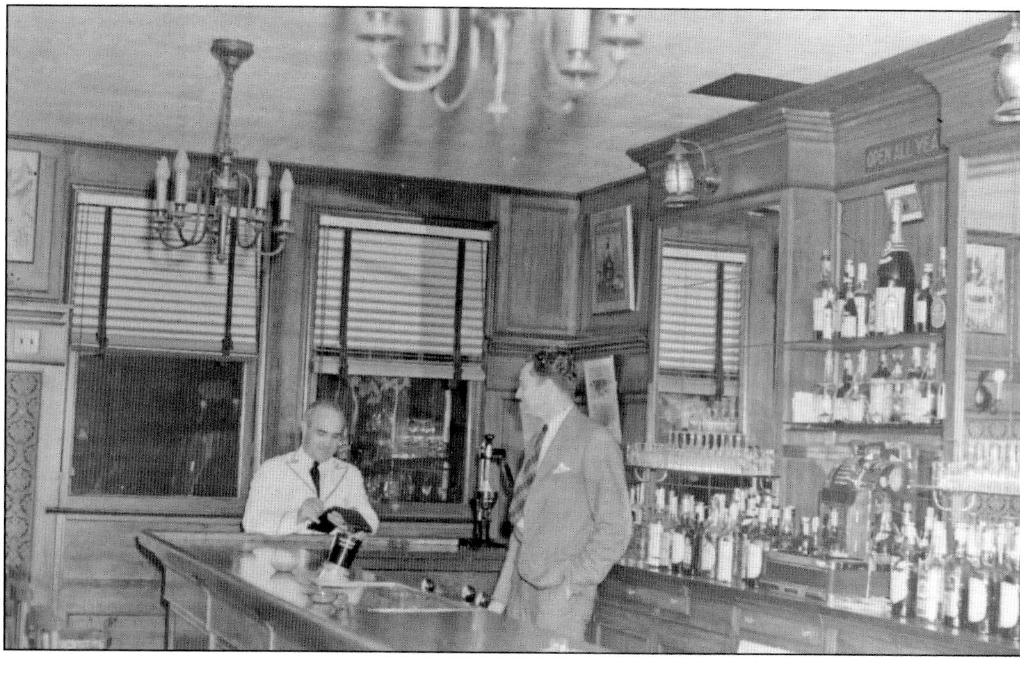

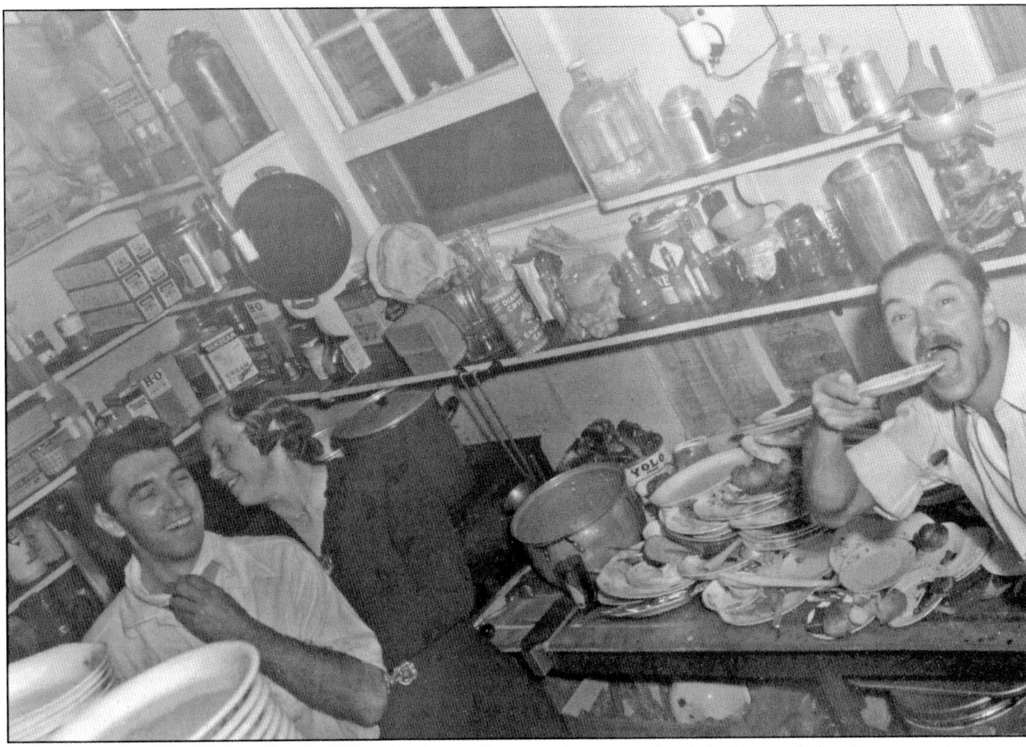

The photograph above dates from 1939 or 1940 and shows the kitchen of the Snapper Inn on a busy night. Pictured are, from left to right, the cook, Henry ?; Louise Remmer; and the dishwasher (or "pearl diver"), Charlie Thompson. The undated photograph below shows the Snapper Inn looking north from the bay. To the right of the restaurant is the entrance to one of William K. Vanderbilt's canals. Just to the north was a turn bridge that allowed boats to transport goods such as coal up to the estate buildings.

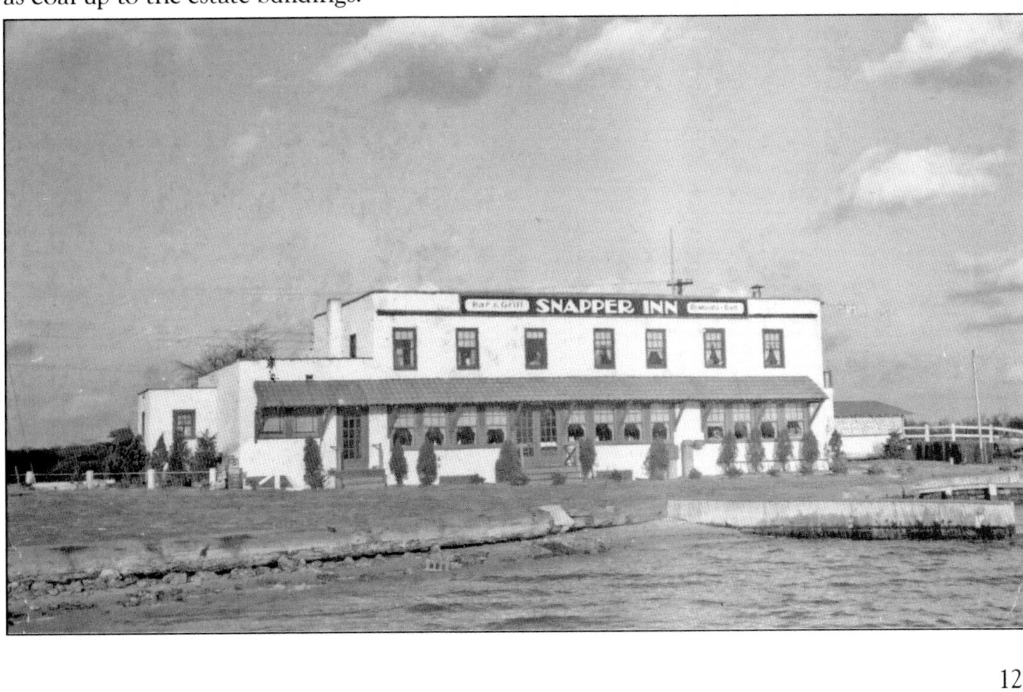

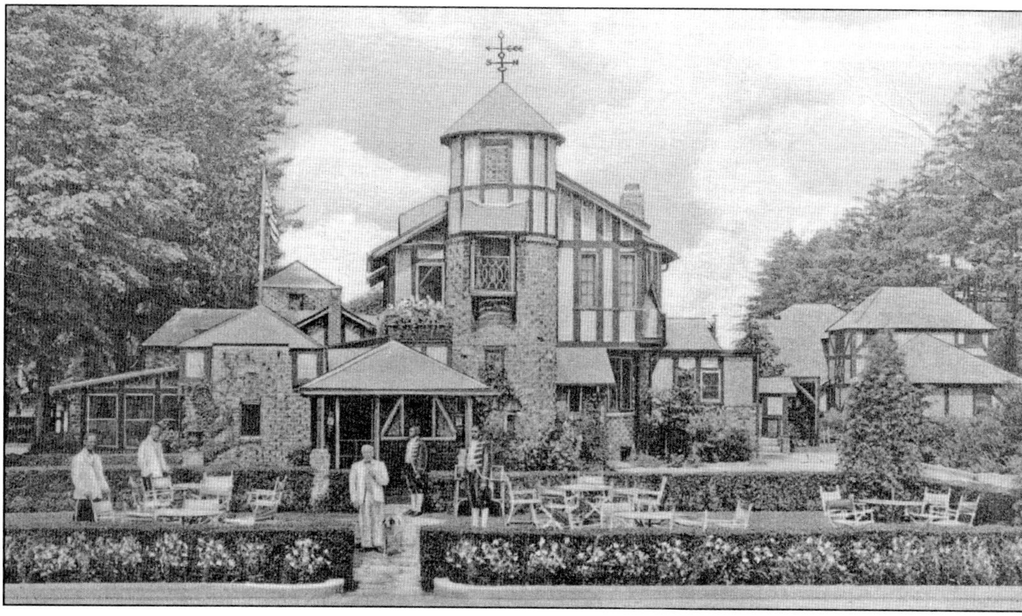

Adolph Klug and his wife, Louise, built and operated the Stirrup-Cup Castle. It was located on the north side of Montauk Highway a little to the east of Oakdale-Bohemia Road. Klug built the restaurant to resemble the Bavarian castles of his homeland, but the food was influenced by Colonial American recipes. The grounds included a floral garden and gazing ball. Shown here are two postcard views around 1940 looking west from the restaurant's parking lot.

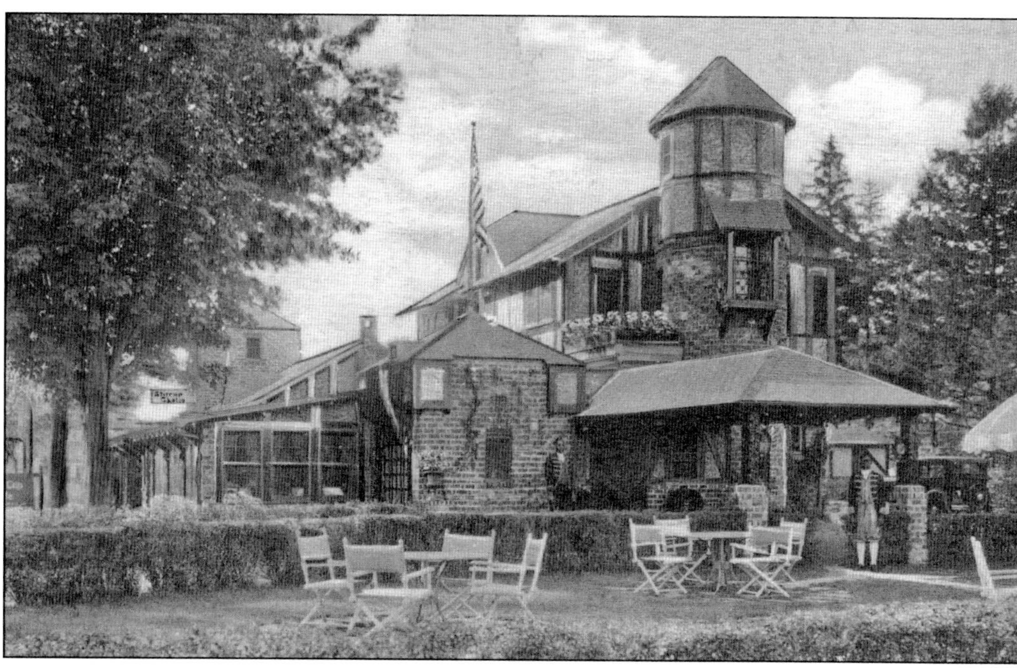

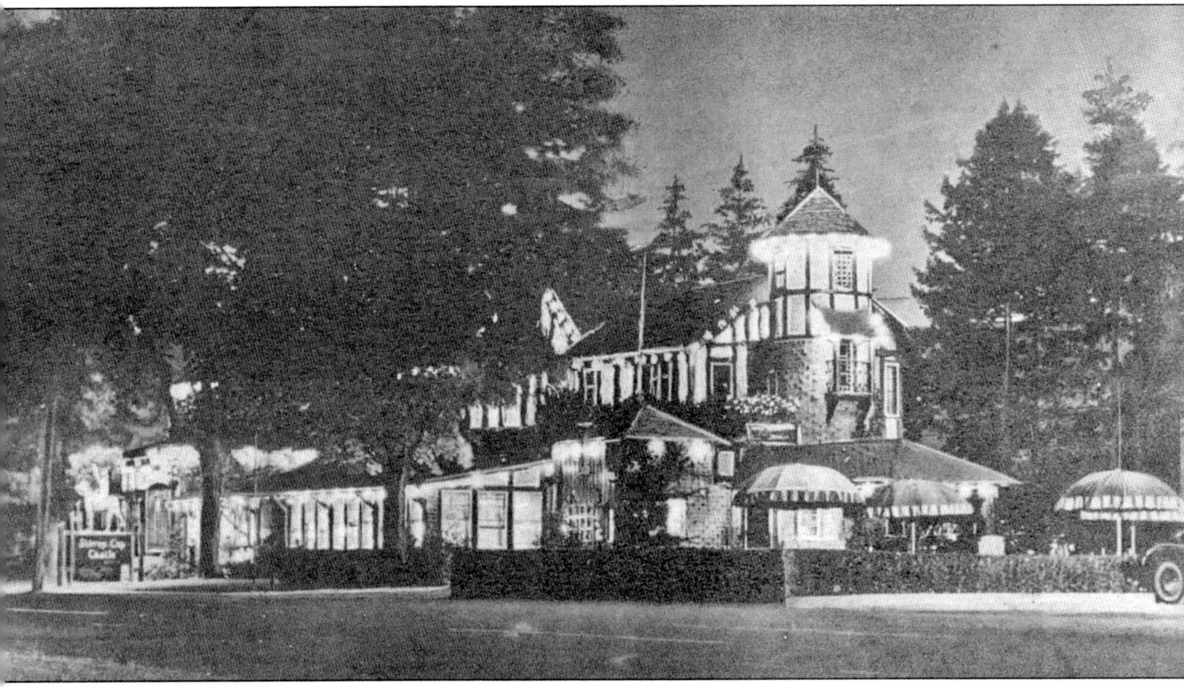

This nighttime view of the Stirrup-Cup Castle from a postcard around 1940 shows the restaurant looking north across Montauk Highway. The tracks of the Long Island Rail Road ran behind the restaurant, screened by a stand of trees. Adolph Klug, the proprietor, established the restaurant around 1935. He had previously operated the Stagecoach Inn in Locust Valley for 10 years. Klug stated that the Stirrup-Cup refers to a potent drink supposedly concocted by Light Horse Harry Lee to "stir up" his soldiers before battle. Klug maintained the restaurant until a fire in 1945 almost completely destroyed it. The property was then sold to August Kappel of Sayville.

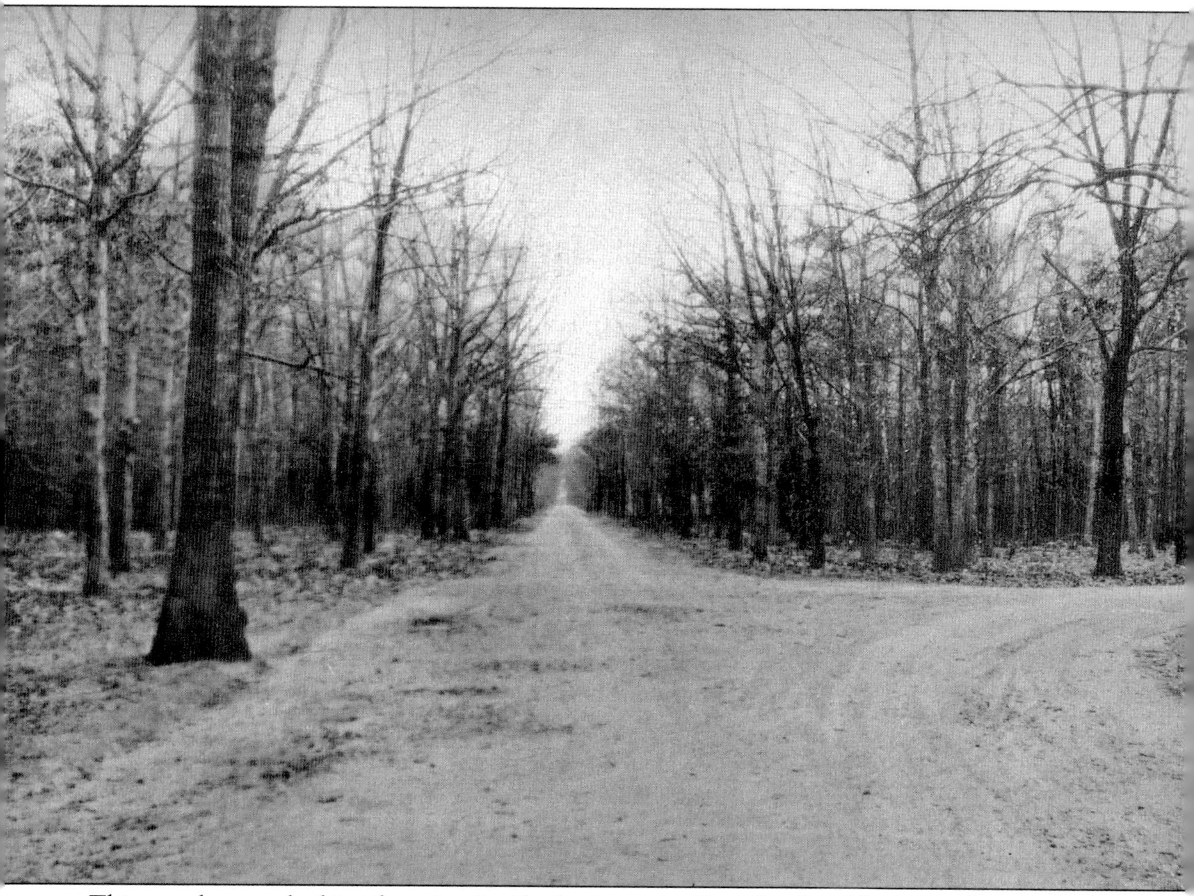

This was the view looking from just inside the east gate. Straight ahead looks south towards the Great South Bay down what is now Vanderbilt Boulevard. The road to the right today is known as Woodlawn Avenue and it leads to Idle Hour Boulevard.

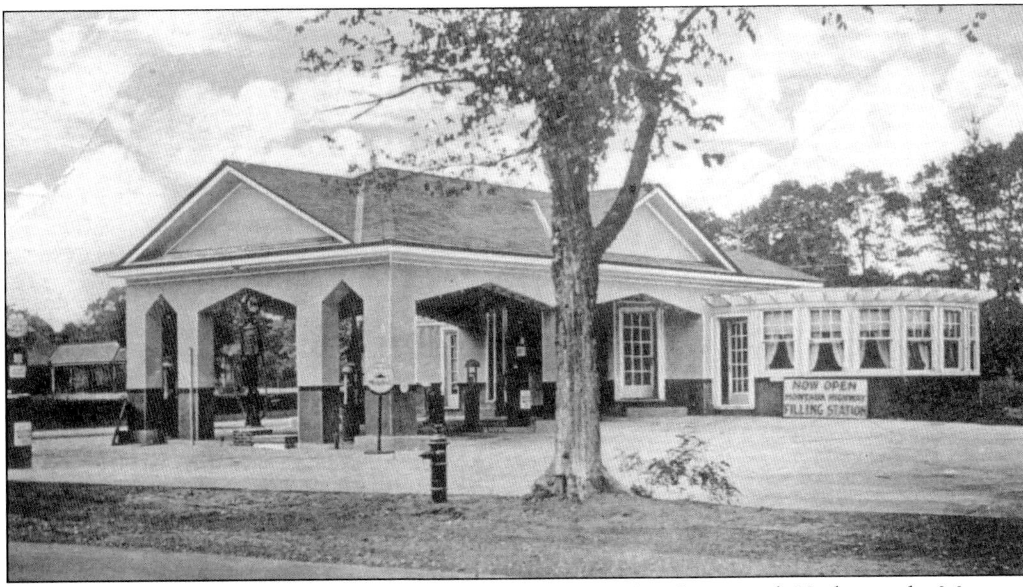

Located on the northeast corner of Oakdale-Bohemia Road and Montauk Highway, the Montauk Highway filling station was owned by Premm Garage Corporation. Premm was also a superintendent of the W. K. Vanderbilt Idle Hour estate. This picture was taken around 1940 when it also housed the Oakdale Post Office for a number of years. Today the post office has moved up the road, and this building it is still in operation as a gas station.

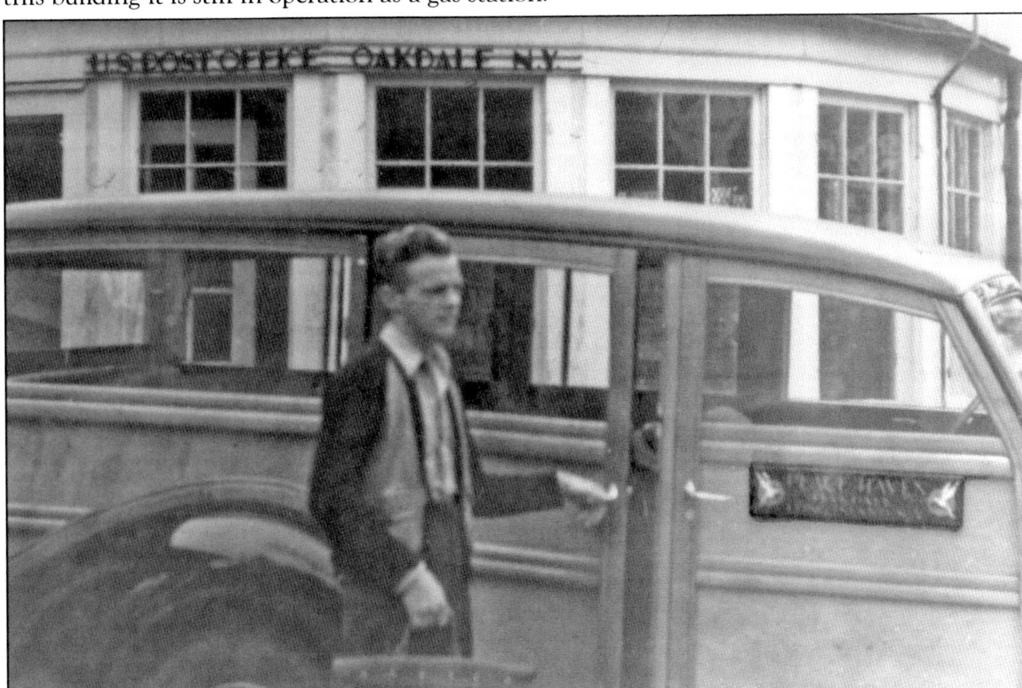

This picture is at the Oakdale Gas Station when it served as the post office. The vehicle is from Peace Haven, the Royal Fraternity of Master Metaphysicians (1938–1942). Earlier in the century, this location was the site of the Oakdale Rest. This restaurant catered to the throngs of avid bicyclists that trekked out to the nearby Vanderbilt well on their century runs from Brooklyn.

Bibliography

Davis, Gherardi. *The South Side Sportsmen's Club of Long Island.* New York: Privately published, 1909.

Havemeyer, Harry W. *Along the Great South Bay: From Oakdale to Babylon the Story of a Summer Spa 1840 to 1940.* Mattituck, NY: Amereon House, 1996.

King, Robert B. *The Vanderbilt Homes.* NY: Rizzoli, 1989.

MacKay, Robert B., ed. *Long Island Country Houses and Their Architects, 1860–1940.* NY: W. W. Norton, 1997.

Old Oakdale History: Volume I. Oakdale, NY: William K. Vanderbilt Historical Society of Dowling College, 1983.

Old Oakdale History: Volume II. Oakdale, NY: William K. Vanderbilt Historical Society of Dowling College, 1993.

Roussos, George. *A History and Description of William Bayard Cutting and his country house: Westbrook, Great River, L. I.* Islip, NY: Board of Trustees of the Bayard Cutting Arboretum; Babylon, NY: Long Island State Park and Recreation Commission, 1984.

Spinzia, Raymond E., and Judith A. Spinzia. *Long Island's Prominent South Shore Families: Their Estates and Their Country Homes in the Towns of Babylon and Islip.* College Station, TX: VirtualBookworm, 2007.

About the Organization

Dowling College serves undergraduate and graduate students through its four schools: Arts and Sciences, Business, Education, and Aviation. The college is located on two campuses—the historic Rudolph Campus in Oakdale and the Brookhaven Center in Shirley. At these locations, students work in a unique setting that blends history, natural beauty, state-of-the-art classroom and library/research technology, championship athletics, and diverse student activities.

The Dowling College Library provides instruction, services, and access to resources that supports the scholarly and informational needs of the college community. To partially fulfill its mission, the library maintains archives and special collections, which contain information relating to the history of Dowling College, the Idle Hour mansion, the Idle Hour Artist Colony, the Oakdale community, Long Island history, Bronco Charlie, and the Vanderbilt family. The college and the library look forward to establishing a South Shore History Center to showcase and share this rich local history collection.

Consistent with our mission to preserve history on a local level, this book was printed in South Carolina on American-made paper and manufactured entirely in the United States. Products carrying the accredited Forest Stewardship Council (FSC) label are printed on 100 percent FSC-certified paper.

MADE IN THE USA